KU-142-157

THE BASICS
For a full list of titles in this series, please visit
www.routledge.com/The-Basics/book-series/B

SEMIOTICS
THE BASICS

THIRD EDITION

Daniel Chandler

Routledge
Taylor & Francis Group

LONDON AND NEW YORK

Third edition published 2017
by Routledge
2 Park Square, Milton Park, Abingdon, Oxon OX14 4RN

and by Routledge
711 Third Avenue, New York, NY 10017

Routledge is an imprint of the Taylor & Francis Group, an informa business

© 2017 Daniel Chandler

First edition published by Routledge 2002

Second edition published by Routledge 2007

British Library Cataloguing-in-Publication Data
A catalogue record for this book is available from the British Library

Library of Congress Cataloging-in-Publication Data
Names: Chandler, Daniel.
Title: Semiotics : the basics / by Daniel Chandler.
Description: Third edition. | New York, NY : Routledge, 2018. |
Includes bibliographical references and index.
Identifiers: LCCN 2016058660| ISBN 9781138232921 (hardback) |
ISBN 9781138232938 (pbk.) | ISBN 9781315311050 (ebook)
Subjects: LCSH: Semiotics.
Classification: LCC P99 .C463 2018 | DDC 302.2—dc23LC
record available at https://lccn.loc.gov/2016058660

ISBN: 978-1-138-23292-1 (hbk)
ISBN: 978-1-138-23293-8 (pbk)
ISBN: 978-1-315-31105-0 (ebk)

Typeset in Times New Roman and Scala Sans
by Florence Production Ltd, Stoodleigh, Devon, UK

Printed and bound in Great Britain by
TJ International Ltd, Padstow, Cornwall

For Jem

'The subtlety of nature is greater many times
over than the subtlety of argument'
Francis Bacon, *Novum Organum*
(1620) Aphorism XXIV

CONTENTS

ILLUSTRATIONS

PREFACE

The first version of this book was written in 1994 as an online hypertext document. Its surprising popularity online eventually led to an invitation from the publisher to produce a printed book version for their series, *The Basics*. Like many other readers driven by a fascination with meaning-making, my forays into semiotics had been frustrated by many of the existing books on the subject which seemed to make it confusing, dull, and deeply obscure, as if designed to keep out those who are not already 'members of the club'. This text was therefore designed to let them in.

Like the original online text, this book has been used around the world as part of university courses in many different subjects, including advertising, aesthetics, art education, art history, brand management, communication theory, consumer behaviour, cultural studies, design, fashion, film studies, journalism, linguistics, literary theory, media analysis, visual communication, visual culture, and visual rhetoric. One of the things that attracts me to semiotics is the way in which it supports my own enjoyment of crossing the 'boundaries' of academic disciplines, and of making connections between apparently disparate phenomena.

No treatment of semiotics can claim to be comprehensive because, in the broadest sense (as a general theory of signs), it embraces the whole field of signification, including 'life, the universe, and everything', regardless of whether the signs are goal-directed (or interpreted as being so). This book has a far more modest scope: it is an introduction to semiotic theories, models, and methods primarily in the context of cultural semiotics, a branch of applied semiotics. The core topics here are communication and representation, which are key themes in the disciplines represented in its existing readership. Even within cultural studies, the coverage is unavoidably selective but the general principles outlined are widely applicable across the cultural domain. Within semiotics, there are competing theories and models of the sign, so it should be noted that considerable attention is given to Saussurean 'semiology' and structuralist methodologies because of their widespread use for textual analysis. This book could almost have been titled *Semiology: The Basics* were it not for the eclipse of that term in current anglophone usage and the emergence of 'social semiotics'. However, the coverage of Peircean concepts has been considerably increased in this edition.

The American semiotician Thomas Sebeok (1920–2001) declares that 'the subject matter of semiotics is, quite simply, messages – any messages whatsoever' (Chatman *et al.* 1979, 222). This book is intended to be of particular value to readers who wish to use semiotics as an approach to textual analysis and the analysis of cultural practices. However, even within the cultural domain, semiotics is far more than a method of textual analysis. For instance, it involves the philosophical exploration of issues of representation and reality, in relation to which I should declare a social constructionist bias. Social constructionism does not entail denying the existence of external reality but it does assume that our sign systems (language and other media) play a major part in 'the social construction of reality' (or at least 'the construction of social reality') and that realities cannot be separated from the sign systems in which they are experienced. It is a fundamental principle of semiotic theory that all human experience is mediated by signs. It has been suggested that 'the basic tenet of semiotics . . . is anti-realist'

(Bal and Bryson 1991, 242). However, it would be more appropriate to suggest that the semiotic principle of mediatedness represents a challenge to 'naïve realism' (as well as to pure idealism, since sign systems depend on shared frames of reference).

To shorten unwieldy referencing, when referring to Saussure's *Cours de linguistique générale*, I have adopted Holdcroft's convention (1991): in references to *CLG*, the first page reference is to the French edition (1995); the second reference is to Baskin's translation (2011). If you use Harris's 1983 translation note he translates *signifiant* as 'signal' and *signifié* as 'signification'. Citations from Peirce's *Collected Papers* (1931–58) follow the standard practice of listing the volume number and section number thus: (CP 2.227). Wherever I include quotations within the current text, it may be assumed that any form of typographic emphasis is that of the original author except where otherwise indicated.

Since the book has been adopted as a textbook in university courses, at the request of classroom users this new edition includes suggestions for review and related reading at the end of each chapter. The independent scholar may of course ignore this pedagogical apparatus. The early hypertext version from which this text originally emerged is still available online, currently at: http://visual-memory.co. uk/daniel/Documents/S4B/. A printed Spanish version of the online text, translated by Vanessa Hogan Vega and Iván Rodrigo Mendizábal, was published by Ediciones Abya-Yala (Quito) in 1998. There are currently two online translations, archived here: Greek (Maria Constantopoulou)

http://visual-memory.co.uk/daniel/Documents/S4B/greek/

and Japanese (Masaya Tanuma)

http://visual-memory.co.uk/daniel/Documents/S4B/japanese/.

Since the previous edition, a number of print translations have been published, including the Korean translation of the first edition by Inkyu Kang (Seoul: Somyong Publishing, 2006) and various translations of the second edition: Arabic by Talal Wehbe (Beirut: Arab

Organization for Translation, 2008), Farsi by Medhi Parsa (Tehran: Soureh Mehr, 2010), Polish by Catherine Hallett (Warsaw: Oficyna Wydawnicza Volumen, 2012) and Spanish by Jorge Gómez Rendón (Quito: Ediciones Abya-Yala, 2014). A Chinese translation by Song Li and Ping Liu was completed in 2014 but has not yet been published. A new Spanish translation is currently in progress with Editorial Trillas in Mexico. If there is a demand for translations into other languages, please approach my British publishers.

ACKNOWLEDGEMENTS

The original online text might not have found its way into print if it were not for the unsolicited encouragement to publish that I received from the philosopher Anthony C. Grayling, to whom I am particularly grateful. For the previous editions, thanks go to Winfried Nöth, David Glen Mick, Jo B. Paoletti, Martin Ryder, Bob Morris Jones, Marilyn Martin-Jones, Maria Constantopoulou, Juan A. Prieto-Pablos, Ernest W. B. Hess-Lüttich, Ed McDonald, Guy Cook, Rod Munday, Osama Ammar, and Tommi Turunen. For the current edition my thanks go to Rod Munday, Ioana Maria Toader, and Rhys Thomas Fowler, for reviewing drafts and offering invaluable feedback, and in particular to Ed McDonald for his extraordinary endurance in the irksome and interminable task of locating lapses. I would also like to thank all of those who urged me to agree to undertake this new edition, including John Hartley, Arthur Asa Berger, Ernest Mathijs, Jim Slevin, Jennifer Slack, and Ian Weber. Gregory Eiselein provided useful comments on the end-of-chapter study suggestions and Torkild Thellefsen kindly checked the list of online links for significant omissions. None of these kind people can be held responsible for any of my authorial decisions.

The image from the plaque on Pioneer 10 shown in Figure 6.1 was produced by the Pioneer Project at NASA Ames Research Center and obtained from NASA's National Space Science Data Center with the kind assistance of John F. Cooper. Figure 3.6 is from an article in *Modern Language Notes* by Victor Larrucia (1975), and is reproduced here under the 'fair use' provisions of US copyright law with the approval of the publisher, the Johns Hopkins University Press.

The publisher and author of this book have made every effort to trace copyright holders and to obtain permission to publish extracts. Any omissions brought to our attention will be remedied in future editions.

INTRODUCTION

If you go into a bookshop and ask an assistant where to find a book on semiotics, you are likely to meet with a blank look. Even worse, you might be asked to define what semiotics is – which would be a bit tricky if you were looking for a beginner's guide. It's worse still if you do know a bit about semiotics, because it can be hard to offer a simple definition that is of much use in the bookshop. If you've ever been in such a situation, you'll probably agree that it's wise not to ask. Semiotics could be anywhere. The shortest definition is that it is *the study of signs*. But that doesn't leave enquirers much wiser. 'What do you mean by a sign?' people usually ask next. The kinds of signs that are likely to spring immediately to mind are those that we routinely refer to as 'signs' in everyday life, such as road signs, pub signs, and star signs. If you were to agree with them that semiotics can include the study of all these and more, people will probably assume that semiotics is about 'visual signs'. You would confirm their hunch if you said that signs can also be drawings, paintings and photographs, and by now they'd be keen to direct you to the art and photography sections. But if you are thick-skinned and tell them that it also includes words, sounds, and 'body language', they may reasonably wonder what all these things have in common and how anyone could possibly study such disparate phenomena. If you get this far, they've probably already 'read the signs' which suggest that you are either eccentric or insane and communication may have ceased.

DEFINITIONS

Beyond the most basic definition as 'the study of signs', there is considerable variation among leading semioticians as to the scope of semiotics. One of the broadest definitions is that of the late Italian semiotician Umberto Eco (1932–2016), who states that 'semiotics is concerned with everything that can be taken as a sign' (1976, 7). A sign is traditionally defined as 'something which stands for something else' (in the medieval formula, *aliquid stat pro aliquo*). All meaningful phenomena (including words and images) are signs. To interpret something is to treat it as a sign. All experience is mediated by signs, and communication depends on them. Semioticians study how meanings are made and how reality is represented (and indeed constructed) through signs and sign systems.

Theories of signs (or 'symbols') appear throughout the history of philosophy from ancient times onwards. The study of signs as medical symptoms originated with Hippocrates (460–377 BCE) and was developed by Galen (*c.*129–200 CE). Plato's *Cratylus* (*c.*360 BCE) featured a famous dialogue on the conventionality of words and the introductory chapter of Aristotle's *On Interpretation* (*c.*350 BCE) proved to be an influential contribution to the theory of signs. The Stoics (*c.*300 BCE–200 CE) are often considered to have produced the first semiotic theory (Bouissac 1998, 568). However, a general theory of signs (both natural and cultural) is commonly traced back to the medieval theologian and philosopher Augustine of Hippo (354–430 CE), who is consequently claimed by some to be the founder of semiotics.

The two primary traditions in contemporary semiotics stem respectively from the Swiss linguist Ferdinand de Saussure (1857–1913) and the American philosopher Charles Sanders Peirce (pronounced 'purse') (1839–1914). They are widely regarded as the co-founders of what is now generally known as *semiotics* – despite the fact that neither of them actually wrote a book on the subject. The first edition of Saussure's *Course in General Linguistics*, published posthumously in 1916, contains the declaration that he could envisage, and staked a claim for, 'a science that studies the life of signs within society'), which he called *semiology*, from the Greek *sēmeîon*, 'sign' (*CLG* 33; 16). His use of the term *sémiologie* dates originally from a manuscript of 1894. Although Saussure was a linguist, he saw linguistics as a branch of the 'general science' of semiology, which was in turn an offshoot of (social) psychology. Across the Atlantic, to the philosopher Charles Peirce the field of study which he calls 'semeiotic' (or 'semiotic') is the 'formal doctrine of signs', which is closely related to logic (2.227). Working quite independently from Saussure, Peirce borrowed his term from the British philosopher John Locke (1632–1704). Saussure's term 'semiology' is sometimes used to refer to the Saussurean tradition, while the term 'semiotics' sometimes refers to the Peircean tradition. However, nowadays the term 'semiotics' is widely used as an umbrella term to embrace the whole field (Nöth 1990, 14). We will outline and discuss both the Saussurean and Peircean models of the sign in the next chapter.

Some commentators adopt a definition of semiotics by Charles W. Morris (1901–79) as 'the science of signs' (1938, 1–2). The term 'science' (used also by Saussure) is misleading. Semiotics is perhaps best thought of as a way of looking at the production of meaning from a particular critical perspective. So far, it involves no widely agreed theoretical assumptions, models, or empirical methodologies. It has tended to be largely theoretical, many of its theorists seeking to establish its scope and general principles. Peirce and Saussure, for instance, were both concerned with the fundamental definition of the sign. Peirce developed logical taxonomies of types of signs. Many subsequent semioticians have sought to identify and categorize the 'codes' or conventions according to which signs are organized.

Semiotics is still not widely institutionalized as an academic discipline (although it does have its own associations, conferences, and journals, and it exists as a department in a growing number of universities). Although there are some self-styled semioticians, those involved in semiotics include linguists, philosophers, psychologists, sociologists, anthropologists, literary, aesthetic and media theorists, psychoanalysts, marketing researchers, and educationalists. Indeed, the impact of semiotics within existing disciplines could be argued to be its greatest contribution to the advancement of knowledge.

RELATION TO PHILOSOPHY AND LINGUISTICS

As the study of signification, semiotics is intrinsically interdisciplinary. It has strong disciplinary ties to both philosophy and linguistics, although such links typically feature more prominently in the semiotic literature than in that of the long-established disciplines of philosophy or linguistics (as in their subject dictionaries and encyclopedias). The theory of signs is mentioned most often in the subdisciplines of logic and theoretical linguistics. The first explicit reference to semiotics, 'the doctrine of signs', as a branch of philosophy, appeared in John Locke's *Essay Concerning Human Understanding* (1690, Book III, ch. xxi, §4), where it was identified with logic. Peirce followed Locke in seeing 'the doctrine of signs' as 'another name for' logic (CP 2.227). However, a broader link between semiotics and philosophy is not with a specific primary branch of philosophy (such as logic, epistemology, or metaphysics) but with a domain of philosophical inquiry, which lies within the scope of more than one of its branches – namely the *philosophy of language* (Eco 1984). This domain, which is also a philosophical sub-discipline in its own right, is concerned primarily with meaning and reference, and especially with relations between language, thought, and the world. From a philosophical perspective, semiotics (as 'the general theory of signs') can be seen as part of the philosophy of language (which can include the study of other symbolic systems); this is loosely related to the study of other forms of abstract structure and tools of thought such as logic (Honderich 1995, 928, 937). However, from a semiotic perspective, it has been argued that the territory of the philosophy of language forms only part of theoretical semiotics, which concerns itself with all kinds of signs and sign systems, whether or not they are linguistic (Pelc 1994, 714), and which has three branches: semantics (the meanings of signs), syntax (the relations between signs), and pragmatics (the use of signs) (Morris 1946, 217–19). Semiotics is also linked to the philosophical domain of *aesthetics*, or the philosophy of art, primarily via shared concerns with issues of sign relations and systems of representation: such as in the work of the American philosopher Nelson Goodman (1906–98), in whose 'theory of symbols' this domain is related to epistemology and metaphysics (1968). Philosophical issues in semiotic theory will be explored at length in Chapter 2 and they will surface throughout in relation to issues of representation and 'the social construction of reality' through the mediation of signs and sign systems.

This book focuses primarily on structuralist semiotics (and its poststructuralist critiques). Linguistic structuralism derived primarily from Ferdinand de Saussure, Louis Hjelmslev (1899–1966), and Roman Jakobson (1896–1982), and it was linguistic structuralism which provided the point of departure for the structuralists and poststructuralists who followed them – including Claude Lévi-Strauss (1908–2009) in anthropology, Roland Barthes (1915–80) in literary criticism and cultural analysis, Algirdas Greimas (1917–92) in literary theory, Jacques Lacan (1901–81) and Julia Kristeva (b. 1941) in psychoanalysis, Louis Althusser (1918–90) in Marxist political theory, Michel Foucault (1926–84) in the history of ideas, and Jacques Derrida (1930–2004) in philosophy, clearly representing a range of disciplines in the humanities and social sciences (see also Figure 7.1). Saussure's theories constituted a starting point for the development of various structuralist methodologies for analysing texts and social practices, but Saussure refers to language as a 'system', not a 'structure', and it was Jakobson (1990, 6) who first coined the term 'structuralism' in 1929.

Structuralism is an analytical method that involves the application of a linguistic model to a much wider range of social phenomena. This is the primary basis of a link between semiotics and the social sciences (especially anthropology). Jakobson (1968a, 703) writes that 'Language is . . . a purely semiotic system . . . The study of signs, however, . . . must take into consideration also applied semiotic structures, as for instance, architecture, dress, or cuisine . . . Any edifice is simultaneously some sort of refuge and a certain kind of message. Similarly, any garment responds to definitely utilitarian requirements and at the same time exhibits various semiotic properties'. For Jakobson (ibid., 698), semiotics 'deals with those general principles which underlie the structure of all signs whatever'. Structuralists search for 'deep structures' underlying the 'surface features' of sign systems: Claude Lévi-Strauss in myth, kinship rules and totemism; Jacques Lacan in the unconscious; Roland Barthes and Algirdas Greimas in the 'grammar' of narrative. Julia Kristeva (1973, 1249) declares that 'what semiotics has discovered . . . is that the *law* governing or, if one prefers, the *major constraint* affecting any social practice lies in the fact that it signifies; i.e. that it is articulated *like* a language'.

Saussure argues that although language is only one particular semiological system, it is the best example of a system based on the arbitrariness of the sign. In this sense, linguistics can be seen as 'le patron général' (the master-pattern or model) for such systems (*CLG* 101; 68). Nevertheless, he subordinates linguistics to semiology as a discipline. Paul Thibault, a social semiotician, insists that to suggest that Saussure is claiming that the language system 'is the model for all other sign systems' (1997, 21) is a common misinterpretation that is then seen as limiting the semiotic scope of the Saussurean model (e.g. Sebeok 1977, 182). Structuralist semiotics has subsequently drawn heavily on linguistic concepts, partly because of Saussure's influence, and also because linguistics is a more established discipline than the study of other sign systems. Roman Jakobson (1970, 455) insists that 'language is the central and most important among all human semiotic systems'. The French linguist and semiotician Émile Benveniste (1902–76) observes that 'language is the interpreting system of all other systems, linguistic and non-linguistic' (1969, 239), while Claude Lévi-Strauss (1972, 48) notes that 'language is the semiotic system *par excellence*; it cannot but signify, and exists only through signification'.

As we have noted, Saussure saw linguistics as a branch of 'semiology', subject to any general laws that might be discovered by the new science that he envisaged. He consequently saw it as important to identify what language has in common with all other 'systems of expression', such as rites and customs (*CLG* 35, 101; 16–17, 68). Like Saussure, the linguist and semiotician Roman Jakobson was in no doubt that 'language is a *system of signs*, and linguistics is part and parcel of the science of signs or semiotics' (1949a, 50). However, even if we theoretically locate linguistics within semiotics, it is difficult to avoid adopting a linguistic model in exploring other sign systems. Thus Roland Barthes (1967b, xi) declares that 'perhaps we must invert Saussure's formulation and assert that semiology is a branch of linguistics'. The American linguist Leonard Bloomfield (1939, 55) asserts that 'linguistics is the chief contributor to semiotics', and Jakobson (1963d, 289) defines semiotics as 'the general science of signs which has as its basic discipline linguistics, the science of verbal signs'.

The ascendency of structuralism can be dated from the publication of Lévi-Strauss's *Tristes Tropique* in 1955 (Jameson 1972, ix). Structuralist methods have been very widely employed in the semiotic analysis of many cultural phenomena. This approach has had considerable influence in contemporary cultural studies, where films, television and radio programmes, advertising posters, and so on are commonly referred to as 'texts' that require 'reading'. It is a common pedagogical strategy to undermine common sense assumptions about what features such media may have in common with a symbolic system like language rather than with what we treat as reality in the everyday world. However, there is a danger of overextending the linguistic metaphor and failing to address the affordances of different semiotic systems. Most contemporary semioticians would argue that a linguistic model can at best only ever form part of a general theory of signification that reaches beyond intentional communication. Useful as it may be in the cultural domain, semiotics cannot be limited to such a model.

WHY STUDY SEMIOTICS?

While Saussure may be hailed as the founder of the form of semiotics known as semiology, semiotics has become increasingly less Saussurean since the late 1960s. The current account takes us beyond early semiological forms, exploring relevant critiques and subsequent developments. But first we need to ask, 'Why should we study semiotics?' This is a pressing question in part because the writings of semioticians have a reputation for being dense with jargon: one critic wittily remarks that 'semiotics tells us things we already know in a language we will never understand' (Paddy Whannel, cited in Seiter 1992, 31).

The semiotic establishment may initially seem to be a very exclusive club but its concerns are not confined to members. Studying semiotics can make us less likely to take reality for granted as something which is wholly independent of interpretive systems. It can assist us to become more aware of the mediating role of signs and of the roles played by ourselves and others in constructing social realities. The technical concept of 'mediation' (from the medieval Latin *mediare*, 'to be in the middle') is central in semiotics and deserves a brief explanation at the outset. Broadly, it refers to any framework or process which 'intervenes' in our perception of the external world and hence contributes to the construction of our conceptual and experiential worlds. For instance, opening a door requires us to approach it with 'preconceptions': we need to recognize that it belongs to the linguistic category of 'doors' (based on what these are for and how they work). It also requires us to relate it to the social system, for instance with reference to whether you own it, whether you are entitled to open it, and so on. Such prior knowledge forms part of a complex interpretive framework that 'mediates' the experience and routinely guides our expectations and behaviour (usually beyond our conscious awareness). If a door is slammed in your face you may care to reflect that we are never dealing with a purely physical phenomenon: someone was sending you a message.

Becoming aware of the processes of mediation involved in constructing the realities of everyday life is both inherently fascinating and intellectually empowering. Exploring semiotic perspectives helps us to realize that information or meaning is not 'contained' in the world, or in books, computers, or other media. Meaning is not 'transmitted' to us – we actively interpret texts and the world according to a complex interplay of frames of reference. Semiotics helps us to take apart what is taken for granted, making our interpretive systems more explicit. In defining realities, sign systems serve ideological functions. Deconstructing and contesting the realities they represent can reveal whose realities are privileged and whose are suppressed. Such a study involves investigating the construction and maintenance of reality by particular social groups. To decline the study of signs is to leave to others the control of the world of meanings that we inhabit.

MODELS OF THE SIGN

As a species we seem to be driven by a desire to make meanings: above all, we are surely *Homo significans* – meaning-makers. We cannot avoid interpreting things, and, in doing so, we treat them as 'signs'. Signs take the form of words, images, sounds, odours, flavours, actions, events, objects, and so on, but these have no intrinsic meaning and become signs only when we invest them with meaning. 'Nothing is a sign unless it is interpreted as a sign', declares Peirce (CP 2.308). Anything can be a sign as long as someone interprets it as 'signifying' something. It is the meaningful use of signs that is at the heart of the concerns of semiotics.

References to the 'meaning' of something have two very different senses which are important for any understanding of signs. These two dimensions (or relations) of meaning are conceptual meaning ('sense' or designation) and referential meaning ('reference' or denotation). In this context, the *sense* is a specific meaning in the mind (a concept) and the *reference* is something in the outside world (an *object* or *referent*). Dictionaries define the various linguistic senses of individual words (many of which have no reference to things to which we can point in the world). Referents can include things or people (real or imaginary) but also more abstract categories within a particular topical domain (a 'universe of discourse'). If we ask what is meant by the word 'semiotician', its *sense* is 'someone who studies signs' (as distinct from say, 'someone who paints signs'), while its *reference* could be to any of its practitioners in the world. If someone asks what you do and you foolishly reply 'I am a semiotician', you have provided a reference but they will probably be none the wiser; the next thing they will expect is some sense. In the broadest usage, a sign is a combination of the form it takes (technically the 'sign vehicle', such as a word or image) and what it is interpreted as meaning (see Figure 1.1).

In the medieval formula already mentioned, *aliquid stat pro aliquo*, *aliquid* is whatever 'stands for' (*stat pro*) something else and *aliquo* is what it stands for. This is a 'dyadic' model, its two 'relata' or correlates being a sign vehicle and a referent. Triadic models account for the dimensions of sense as well as reference, the three relations being commonly referred to as sign–object, sign–mind, and object–mind (usage which can lead to confusion of the sign as a whole with the part which is simply its vehicle). Even ostensibly dyadic models are implicitly triadic insofar as they presuppose an interpreter. We begin our exploration of the most influential contemporary models with one which involves a radical challenge to the traditional 'standing for' relation or 'representational' model.

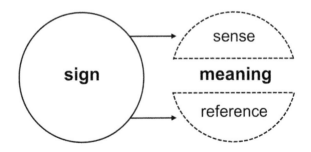

FIGURE 1.1 Sense and reference

Source: © 2016 Daniel Chandler

THE SAUSSUREAN MODEL

For the Swiss linguist Ferdinand de Saussure, who is regarded as the founder of modern linguistics, language is a *system* of signs, and linguistic signs make sense only as part of a language's sign system. Within such a system, a sign has two aspects: a *signifiant* (usually rendered in English as a 'signifier') and a *signifié* (a 'signified') (see Figure 1.2). Although in contemporary discourse the term *signified* is often used to refer generally to 'meaning', and in loose usage may involve reference, Saussure makes it very clear that he is *not* dealing with the dimension of reference: 'The linguistic sign unites, not a thing and a name, but a concept and an acoustic image' (*CLG* 98; 66). Thus, for Saussure, words do not 'stand for' things, and his signifier and signified are *not* to be understood dualistically as 'sign' (vehicle) and 'referent' (a common misinterpretation).

Within the Saussurean linguistic model, the *sign* is the unified whole that results from the association of a sound with a concept (ibid. 99; 67). This is a relationship in which the two layers are as inseparable as the two sides of a piece of paper (ibid. 157; 113). A linguistic sign could not consist of sound without sense or of sense without sound (ibid. 144; 102–3). Although the signifier and the signified can be distinguished for analytical purposes, Saussure defines them as wholly interdependent, neither pre-existing the other (a concept which later proved challenging for his 'deconstructionist' critics, as

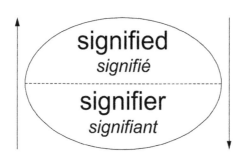

FIGURE 1.2 Saussure's dyadic model of the sign

Source: Adapted from Saussure 1916/1995, 158

we shall see). The two arrows in the diagram represent their interaction. Roland Barthes comments that 'signification can be conceived as a process; it is the act which binds the signifier and the signified, an act whose product is the sign' (1964, 48).

Any individual sign is a recognizable combination of a signifier with a particular signified. For instance, the spoken word 'duck' is a *sign* consisting of:

- a *signifier*: a mental representation of a perceptible pattern of sound, and
- a *signified*: the relational concept of a species of waterbird – not a pictorial 'mental image' but a linguistic 'value' (a notion to be discussed shortly).

Both the signifier and the signified are purely psychological, united in the mind by an associative link. Although the 'acoustic image' is less abstract than the concept, it is 'not the material sound, a purely physical thing' but the impression made on our senses or its 'psychological imprint' (*CLG* 98; 65–6). For Saussure, neither of these are material 'things'. Both elements consist of non-material *form* rather than substance. As we shall see, this immateriality derives from Saussure's radical conception of language as a *system* of signs (a network of pairings of sounds with concepts). Note that in post-Saussurean semiotics (originally in Hjelmslev), the *signifier* is commonly interpreted as the material (or physical) form of the sign – it is something which can be seen, heard, touched, smelled, or tasted – as with Roman Jakobson's *signans*, which he describes (more traditionally) as the external and perceptible part of the sign (1963b, 111; 1984, 98).

Saussure was a linguist, and his focus was understandably on linguistic sign systems. As we have noted, he refers specifically to the signifier as an 'acoustic image' (*image acoustique*). In the *Cours* writing is referred to as a separate, secondary, dependent, but comparable sign system (*CLG* 32, 46ff., 165–6; 15, 24ff., 119–20). Within the system of written signs, a signifier such as the written letter 't' signifies a sound in the primary sign system of language (and thus a written word would also signify a sound rather than a concept). Jacques Derrida famously argues that, from this perspective, writing relates to speech as signifier to signified and writing is 'a sign of a sign' (1967a, 43). Most subsequent theorists who have adopted (or adapted) Saussure's model tend to refer to the form of linguistic signs as either spoken or written (e.g. Jakobson 1970, 455–6).

Saussure's model of the linguistic sign as part of the language system (*langue*) is not based on the notion of reference to extra-linguistic reality. The linguistic sign does not 'represent reality'. The language system has no referents. Cultural theorists often refer to this as 'bracketing the referent' (a phenomenological concept), but for Saussure reference is simply not relevant to his objective in describing the language system. As we shall see, for him, meaning is derived from the way each language imposes its relational system on the continuum of thought and not directly from things in the world. This is radically different from traditional models of the sign – in which meaning is tied to representation. Saussure's signified is a *concept* in the mind – not a thing but the notion of a thing. Some may wonder why his model of the sign refers only to a concept and not to a thing (the 'common sense' view). The philosopher Susanne Langer (1957, 60) notes that symbolic signs 'are not proxy for their objects but are *vehicles for the conception of objects* . . . In talking *about* things we have conceptions of them, not the things themselves'. Words normally evoke 'behaviour towards conceptions'. She adds that 'If I say "Napoleon", you do not bow to the conqueror of Europe as though I had introduced him, but merely think of him'.

Thus, for Saussure, linguistic signs are wholly immaterial – although he dislikes referring to them as 'abstractions' (*CLG* 32; 15). The immateriality of the Saussurean sign is a feature that tends to be neglected in many popular commentaries. If the notion seems strange, we need to remind ourselves that words have no value in themselves – that is their value. Saussure notes that it is not the metal in a coin that fixes its value (ibid. 164; 118). Several reasons could be offered for this. For instance, if linguistic signs drew attention to their materiality this would hinder their communicative transparency. Furthermore, being immaterial, language is an extraordinarily economical medium and words are always ready to hand. Nevertheless, a principled argument can be made for the revaluation of the materiality of the sign, as we shall see in due course.

Jacques Derrida criticizes Saussure for his 'psychologism', dismissing the Saussurean model as simply replacing with a mental representation the referent associated with traditional dyadic models of the sign (1981, 22–3) – a wilful misrepresentation of Saussure's radical conception. Of course we have seen that his linguistic sign is psychological. A subject who makes the connection between the signifier and the signified is a notable absence from his formal model of signification (Figure 1.2), but subjects are featured in his 'speech circuit' (Figure 6.2). It is possible to decompose his model into a binary structure with two pairs of terms (signifier–signified, sign–subject) (Figure 1.3), and we may also interpret his ostensibly dyadic model as implicitly triadic (see Langer 1957, 57–8).

However, the Saussurean model is not reducible to a matter of individual psychology. Saussure sees linguistics as closely related to social psychology (*CLG* 33; 6). Language has a 'social side' as well as an 'individual side' (ibid. 24; 8). 'Speaking is an individual act', but 'language is not a function of the speaker' (ibid. 30; 14). It is a

FIGURE 1.3 Signification and the subject

Source: © 2016 Daniel Chandler

social institution which is 'independent of the individual' (ibid. 37; 18). The language system is reflected as a cognitive system in the minds of individuals but it exists in its entirety only in the community of speakers (ibid. 30; 14). The linguistic sign system is socially grounded and functions as an *intersubjective* mediator between individuals in society. As Thibault puts it, 'Meaning is always the *social* product of the language system' (1997, 40).

THE RELATIONAL SYSTEM

For Saussure, meaning is dependent on *relations* within the language *system*. Linguistic signs make no sense as isolated elements but only as part of an abstract, transindividual system (*CLG* 179; 130). Thibault (1997) observes that signifier–signified sign relations are dependent on higher-order systemic relations such as rules or conventions. Saussure prioritizes the *system* rather than the *sign*. The relational system allows scope for signifier–signified relations to change (*CLG* 113; 78). None of this is obvious from the signifier–signified model of a single sign illustrated in the *Cours* (Figure 1.2; cf. Figure 1.5). In treating languages as sign systems, Saussure's approach is a radical departure from linguistic tradition. He is a relational thinker. His conception of meaning is purely *systemic* and *relational* rather than *referential*: primacy is given to relationships rather than to things (the meaning of signs is seen as lying in their systematic relation to each other rather than deriving from any inherent features of sign vehicles or any reference to material things). Language is a system of signs within which 'everything is based on relations' (ibid. 170; 122). No sign makes sense on its own but only in relation to other signs. Both signifier and signified are purely relational entities, correlated by the language system (ibid. 163; 117–18). They are nodes within a network. Each language has its own relational structure. This radical notion is counterintuitive and difficult to understand since, in the common-sense view, words seem to refer directly to things in the world – as if reality were pre-packaged in tidy boxes to which each language simply attaches labels (see Chapter 2).

Saussure rejects any one-to-one correspondence between language and external reality. Common sense suggests that the existence of things in the world precedes our apparently simple application of 'labels' to them. Linguistic categories are not a consequence of some predefined structure in the world. There are no natural concepts or categories that are simply reflected in language; to think otherwise has been described as 'a naïve belief in the divinity of one's own language' (Haas 1962, 222–3). Saussure notes that if words stood for pre-existing concepts they would all have exact equivalents in meaning in every language, which of course is not the case (*CLG* 161; 116). Reality is divided up into arbitrary categories by every language and the conceptual world with which each of us is familiar could have been divided up very differently. No two languages categorize reality in the same way. As John Passmore (1985, 24) puts it, 'Languages differ by differentiating differently'.

Saussure refers to *sound* and *thought* as two distinct but correlated planes (see Figure 1.4). Later, the Danish linguist Louis Hjelmslev (1961, 59) refers to these as the 'expression plane' and the 'content plane'. Language, we are told in the *Cours*, 'can . . . be pictured in its totality . . . as a series of contiguous subdivisions marked off on both the indefinite plane of jumbled ideas (A), and the equally vague plane of sounds (B)' (*CLG* 155–6; 112). The arbitrary division of the

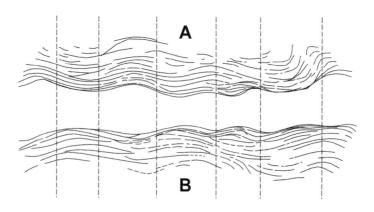

FIGURE 1.4 Planes of thought and sound

Source: Based on Saussure 1916/1995, 156

two continua into signs is represented by the dotted lines while the wavy, non-parallel edges of the two 'amorphous' masses suggest the lack of any natural fit between them (of which we are sometimes aware, as in where 'there are no words . . .'). There is no isomorphic mapping or tidy correlation between the world of words and the world of things. The structure of language is not a reflection of anything external to it. The relationship between words does not reflect the relationship between things. If reality is perceived as a seamless continuum, which is how Saussure sees the initially undifferentiated realms of both thought and sound, there is nothing natural about the way language fragments it. Where, for example, does a 'corner' end?

The American literary theorist Fredric Jameson suggests that:

> It is not so much the individual word or sentence that 'stands for' or 'reflects' the individual object or event in the real world, but rather that the entire system of signs, the entire field of the *langue*, lies parallel to reality itself; that it is the totality of systematic language, in other words, which is analogous to whatever organized structures exist in the world of reality, and that our understanding proceeds from one whole or Gestalt to the other, rather than on a one-to-one basis.
>
> (Jameson 1972, 32–3)

Saussure prefers the term *signifié* ('signified') to 'concept', which lacks relational connotations (*CLG* 99; 67). It cannot be equated with the related term 'sense' either (Holdcroft 1991, 51, 108, 120). A language system is nothing like a dictionary. It is a distinctively Saussurean notion that the meaning of a linguistic sign is dependent on its 'value' (*valeur*), which functions as a systemic constraint on its potential meaning. Saussure uses an analogy with the game of chess, noting that the value of each piece depends on its position on the chessboard (*CLG* 125–6; 88). Values are the holistic products of a system and do not exist independently of it (Holdcroft 1991, 130). The value of any sign (and of signifiers and signifieds) depends not on the sign itself but on reciprocal relations with other signs within the system as a whole (*CLG* 157–9, 162; 113–15, 117; see Figure 1.5). *Valeur* is a principle of internal organization within the language system.

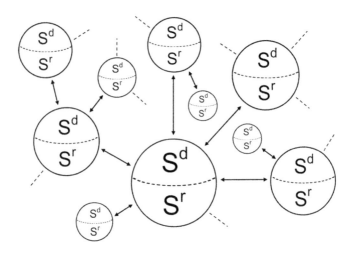

FIGURE 1.5 The relations between signs

Source: © 2016 Daniel Chandler

This is a radical notion. The linguistic value of a word is determined by systemic contrasts with related words. This is what is 'lost
in translation'. Saussure notes that the French word *mouton* has the
same sense as the English word *sheep* but it does not have the same
value because in English there is a distinction between *sheep* (the
animals) and *mutton* (the butchered meat) whereas in French there is
no such distinction (ibid. 160; 115–16). Linguistic values thus arise
from within the linguistic system (which is a system of values).
Saussure's principle of systemic values ensures that no linguistic sign
can be considered in isolation from the system to which it belongs
(ibid., 124; 87). A sign has no 'absolute' value independent of this
internal context – a notion which undermines the traditional model
of language as representation (based on the 'standing for' relation).
Linguistic values are relative (which is why the relation between
sound and concept is arbitrary). Linguistic values are established by
social usage and general agreement in the community (ibid., 157; 113).
Valeur is abstracted from specific instances of use but it serves as a
meaning-making resource which both enables and constrains such acts.

Significance thus lies not in individual signs, but in relational patterns of likeness and contrast within a sign system. Saussure's relational conception of meaning is specifically *differential*: he emphasizes the differences between signs. 'In language there are only differences' (ibid. 166; 120). This 'principle of difference' is generally regarded as one of Saussure's most distinctive contributions to the theory of signs. Language for him is a system of functional differences and oppositions. 'In language, as in any semiological system, whatever distinguishes one sign from the others constitutes it' (ibid. 168; 121). It has been noted that 'a one-term language is an impossibility because its single term could be applied to everything and differentiate nothing; it requires at least one other term to give it definition' (Sturrock 1979, 10).

Marketing furnishes a good example of this notion of differential relations, since what matters in 'positioning' a product in the market and in relation to its rivals is *not* the relationship of advertising signs to real-world referents, but the differentiation of each sign from the others to which it is related (Leymore 1975, Oswald 2012). The logos, slogans, colours, fonts, packaging, campaigns, and individual advertisements of rival brands need to be understood within a system of relationships. These are often represented in brand positioning grids with key dimensions (such as low price–high price, or traditional–modern, against high quality–low quality) on the horizontal and vertical axes, with the perceived positions of the product and its rivals mapped onto its quadrants (see Figure 1.6).

Saussure's concept of the relational identity of signs is at the heart of subsequent structuralist theory. He emphasizes in particular negative, oppositional differences between signs. They are defined not by their content but by relations of contrast with other terms within the system. They are *what the others are not* (*CLG* 162; 117). Saussure adds that the entire mechanism of language is based on phonic and conceptual differences and oppositions (ibid. 165, 167; 119, 121). Each language system is a unique network of contrastive sound–concept pairs. David Holdcroft argues that such a system must be dependent on a principle of relevance (even oppositions have something in common), since otherwise we would be 'adrift in a sea of differences' (1991, 126).

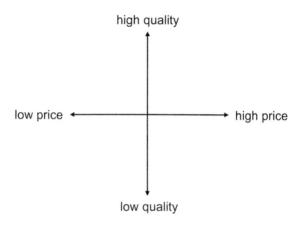

FIGURE 1.6 A brand-positioning grid

This system of differences, in which meaning depends on contrasts, is not limited to verbal language. Colours are frequently used in this way in particular codes and contexts. The British anthropologist Edmund Leach (1910–89) emphasizes that 'it is the *set* of contrasts that invites interpretation not the individual colour usage' (1976, 58–9). The most elementary system represents a contrastive relationship between two different signs. In such binary sets, where one signifier is used the other is an absent presence: meaning depends on what isn't there. In traffic control, red signifies 'stop' only as part of a relational system in which green is taken to signify 'go'. The same colours are used on boats for 'port' and 'starboard', on football substitution boards for 'out' and 'in', and on electrical devices for 'off' and 'on'. Black and white are frequently paired to represent some strong contrast (such as life–death), but what they signify varies greatly by cultural context. Pink and blue have been used in complementary (but unstable) relations in modern times to signify female and male, or feminine and masculine (Paoletti 2012). Such colours carry cultural meanings only as part of a conventional system of differential relations. Because of this system of contrasts, in countries with red, white, and blue national flags, when one political party adopts the colour red, it feels natural for an opposing party to adopt the colour blue; the arbitrary nature of such associations was illustrated in 2000 in the USA when, despite the long and widespread association of red with the political left, the television news networks began to reverse the traditional associations in their election maps, associating blue with the Democrats and red with the Republicans (Bensen 2004). Just as with black and white, such linkages are in principle interchangeable.

ARBITRARINESS

Traditionally, in the theory of signs (before and after Saussure), the term 'arbitrary' refers to sign–object relations, where it is conventionally contrasted with 'natural' relations. In this context, the issue is whether a sign vehicle has some inherent connection to a referent (as with a shadow) or whether the connection is purely conventional (as with the word *shadow*). In Plato's dialogue *Cratylus*, set in the fifth century BCE, the issue of 'the correctness of names' is debated. This debate produced the first known formulation of an opposition between resemblance and conventionality as the basis of signs. Although Cratylus defends the notion of a natural relationship between words and what they represent, Hermogenes declares that 'no one is able to persuade me that the correctness of names is determined by anything besides convention and agreement . . . No name belongs to a particular thing by nature' (Plato 1998, 2). While Socrates rejects the absolute arbitrariness of language proposed by Hermogenes, he does acknowledge that convention plays a part in determining meaning. In his work *On Interpretation*, Aristotle (2004, 2) went further, asserting that there can be no natural connection between the sounds of a language and the things signified. 'By a noun [or name] we mean a sound significant by convention . . . The limitation "by convention" was introduced because nothing is by nature a noun or name – it is only so when it becomes a symbol'. The issue even enters into everyday discourse via Shakespeare: 'That which we call a rose by any other name would smell as sweet' (*Romeo and Juliet* II, ii).

Saussure rejects the common-sense (naïve realist) assumption that there is a natural relationship between words and things. Language is not based on the mimetic representation of independently identifiable 'things'. There is nothing tree-like about the word 'tree'. Even onomato-poeic words (such as words for the sounds made by familiar animals) are more conventional than is often supposed, as is demonstrated by the variability between different languages in their words for the same sounds (*CLG* 101–2; 69). The principle applies as much to writing as it does to speech: there is no inherent connection between any letter and the sound that it denotes (ibid. 165; 119). Counter-intuitively, words do *not* 'refer to', 'correspond to', or 'stand for' things. Saussure's reconceptualization of the traditional notion of the arbitrariness of the linguistic sign is non-referential. His signified is *not* to be identified with a referent (a common misinterpretation). He rejects the whole notion of linguistic 'reference'.

Saussure emphasizes that words are arbitrary signs. However, the *Cours* does not relate the principle of arbitrariness to the relationship between language and an external world. Saussure's radical recon-ceptualization of arbitrariness does not relate to sign–object relations but to there being no intrinsic, direct, or self-evident relationship between the signifier and the signified (the link between which is arbitrary). The relation between them is an internal link within the linguistic system. For Saussure, the arbitrariness of the sign (*l'arbitraire du signe*) in this sense is the 'first principle' of language (ibid. 100ff.; 67ff). The connections between words and ideas have no natural basis. The linguistic sign is 'unmotivated' (ibid. 101–2; 69). This point had been anticipated by John Locke. Writing in 1690, Locke noted that signification works 'not by any natural connexion that there is between particular articulate sounds and certain ideas . . . but by a voluntary imposition whereby such a word is made arbitrarily the mark of such an idea' (1690, Book III, ch. x, §5). Nothing prevents any idea from being associated with any sequence of sounds whatsoever; such associations are completely arbitrary (*CLG* 110, 157; 76, 113). In language, the form of the signifier is not determined by what it signifies. No specific signifier is naturally more suited to a signified than any other signifier; in principle any signifier could represent any signified.

The Saussurean system is thus based on *signification* rather than *reference*. Many critics have found this crucial part of Saussure's theory difficult if not impossible to accept (or even to understand). In their book *The Meaning of Meaning*, Charles Ogden (1889–1957) and Ivor Richards (1893–1979) criticize Saussure for 'neglecting entirely the things for which signs stand' (1923, 8), but he did not regard linguistic signs as 'standing for things' at all. Heretically, Benveniste (1939, 44) argues that a referential third term – 'the thing itself, reality' – is an implicit element in Saussure's model (and a necessary one in any model of the sign), and that it is the link between the signifier and its *referent* (rather than its signified concept) which is arbitrary. Saussure's critics are quick to suggest that that reality seeps into his system and that what he called *un rudiment de lien naturel* (the vestige of a natural bond) is detectable within it (*CLG* 101; 68). Lest any be misled by any of Saussure's critics or postmodernist interpreters, let us be clear that Saussure denies the referent any place in his model of the language system but also that this does not involve a denial of the existence of external reality. For instance, he insists that language is a 'social institution' and that it cannot be divorced from 'social reality': it is a 'social fact' that language depends on a *masse parlante* (community of speakers) (ibid. 33, 112; 15, 77). Furthermore, he acknowledges that we cannot conceive of things such as a street or a train outside their material realization (ibid. 151–2; 109). It is understandable that the Saussurean model of the sign is criticized by realists as philosophically idealist (excluding the reality of anything beyond what is created in the mind). However, like most of us, Saussure himself takes the reality of the objective world for granted, though he sees it as unavoidably mediated through languages and their categories. In reading and interpreting Saussure, it is all too easy for the unwary to slip into treating arbitrariness as a matter of reference. After all, how can we assess whether or not the word 'tree' is 'treeish' without reference to some kind of mental representation of a tree, which (however mediated) must surely derive from some experience of trees in the living world? Surely such concepts cannot be wholly divorced from reality? Indeed, in the *Cours* the signified for the word 'tree' is illustrated by its editors with a schematic drawing of a tree (ibid. 99; 67). Nevertheless, if we wish to understand Saussure's conception of the language system in accord with his own intentions, we must attempt to exclude the concept of reference. This demanding task may also assist us to recognize the (counter-intuitive) mediatedness of all experience.

The Saussurean model, with its emphasis on internal structures within a sign system, supports the notion that rather than reflecting reality, language plays a major role in *constructing* it (a contention challenged by naïve realists). Insofar as we live within the realities constructed by language, rather than excluding 'reality', the Saussurean model embodies much of what is real and meaningful to those within a speech community. What is signified is part of the collective consciousness of such a community rather than part of the material world. The ontological arbitrariness that the language system involves becomes invisible to us as we learn to accept it as natural. As the anthropologist Franz Boas notes, to native speakers of a language, none of its classifications appear arbitrary (Jakobson 1943, 483). We shall return to the relationship between language and reality in Chapter 2.

Saussure illustrates the principle of arbitrariness at the lexical level – in relation to individual words as signs. He does not, for instance, argue that syntax is arbitrary. However, he declares that the entire system of language is based on 'the irrational principle' of the arbitrariness of the sign. This provocative declaration is followed immediately by the acknowledgement that this would result in fatal complications if applied without restriction (*CLG* 182; 133). If linguistic signs were to be *totally* arbitrary in every way, language would not be a system and its communicative function would be destroyed. He concedes that there is no language in which nothing is motivated. Saussure admits that language is not completely arbitrary but has a certain logic (ibid. 183, 107; 133, 73). The principle of arbitrariness does not mean that the form of a word is accidental or random, of course. While the sign is not determined *extralinguistically*, it is subject to *intralinguistic* determination. For instance, combinations of sounds must conform with existing patterns within the language in question. Furthermore, we can recognize that a compound noun such as 'screwdriver' is not wholly arbitrary since it is a meaningful combination of two existing linguistic signs. Saussure introduces a distinction between *degrees* of arbitrariness. While repeating that the linguistic sign is fundamentally arbitrary, he acknowledges that (even within language) not all signs are 'radically arbitrary' (unmotivated) and that the sign may be 'relatively motivated' (ibid. 180–1; 131). Here, then, Saussure modifies his stance somewhat and accepts that signs may be *relatively arbitrary* (a concept to which we will return shortly). Social semioticians have subsequently argued that we should not underestimate the situational motivation of signs in their social context of use.

It should be noted that, while the relationships between signifiers and their signifieds are *ontologically* arbitrary (philosophically, it would not make any difference to the status of these entities in 'the order of things' if what we call 'black' had always been called 'white' and vice versa), this is not to suggest that signifying systems are *socially* or *historically* arbitrary. Natural languages are not, of course, arbitrarily established (unlike inventions such as Morse Code). Even in the case of the colours of traffic lights, the original choice of red for 'stop' was not entirely arbitrary, since it already carried relevant associations with danger. The art historian Ernst Gombrich (1909–2001) notes that 'Red, being the colour of flames and blood, offers itself as a metaphor for anything that is strident or violent. It is no accident, therefore, that it was selected as the code sign for "stop" in our traffic code and as a label of revolutionary parties in politics' (1963, 13).

After the sign has come into historical existence, it cannot be arbitrarily changed. As part of its social use within a sign system, every sign acquires a history and connotations of its own which are familiar to members of the sign-users' culture. Saussure remarks that although the signifier appears to be freely chosen, from the point of view of the linguistic community, it is *imposed* – because a language is a legacy of the past, which its users have no choice but to accept. Saussure declares, paradoxically, that it is because the sign is arbitrary that the only law it follows is that of tradition, and because it is based on tradition, it is arbitrary (*CLG* 104, 108; 71, 74). The arbitrariness principle does *not*, of course mean that an individual can arbitrarily choose any signifier for a given signified. The relation between a signifier and its signified is *not* a matter of individual choice; if it were, then communication would become impossible. Individuals have no power to change a sign in any way once it has become established in the linguistic community (ibid. 101; 69). From the point of view of individual language-users, language is a 'given' – we don't create the system for ourselves.

For Saussure, the arbitrariness of the linguistic sign (the whole ensemble as well as the sign relations between signifier and signified) is related to the dependence of language on cultural convention. Saussure notes that in principle, every means of expression used in society is based on collective behaviour or convention (ibid. 101–2; 68). A word means what it does to us only because we collectively agree to let it do so. As long as there is such an agreement, in principle anything can signify anything. In cultural studies, the Saussurean emphasis on arbitrariness and conventionality has been widely employed to alert us to 'the familiar mistake of assuming that signs which appear natural to those who use them have an intrinsic meaning and require no explanation' (Culler 1975, 5). A valuable function of the Saussurean concepts is to undermine our taken-for-granted, common-sense beliefs in the naturalness of the links between our interpretive systems and the world. Although, of course, we use language to talk about the world, Saussure's radical stance is that the language *system* does not need to refer to extralingual reality.

Saussure felt that the main concern of semiotics should be all systems that are grounded in the arbitrariness of the sign. For him, it is signs that are wholly arbitrary that epitomize 'the semiological process', and of course he sees this as characteristic above all of language (*CLG* 101; 68). The *Cours* does not in fact offer many examples of sign systems other than spoken language and writing, mentioning only the deaf-and-dumb alphabet, social customs, etiquette, religious and other symbolic rites, legal procedures, military signals, and nautical flags (ibid. 33, 35, 101, 107; 16, 17, 68, 73). Saussure is clearly interested in the arbitrariness of signs in general. However, his critics see the Saussurean model as excluding signs that are not as arbitrary, unmotivated, and conventional as words.

THE PEIRCEAN MODEL

Saussure began formulating his model of the sign and of 'semiology' in the early 1890s. Unknown to him, across the Atlantic in the late

1860s, the American pragmatist philosopher and logician Charles Sanders Peirce had already begun to formulate his own model of the sign, of 'semeiotic' (as he called it), and of the taxonomies of signs. In contrast to Saussure's dyadic model of the linguistic sign, Peirce offered a triadic (three-part) model consisting of these functions:

1 The *representamen*: the form that the sign takes – the 'sign vehicle'.
2 An *object*: something to which the sign refers (a referent), or which it represents.
3 An *interpretant*: the effect produced by the sign or the *sense* made of it.

As Price (1969, 92) puts it, ' "Being a sign of" is a three-term relation'. '**A** is not a sign of **B** *per se*, but only to someone – to some conscious being' (ibid.). As in Saussure's model, the sign is an indivisible whole, and it signifies only when interpreted. It is important to be aware that semioticians usually make a distinction between the sign (the whole meaningful ensemble), which as Peirce (1992, vol. 2, 303) notes 'is not a real thing', and its *sign vehicle* – the perceptible form it takes (such as a word or image), which more strictly is a *signifier* in structuralist usage and a *representamen* for Peirceans. However, the term 'sign' is often used loosely, so that this distinction is not always preserved (including here, where it is sometimes a useful philosophical shorthand term, as in generic references to a *sign–object* relation). It is easy to be found guilty of such a slippage, perhaps because we are so used to 'looking beyond' the form that the sign happens to take.

In Peirce's words:

> A sign . . . is something which stands to somebody for something in some respect or capacity. It addresses somebody, that is, creates in the mind of that person an equivalent sign, or perhaps a more developed sign. That sign which it creates I call the *interpretant* of the first sign. The sign stands for something, its *object*. It stands for that object, not in all respects, but in reference to a sort of idea, which I have sometimes called the *ground* of the representamen.
>
> (CP 2.228)

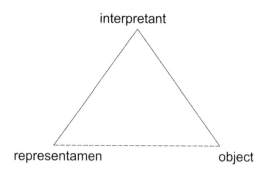

FIGURE 1.7 Peirce's model as a semiotic triangle

Source: Adapted from Ogden and Richards 1923, 11, and Nöth 1990, 89

The 'ground' is the particular context or framework with reference to which the sign is interpreted. We may note the traditional 'standing for' sign–object relation that is radically rejected by Saussure. However, Peirce's model is no less groundbreaking than that of Saussure. For Peirce, the sign is a unity of the thing that does the representing (the representamen), what is represented (the object), and how it is interpreted (the interpretant). To qualify as a sign, all three functions are essential. Peirce did not himself offer a visualization of his model but Figure 1.7 shows the Peircean terms in a conventional *semiotic triangle* (Ogden and Richards 1923, 11; Eco 1976, 59). The broken line at the base of the triangle is intended to indicate that there is not necessarily any direct relationship between the sign vehicle and the referent. Many Peirce scholars prefer to visualize Peirce's model using a tripod or pinwheel shape with a central node (along the lines of Figure 1.8; for a visual precursor, with different relata, see Bühler 1933, 147). Floyd Merrell (1997, 133) argues that the triangular form 'evinces no genuine triadicity, but merely three-way dyadicity'. In other words, the triangular form gives the misleading impression that the model could be broken down into three pairs of relations: sign–object, sign–mind, object–mind, whereas Merrell stresses that the three components are interdependent and interrelated, each acting as an intermediary between the others. They function only in relation to each

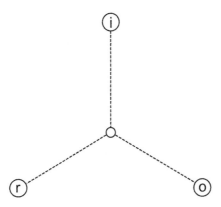

FIGURE 1.8 Peirce's model as a semiotic tripod

Source: © 2016 Daniel Chandler

other. The interaction between the *representamen*, the *object*, and the *interpretant* is referred to by Peirce (CP 5.484) as 'semeiosis' or *semiosis* (Greek, 'the process of making meaning'). Semiosis involves dynamic processes of mediation:

> The sign [representamen] as the conveyer of meaning mediates between the object and the interpretant; the interpretant mediates between the sign and the object to interpret the meaning; the object mediates between the interpretant and the sign to ground the meaning.
>
> (Daniel 2008, 437)

Peirce offers a general model of all kinds of signs whereas the model in the *Cours* is of the linguistic sign (which makes sense only as part of a language system). The Peircean and Saussurean models are often compared and more often contrasted (sometimes in rather heated debates between rival factions). It is not a question of whether one is 'better' than the other. We need to bear in mind that whereas Saussure was a linguist, Peirce was a logician, and they were engaged in very different projects. Saussure focuses on the social function of the linguistic sign and Peirce on the logical function of signs in general. While Saussure seeks to demolish the myth that the language system is based on reference to the 'real world', for Peirce theorizing reference to the world is of course a central concern. As Russell Daylight puts it, 'It is impossible for Peircean semiotics to do without the "stand-for" relation, and impossible for Saussurean linguistics to accept it' (2011, 107).

The representamen is generally regarded as equivalent to Saussure's signifier and many commentators treat the interpretant as roughly analogous to the Saussurean signified. However, attempting to 'translate' between a two-term and three-term system is, to say the least, problematic. A salient dimension in the triadic model, notable by its absence from the dyadic one, is the sign–object relation, but this referential feature is not what is most distinctive about the Peircean model. It is not Saussure's model with an extra leg of referentiality (signifier, signified, and 'thing'), any more than Saussure's is Peirce's model with that leg lopped off (leaving only the representamen and the interpretant). Peirce (CP 2.274) insists that his triad cannot simply be reduced to dyads (sign–object, sign–mind, object–mind). Representation is irreducibly triadic, involving a representamen, an object, and an interpretant. Only in relation to each other can these operate as a sign; a dyad is not a genuine sign (1.346). Peirce rejects Cartesian dualism, and the primacy of *relations* functions to counter the duality of mind and matter (Lidov 1999, 34). The Peircean model is a triadic 'sign relation' in which signs mediate between objects in the world and concepts in the mind. 'The object of a sign is one thing; its meaning is another' (CP 5.6). The 'representing relation' involves *the sign representing an object to the mind* (the *representamen* representing an *object* to the *interpretant*). The interpretant is a 'mediating representation' (1.553). Without it, there is no sign. It mediates between the representamen and the object: this is what gives the sign meaning. Interpretants are the 'proper significate effects' of the sign (5.475); these are not limited to mental concepts but can include actions and experiences (8.332). Peirce distinguishes between various forms of interpretant, in particular between the *immediate* interpretant (the representation within the sign), the *dynamical* interpretant (the actual reaction produced), and the *final* interpretant (its significance) (4.536, 8.315).

What gives the interpretant a quality unlike that of the Saussurean signified is that it is itself a sign. The interpretant function involves a dynamic process. Some contrast this processual model with structuralist models of 'decoding', which are widely seen as based on a one-to-one correlation of signifier and signified (though the concepts of 'decoding' and one-to-one correspondence owe nothing to Saussure). The Peircean sign always has more than one interpretant. The interpretants of a sign include all of the other signs to which it is related (an obvious similarity to Saussure's system, albeit in a more dynamic form). Peirce writes that 'the meaning of a sign is the sign it has to be translated into' (4.132) and that 'the meaning of a representation can be nothing but a representation' (1.339). Indeed, 'a sign is not a sign unless it translates itself into another sign in which it is more fully developed' (5.594). So in an ongoing process of semiosis, the interpretant of a sign spawns a further triadic sign, which is a sign of the same object represented by the original sign, and which has its own interpretant – and so on (see Figure 1.9). Umberto Eco (1976, 68–9) uses the phrase 'unlimited semiosis' to refer to the way in which this could lead to a series of successive interpretants (potentially) *ad infinitum*. Any initial interpretation can be reinterpreted (leading to a 'hermeneutic circle' which resists closure). This feature of apparently infinite regress appeals to deconstructionists such as Derrida in his critique of what he (mistakenly) sees as the 'static' system of Saussure (Derrida 1967a, 48–50), although it has been suggested that a similar potential exists within the Saussurean model, where 'the signifier is always already a signified' and 'the signified . . . is always another signifier' (Meisel and Saussy 2011, xxxiii).

The epistemological idealism and radical relativism of the deconstructionists (in its most extreme form, that reality is wholly a product of our interpretive systems) is not compatible with Peirce's referential realism (in which the external world exists independently of such systems). It is in the sense of deepening understanding that 'a sign is something by knowing which we know something more' (CP 8.332). The object constrains or 'grounds' the meaning and 'an endless series of representations . . . may be considered to have

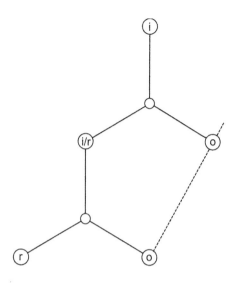

FIGURE 1.9 Peirce's successive interpretants

Source: © 2016 Daniel Chandler

an absolute object as its limit' (1.339). The elusiveness of the object is alluded to in this book's epigraph – Francis Bacon's aphorism that 'The subtlety of nature is greater many times over than the subtlety of argument' – which Peirce cites with approval (2.638, in a variant form). The material world acts as a constraint on interpretation. Another constraint is social: the subtlety of argument is limited by collective 'habits of mind' (7.358), which can terminate a process of semiosis (e.g. on the basis of pragmatic sufficiency). Such habits are inculcated within a community as conventions (a notion not unlike Saussure's concept of the social grounding of sign systems).

> The real . . . is that which, sooner or later, information and reasoning would finally result in, and which is therefore independent of the vagaries of me and you. Thus, the very origin of the conception of reality shows that this conception essentially involves the notion of a COMMUNITY.
>
> (CP 5.311)

Peirce adds that 'reality depends on the ultimate decision of the community' (5.316). Reality is thus ratified by consensus. Semiosis is socially regulated, transcending individuals. In the physical world, the counterparts of habits are natural laws or regularities. Peirce thus proposes that limits to interpretation derive from both nature and culture.

Peirce's model of the sign represents a dynamic chain-like process rather than a system correlating signifiers and signifieds. His emphasis on sense-making involves a rejection of the simplistic metaphor of form as container and meaning as content (which is also rejected by Saussure); the meaning of a sign is not 'contained' within it, but arises in its interpretation. The 'standing for' sign–object relation requires an active agent, such an individual or a community. Although Peirce declares that 'a sign . . . is something which stands to some-body for something in some respect or capacity' (2.228), his model refers to an 'interpretant' (the sense made of a sign) rather than to an individual interpreter. It is not surprising that the term causes some confusion, since 'no single, canonical definition of it is to be found in his writings' (Sebeok 1994a, 12). Of course the interpretant is an interpretive dimension. An interpretant can be seen as an interpre-tation, but the term does not represent, and should not be taken to imply, 'the interpreter' (as it does in Charles Morris's version of semiotics). The concept of 'interpretation' has Cartesian and indi-vidualistic connotations (of the knower–known dichotomy), which Peirce rejects. Peirce's model is not a psychological model (unlike that of Saussure, whose social emphasis nevertheless reflects his own antipathy to an individualistic perspective): the interpretant has an abstract logical function rather than a subjective one. 'The interpretant is that which guarantees the validity of the sign, even in the absence of the interpreter' (Eco 1976, 68). It is a sign that translates, explains, makes clear, analyses, or substitutes for the sign which gave rise to it (Eco 1973, 57, 71). It helps to generate a 'habit' that guides current reactions to the object, and future reactions to others like it (Hauser 1992, xxxix). Interpretation is a collective social activity, and as we shall see, it is possible for a social convention to serve as an interpretant (Peirce CP 5.402). However abstract it may seem to be, the Peircean model is well-adapted to the socio-semiotic principle that interpretations take place in real-world situations and that the meanings of signs arise in the context of use. Again it should be added that, for Saussure, the sign system as a whole is no less grounded in the social context.

On a macro level, 'semiosis can also be taken to refer to the processes of communication by which cultures are maintained and societies reproduced' (Jensen 2001, 13888). On a micro level, the notion of *dialogical thought* is also related to the concept of the interpretant. Peirce argues that 'all thinking is dialogic in form. Your self of one instant appeals to your deeper self for his assent' (6.338). This notion resurfaced in a more developed form in the 1920s in the theories of Mikhail Bakhtin (1981). Some writers have experienced revision as a process of arguing with themselves – as I have when revising this text (Chandler 1995a, 53). One important aspect of this is its characterization even of internal reflection as fundamentally social.

The most obvious difference between the Saussurean and Peircean models is of course that Peirce's model of the sign features a third term representing an *object* (or referent) beyond the sign itself. Peirce explicitly allocates a place in his model for reference to reality outside the sign system, though he is not a naïve realist, and he argues that all experience is mediated by signs. Note that we should beware of regarding Saussure's model as 'deficient' in this regard; he was a linguist, dealing solely with the language system (a specific form of mediation). For Peirce the object was not just 'another variety of "interpretant"' (Bruss 1978, 96), but was crucial to the meaning of the sign: as we have noted, 'meaning' within his model includes both 'reference' and (conceptual) 'sense' (or more broadly, representation and interpretation).

Most contemporary semioticians argue that a theory of the sign that does not theorize the referent cannot form the basis of a general semiotics that seeks to identify common laws for all kinds of signs and sign systems. Advocates argue that the triadic basis of the Peircean model enables it to operate as a more general model of the sign than a dyadic model can (ibid., 86). Clearly, its scope includes both motivated and unmotivated sign relations. It is concerned with signification in any form whatsoever and can be applied not only to 'artificial signs', but to anything that is capable of interpretation, including 'natural signs'. Umberto Eco argues that it is not subordinated to a linguistic model and is not restricted to codified *systems* (1976, 15–16). Roy Harris (1987, 28) acknowledges that 'there is no doubt that Saussure's semiology falls far short of being a general science of signs in the sense later defined by semioticians such as Charles Morris: it does not deal with "signs in all their forms and manifestations, whether in animals or men, whether normal or pathological, whether linguistic or nonlinguistic, whether personal or social" (Morris 1964: 1)'. However, this is a case where 'comparisons are odious'. Although Saussure did of course envisage linguistics as part of the larger project of semiology, which he saw as investigating the laws governing signs (*CLG* 33; 16), his own model of the sign was intended to be applied only to language systems (and can be reasonably extended only to language-like systems).

Like Saussure, Peirce does not doubt the independent existence of an objective world in which there are real things (CP 6.349), and in this sense he is a referential realist. He declares that 'we may define the real as that whose characters are independent of what anybody may think them to be' (5.405). He does not exclude our experience of the world from his model of the sign. For him, every sign has an object. There is an objective (though not necessarily physical) referent. His model is thus not open to the philosophical criticisms of idealism levelled at the Saussurean model. The Peircean sign is part of the experiential world. It is open to materiality in a way that the original Saussurean model is not. However, the referential element is as mediated as any signified concept: the sign is not the thing. The referent is not the actual object to which the sign refers. The objective world is not part of the sign. The object is mediated by the interpretant. For Peirce, the object is not identical to the 'real' one because this can never be fully known, and he makes an analytical distinction between the object as it is in the real world outside a particular process of semiosis (the *dynamic object*) and as it is represented by a sign (the *immediate object*). We have no direct access to dynamic objects but only to immediate objects. An actual object does not even have to exist. Nor does the object determine meaning.

The inclusion of a referent does not make a triadic model inherently less problematic than a dyadic one. John Lyons (1977, 99) notes that 'there is considerable disagreement about the details of the triadic analysis even among those who accept that all three components . . . must be taken into account'. Aptly, in the manner of the interpretant, Peirce himself produced three dozen different definitions of a sign, so it is hardly surprising that reading any selection of accounts by Peircean scholars quickly reveals a great diversity of interpretations. Consequently, the question of which version of Peirce we are dealing with on any occasion is a pertinent and pressing one.

JAKOBSON'S MODEL

One modern commentator argues that:

> Saussurean semiology is supposedly constrained by a bipartite relationship between signifier and signified. However, it would be very easy to restore triadicity to the Saussurean sign, if one wished. The Saussurean sign would merely take for granted the interpretant of 'social agreement'. The verbal representamen 'tree' would stand for the object 'tree' through the interpretant of 'social agreement'.
>
> (Daylight 2014, 48)

This notion had long ago been anticipated by one of the foremost post-Saussurean structuralists, whose inflection of structuralism had important consequences for the evolution of the European semiotic tradition. Prior to his discovery of Peirce's work, Roman Jakobson, a consistent exponent of binary structures in language, had clearly adopted (or adapted) the Saussurean sign – despite his critique of Saussure's analytical priorities: 'The constitutive mark of any sign in general or of any linguistic sign in particular is its *twofold* character: every linguistic unit is bipartite and involves both aspects – one sensible (i.e., perceptible) and the other intelligible, or in other words, both the "signifier" and the "signified"' – his preferred terms (adopted from Augustine) usually being *signans* and *signatum*. The key difference, of course, is that whereas Saussure's signifier is a mental representation, Jakobson's *signans* is, more traditionally, a directly perceptible material form. Jakobson (1949a, 50) adds that the linguistic sign involves 'the indissoluble dualism of . . . *sound* and *meaning*'. After his encounter with Peirce's work in the early 1950s, Jakobson became and remained a key adopter and promoter of Peircean ideas, yet in 1958 he still accepted that the signified/*signatum* 'belonged to' linguistics and the referent/*designatum* to philosophy (1973, 320). Even when he came to emphasize the importance of *context* in the interpretation of signs, he did not directly incorporate a referent into his model of the sign, referring to the term as 'somewhat ambivalent' (1960, 353). By 1972, he had granted the referent (in the form of contextual and situational meaning) a more explicit status within linguistics (1973, 320), but his model of the sign still remained formally dyadic. Nevertheless, he had come to equate the signified with Peirce's 'immediate interpretant' (1966, 409), and on one occasion he referred to there being 'two sets of *interpretants* . . . to interpret the sign – one [referring] to the code, and the other to the context' (1956, 61). Clearly, Jakobson sought to incorporate into the dyadic model the special quality of Peirce's interpretant, referring to the signified as the 'translatable' (or interpretable) part of the sign (e.g. 1958, 261, 1963b, 111, and 1966, 408). Thus, a major semiotician felt able to accommodate reference (indirectly) without abandoning a dyadic model. Whereas Roland Barthes (1977b, 166) acknowledges that 'in signification, as it has been conceived since the Stoic philosophers, there are three things: the signifier, the signified, and the referent', Jakobson insists that 'in spite of . . . attempts' to revise the 'necessarily twofold structure' of the sign or its constituent parts (the signifier/*signans* and the signified/*signatum*), 'this more than bimillenary model remains the soundest and safest base' for semiotic research (1968a, 699). Readers need to be alert for semantic slippage because he often employs the Saussurean terms in describing both the Saussurean and Peircean models. Jakobson was a key propagator of Peircean concepts in the European semiotic tradition (Umberto Eco was another), and although his structuralism was in many ways markedly different from Saussure's principles, his stance on the sign model enabled cultural theorists to absorb Peircean influences without a fundamental transformation of the dyadic model.

Roman Jakobson's model (explored further in Chapter 6) represents an attempt at a synthesis of the Saussurean and Peircean models. The differences between – or even, according to some (e.g. Deledalle 2000, Short 2007), the incompatibility of – these models, have led some scholars to take sides, but a binary either/or choice is not the only option. Pragmatic scholars and practitioners of applied semiotics (such as in marketing semiotics) have employed concepts and tools drawn from both traditions, depending on their priorities in particular analytical tasks. A focus on structure and syntax (the relations between signs) favours structuralist methodologies, while a focus on processes and pragmatics (the use of signs) favours Peircean concepts. Whether or not both approaches are adopted by the same investigators, in the domain of communication and representation it seems foolish not to explore their potential to perform complementary functions.

SIGN RELATIONS

Signs vary in their referentiality. A common-sense distinction between 'conventional signs' (the names we give to people and things) and 'natural signs' (pictures resembling what they depict) dates back to ancient Greece (Plato's *Cratylus*). Writing in 397 CE, Augustine distinguishes 'natural signs' (*signa naturalia*) from conventional signs (*signa data*, 'given signs') on the basis that natural signs lack intentionality and are interpreted as signs by virtue of an immediate link to what they signified (he instances smoke indicating fire and footprints indicating that an animal had passed by) (*On Christian Doctrine*, Book II, Chapter 1). Both of these types of 'natural' signs (respectively iconic and indexical) as well as 'conventional' (symbolic) signs feature in Charles Peirce's influential tripartite classification.

Peirce (CP 1.291, 2.243) offers several typologies of signs. What he himself regards as 'the most fundamental' division of signs (first outlined in 1867) has been very widely cited in subsequent semiotic studies (2.275). Although this is often referred to as a classi-fication of distinct 'types of signs', it is usually interpreted in terms of differing *relationships* between a sign vehicle and what it refers to – which in Peircean terms are relationships between a *representamen* and its *object*. Whereas Saussurean 'sign relations' are between the signifier and the signified (and internal to the language system), in the Peircean model the concept is referential. Here then are the three different relations:

1   *Symbolic*: based on a relationship which is fundamentally *unmotivated*, arbitrary, and purely conventional (rather than being based on resemblance or direct connection to physical reality) – so that it must be agreed upon and learned: e.g. language in general (plus specific languages, alphabetical letters, punctuation marks, words, phrases, and sentences), numbers, Morse code, traffic lights, national flags.

2   *Iconic*: based on perceived *resemblance* or imitation (involving some recognizably similar quality such as appearance, sound, feeling, taste, or smell) – e.g. a portrait, a cartoon, a scale-model, onomatopoeia, metaphors, realistic sounds in 'programme music', sound effects in radio drama, a dubbed film soundtrack, imitative gestures.

3   *Indexical*: based on *direct connection* (physical or causal). This link can be observed or inferred: e.g. 'natural signs' (smoke, thunder, footprints, echoes, non-synthetic odours and flavours), medical symptoms (pain, a rash, pulse-rate), measuring instruments (weathercock, thermometer, clock, spirit-level), 'signals' (a knock on a door, a phone ringing), pointers (a pointing 'index' finger, a directional signpost), recordings (a photograph, a film, video or television shot, an audio-recorded voice), personal 'trademarks' (handwriting, catchphrases).

These three well-established forms of relations between sign vehicle (representamen) and referent (object) form part of Peirce's triadic model of the sign. Once again we need to remind ourselves that, for Peirce, signification is a three-way relation (requiring an interpretant) rather than simply a two-way sign–object relation. Nothing is intrinsically a symbol, an icon, or an index. The same sign vehicle can, in different contexts, involve different sign relations (Sebeok 1994a, 67). The sign relations differ according to the type of interpretant functioning in the context of the process of semiosis on any particular occasion (Deledalle 2000, 19). However, the use of these distinctions is not limited to Peircean semioticians. In structuralist and poststructuralist discourse, these sign–object relations are often imported into a dyadic framework employing the Saussurean terms *signifier* and *signified* – where *sign vehicle* and *referent* (or *object*) would be less misleading.

Even if we are not embracing a wholly Peircean approach, as soon as we adopt the concepts of iconicity and indexicality we need to remind ourselves that neither of these forms of sign relations can be accommodated within the original Saussurean linguistic model because they depend on some kind of referential context (beyond the sign system itself). Iconicity is based on (at least perceived) 'resemblance' and indexicality is based on (at least perceived) 'direct connection' (completing the relational base of the semiotic triangle). Even arbitrariness in the Peircean model admits a relation to reference (albeit a relation by contrast).

Whereas Jakobson absorbs the Peircean sign relations into his own dyadic model, the late Italian semiotician, Umberto Eco, challenges them. Eco was greatly influenced by Peirce, but he criticizes Peirce's referential realism and, like Saussure, excludes referentiality from his own communicational 'theory of codes' (1976, 58ff.). For Eco, 'assuming that the "meaning" of a sign-vehicle has something to do with its corresponding object' is a 'referential fallacy' (ibid., 62). 'The real object corresponding to the sign is absolutely irrelevant to any semiotic purpose' (1973, 69). He adds that 'the referent of a sign is . . . an abstract entity which moreover is only a cultural convention' (ibid., 66; wholly italicized in the source). Reference is to a *cultural* world (ibid., 61–2). In relation to 'iconism', he insists that perception itself is coded and that so too is the relation of 'resemblance' between an image and its referent. As for indexes (or indices), the 'conventional' correlations are inferred from repeated experiences associating the index with its object (ibid., 222–3). Eco is a conventionalist, seeing all signs as conventionally coded and regarding meanings as 'cultural units', which together form a semantic universe. He consequently chooses to 'disregard the difference between motivated and arbitrary signs' (1976, 121).

Peirce explains the irreducible triadic basis of signs in terms of three fundamental ontological categories, which he called *firstness*, *secondness*, and *thirdness*. All phenomena have these three aspects. Note that beyond this brief summary, Peircean scholars differ greatly in how they interpret and apply these categories (Goudge 1950, 85–95). Firstness is reflected in a sign's reference to itself, secondness in its reference to its object (as in the three sign relations), and thirdness in its reference to the mediating role of its interpretant (CP 1.541). Firstness is exhibited in the inherent qualities of a sign, independent of its object and its interpretant (1.25, 8.329). Secondness is exhibited in the hard 'brutal fact' of 'the hæcceities [the 'thisness'] of things, the hereness and nowness of them' (1.405; [my comment]), in their actual, existential reality (8.330). Furthermore, *this* is not-that: we conceive of the existence of things in terms of their relations or 'their reactions against each other' (1.324). Secondness thus also involves *notness* (a very Saussurean notion). Thirdness is the process of mediation, which is involved in all processes of representation (1.328, 1.532, 3.423, 5.72, 5.104, 5.105, 7.630). Whereas firstness and secondness are 'given in perception' (5.194), thirdness is the conceptual realm of inference, thought, and generality. While firstness is monadic and secondness is dyadic, thirdness is 'the triadic relation existing between a sign, its object, and the interpreting thought' (8.332).

Within the category of firstness there are three kinds of signs: a *qualisign* (a 'mere quality'), a *sinsign* (an 'actual existent'), and a *legisign* (a 'general law'). Within that of secondness are the three sign relations: *iconic*, *indexical*, and *symbolic*. Within thirdness, there are three forms of representation: *rheme* (possibility), *dicisign* (fact), and *argument* (reason). A qualisign can only be an icon; a sinsign can be an icon or an index; only a legisign can be a symbol. A colour sample is a qualisign; any indexical sign is a sinsign; conventional signs such as words and traffic lights are legisigns. Limitations of space prohibit the exploration of these Peircean refinements, and of the ten classes of sign to which they give rise (2.264).

Sign relations are typically ranked in terms of relative conventionality or motivation: primarily symbolic forms such as language are highly conventional or 'unmotivated'; iconic forms always involve some degree of conventionality; indexical forms 'direct the attention to their objects by blind compulsion' (2.306). Indexical and iconic sign vehicles can be seen as constrained by their referents. Within each form particular signs also vary in their degree of conventionality or motivation. Such characteristics have implications for their

sign relations	*based primarily on*	*forms of knowledge needed*	
		representational knowledge	*situational knowledge*
symbolic	convention	interpreters need to have learned the relevant representational forms and conventions	
iconic	similarity		interpreters can infer likely meanings on the basis of analogous real-world situations and objects
indexical	connection		

TABLE 1.10 Knowledge needed for interpreting sign relations

Source: © 2016 Daniel Chandler

interpretation (see Table 1.10). For instance, it is widely argued that while symbolic and (to a lesser extent) iconic signs require 'decoding' (as structuralists put it), indexical signs are not part of a system of signs and depend primarily on inference, though Jakobson (1968b) notes that even the interpretation of indexes can involve learning conventional rules (as in the case of medical symptoms). The overlaps between the three forms of sign relations underline the fact that conventional, coded, symbolism cannot be tidily divorced from other modes of sign relations.

Before discussing these forms of sign relations in detail, three British road signs will serve as examples which represent the relative dominance of each. All three are official blue informational signs with white borders. An example of the primacy of symbolic relations is a round-cornered square with a bold white letter P, signifying 'Parking' (viewers would need to understand the convention in order to know what the 'P' stood for). A circular sign with a generic bicycle shape is an example of iconic relations based on perceived similarity and signifying a 'recommended route for pedal cycles'. A round-cornered square sign with generic knife and fork shapes in white refers indexically to the associated concept of 'eating place' and indicates that there is a motorway café ahead. As part of the sign system in the British *Highway Code* all such road signs also have a conventional symbolic dimension, and as individual objects in specific roadside contexts they also have an indexical dimension (connecting their intended meaning with their location).

SYMBOLICITY

Language is a (predominantly) symbolic sign system and it is widely seen as the pre-eminent symbolic form. Peirce declares that 'All words, sentences, books and other conventional signs are symbols' (CP 2.292), and we shall follow his usage here. Saussure avoids referring to linguistic signs as 'symbols' because of the danger of confusion with popular usage, noting that symbols in the popular sense are never wholly arbitrary: they show the vestige of a 'natural bond' with what they signify (*CLG* 101, 106; 68, 73). For instance, if we joke that 'a thing is a phallic symbol if it's longer than it's wide', this would allude to *resemblance*, making it at least partly iconic – Jakobson (1968a, 702) suggests that such examples may be best classified as 'symbolic icons' (see also Figure 1.11 for hybrid signs).

In a rare direct reference to the arbitrariness of symbols (which he then called 'tokens'), Peirce notes that they 'are, for the most part, conventional or arbitrary' (3.360). A symbol is a sign 'whose special significance or fitness to represent just what it does represent lies in nothing but the very fact of there being a habit, disposition, or other effective general rule that it will be so interpreted. Take, for example, the word "*man*". These three letters are not in the least like a man; nor is the sound with which they are associated' (4.447). Arbitrariness refers here, of course, to the sign–object relation. Peirce adds elsewhere that 'a *symbol* . . . fulfils its function regardless of any similarity or analogy with its object and equally regardless of any *factual* connection therewith' (5.73). The lack of dependence on resemblance or direct connection contributes to the power and flexibility of symbols in this sense.

While arbitrariness is regarded as a key 'design feature' of language, *displacement* is another key property that enables linguistic signs to be used to represent objects in their physical absence, including entities that exist only in our imaginations (Hockett 1958). Symbolic forms of this kind can thus transcend the contextual 'here and now' to which other animals are confined. Such qualities enable symbols to be good to think with. 'Though what we call reality is too rich and too varied to be reproducible at will, symbols can be learned and recalled to a surprising extent' (Gombrich 1982, 16).

'The symbol,' says Peirce, 'is connected with its object by virtue of the idea of the symbol-using mind, without which no such connection would exist' (2.299). It 'is constituted a sign merely or mainly by the fact that it is used and understood as such' (2.307). Symbolic signs are usually understood to be *intended* to communicate something. Their intended meanings are not intuitively obvious: understanding symbolic signs depends wholly on our familiarity with the relevant conventions (without which they may fail to signify or be misinterpreted). We interpret symbols according to 'a habitual connection', 'a rule', or 'a law, usually an association of general ideas, which operates to cause the symbol to be interpreted as referring to that object' (2.292, 2.297, 1.369, 2.249). Consequently, the symbol needs to exist in 'constant conjunctions whereby it is linked to something other than itself' (Price 1969, 213).

The symbolic mode is the most effective in communicating abstract concepts and generalizations. Peirce observes that 'A genuine symbol is a symbol that has a general meaning' (2.293), signifying a *kind* of thing rather than a particular thing (2.301). Linguistic categories perform this key function. Symbols are widely regarded by semioticians as best exemplified by words but they are not limited to this form. Symbols include any conventional signs which signify concepts, and any form of signifier has the potential to be used symbolically. As the Irish philosopher George Berkeley notes (1713), images cannot 'resemble' the referents of abstract ideas. However, images can be used symbolically to represent objects associated with abstract concepts.

Public signage often depends on visual symbols which are intended to achieve generality of reference and to carry authority. For instance, in a 'no dogs allowed' sign, a simple, schematic representation of a prototypical dog is likely to be more effective as a general symbol than an image of a particular type of dog – although, unlike the word 'dog', any depiction of a dog unavoidably resembles some kinds of dogs more than others. Symbolic forms are often more indirect. In some contexts, an image of a lion may function as a metaphorical symbol for abstract concepts such as power or courage (which are of course conventional associations rather than zoological features of lions). Thus, in different contexts, an image may iconically represent the individual it resembles, may be a symbolic icon of a general type, or may symbolize more indirectly some associated concept. Even a photograph can have a symbolic function, as when images of coinage are used to signify 'the economy' when that is the topic of a TV news item. It is thus possible for images to attain some of the symbolic status of words, though their scope and flexibility are limited. Only context and convention can determine whether a sign featuring a generic image of a male figure is intended to symbolize people in general (as on a 'no admittance' sign), or males only (as on the door of a public toilet).

ICONICITY

Unfortunately, as with 'symbolic', the terms 'icon' and 'iconic' are used in a technical sense in semiotics which differs from its everyday meanings (Chandler and Munday 2011, 195). Despite the name, in semiotics icons are not necessarily visual but may involve any sensory mode. For Peirce, the basis of iconic relations lies in any (perceived) resemblance to (or analogy with) what is signified. He declares that an iconic sign represents its object 'mainly by its similarity' (CP 2.276). A sign is an icon 'insofar as it is like that thing and used as a sign of it' (2.247). Peirce originally termed such sign relations, 'likenesses' (e.g. 1.558). Icons have qualities that 'resemble' those of the objects they stand for, and they 'excite analogous sensations in the mind' (2.299).

Since at least the ancient Greeks, resemblance has been regarded as the 'natural' basis of depiction in contrast to the conventionality of words. To the extent that we are able to recognize something familiar in a particular image (even cross-culturally and across the centuries), it is understandable that iconic relations are widely perceived as more 'natural' than symbolic relations. Iconic forms do not draw our attention to their mediation, seeming to present reality more directly or transparently than symbolic forms. Ernst Gombrich refers to 'the beholder's capacity to read "iconicity" *into* . . . [the] sign' (1949, 248), 'seeing' the referent in the sign vehicle (Sonesson 1989, 343) – even in a highly conventionalized iconic symbol such as the heart on a playing card (which bears very little anatomical relation to a human heart). We routinely underestimate the importance of our active contribution to sense-making, but images in particular do not usually seem to need 'reading' at all.

Semioticians generally maintain that there are no pure icons. Iconicity is 'a matter of degree' (Morris 1971, 273). As we have noted, images are frequently used symbolically in public signs. On the internet, simple house-like images signifying a link to a website's homepage are primarily symbolic: they do not resemble a particular house but conventionally signify the concept 'home'. Even a representational picture which is perceived as resembling that which it depicts is not purely iconic. However, Saussure's stance in relation to language can be seen as no less applicable to pictures: 'The notion of matching to the real world is insufficient to explain how pictures mean . . . Correspondence . . . is not . . . to "reality", but rather . . . to conventions' (Worth 1981, 181). The most radical 'conventionalist' is the philosopher Nelson Goodman, who argues (1968) that pictures do not signify through resemblance but through the way they select and combine conventions from existing systems of representation within the medium. As Flint Schier (1986, 179), another philosopher, puts it, 'The real contrast between . . . a linguistic symbol system and an iconic one does not consist in the conventional nature of the former and the non-conventional nature of the latter but in the nature of the conventions involved in each'.

Peirce (CP 2.276) acknowledges this dimension: although 'any material image' (such as a painting) may be perceived as looking like what it represents, it is 'largely conventional in its mode of representation'. All artists employ stylistic conventions and these are, of course, culturally and historically variable.

> We say that the portrait of a person we have not seen is *convincing*. So far as, on the ground merely of what I see in it, I am led to form an idea of the person it represents, it is an icon. But, in fact, it is not a pure icon, because I am greatly influenced by knowing that it is an *effect*, through the artist, caused by the original's appearance . . . Besides, I know that portraits have but the slightest resemblance to their originals, except in certain conventional respects, and after a conventional scale of values, etc.
>
> (CP 2.92)

Peirce nevertheless asserts that 'every picture (however conventional its method)' is an icon (2.279), though we should note that not all visual signs are 'pictures' and although in cases such as the symbolic lion, the sign vehicle must be perceived as resembling that animal, it does not (and cannot) 'resemble' the abstract qualities that it is intended to signify. If a sign resembles something but is intended to signify something else it is not primarily iconic. In the case of the British road sign where a simple schematic image of an elephant on a directional sign signifies a nearby zoo, the sign might best be described as indexically symbolic, since the elephant is part of, and here stands for, the animal kingdom as a whole.

However 'natural' the resemblance may seem, pictures resemble what they represent only in some respects. What we tend to recognize in an image are analogous relations of parts to a whole. For Peirce, icons included 'every diagram, even although there be no sensuous resemblance between it and its object, but only an analogy between the relations of the parts of each' (2.279). 'Many diagrams resemble their objects not at all in looks; it is only in respect to the relations of their parts that their likeness consists' (2.282). Even the most realistic image is not a replica or even a copy of what is depicted. It is not often that we mistake a representation for what it represents. Unlike the index, 'the icon has no dynamical connection with the object it represents' (ibid., 2.299) and consequently 'gives no assurance that any such object as it represents really exists' (Peirce 1976, 242–3).

An extended critique of 'iconism' can be found in Eco (1976, 191ff.). The linguist John Lyons (1977, 105) notes that iconicity is 'always dependent upon properties of the medium in which the form is manifest'. He offers the example of the onomatopoeic English word *cuckoo*, noting that it is only (perceived as) iconic in the phonic medium (speech) and not in the graphic medium (writing). While the phonic medium can represent characteristic sounds (albeit in a relatively conventionalized way), the graphic medium can represent characteristic shapes (as in the case of Egyptian hieroglyphs) (ibid., 103). We will return shortly to the importance of the materiality of the sign.

INDEXICALITY

Indexicality is perhaps the most unfamiliar concept, though its links with everyday uses of the word 'index' ought to be less misleading than the terms for the other two forms of sign relations. An index 'indicates' something: for example, 'a sundial or clock *indicates* the time of day' (CP 2.285). Indexicality is quite closely related to the way in which the index of a book or an 'index' finger point directly to what is being referred to (Latin *index* 'forefinger', 'pointer'). Unlike symbolic and iconic sign relations, indexical relations do not represent or symbolize things but act as a stimulus directing our attention towards them. 'The index, . . . like a pointing finger exercises a real physiological force over the attention . . . and directs it to a particular object' (8.41). Although an example such as pointing is an indexical signal, intentional communication is not a necessary feature of indexical sign relations.

As already noted, Augustine, who regards both words and pictures as conventional signs, distinguishes from these as *natural signs* 'those which, apart from any intention or desire of using them as signs, do yet lead to the knowledge of something else, as for example, smoke when it indicates fire' (2009, 32). In indexical relations, the sign vehicle and the referent 'go together'. Black clouds are a natural sign of rain, not a symbol of it (except as iconic symbols on a weather map, which allude indirectly to the indexicality of the real thing). 'There is nothing conventional or arbitrary about the fact that cumulo-nimbus clouds are a sign of a thunderstorm' (Price 1969, 173). Nor do they signify rain iconically by resembling it or by similarity of attributes. Experience shows that we are justified in treating such natural clouds as indexical signs indicating impending rainstorms in the vicinity. As Susanne Langer (1957, 57) puts it, a natural sign 'indicates the existence – past, present, or future – of a thing, event, or condition. Wet streets are a sign that it has rained. A patter on the roof is a sign that it is raining. A fall of the barometer or a ring around the moon is a sign that it is going to rain'. Such a sign is symptomatic of a state of affairs. Such natural, motivated signs are clearly meaningful but they are not in themselves part of an interpretive *system* – although this does not prevent them from being interpreted according to conventions (as in weather forecasts).

As the most directly referential of the sign relations, indexical relations clearly cannot be accounted for within the original Saussurean model, which of course does not include object–object (or part–whole) relations positing a logical or interpretive relationship between two referents (Daylight 2011, 142). Although natural signs had long been acknowledged, Peirce's concept of the index is nevertheless distinctive. Peirce offers various criteria for what constitutes an index: a somewhat broad and untidy category which is sometimes divided into sub-categories. Indexical signs 'direct the attention to their objects by blind compulsion' (2.306). 'Anything which focuses the attention is an index. Anything which startles us is an index' (2.285). Indexical relations offer the most direct connection with a referent, in strongest contrast to symbolic relations. Jakobson asserts that 'the index, in contradistinction to the icon and symbol, is the only sign which necessarily involves the actual copresence of its object' (Jakobson 1963c, 335). For Peirce, indexical relations are found in signs where there is a direct relation in fact with what is signified. Peirce refers to a 'genuine relation' between the 'sign' and the *object* which does not depend purely on 'the interpreting mind' (2.92, 2.98). The object is 'necessarily existent' (2.310). The index is connected to its object 'as a matter of fact' (4.447). There is 'a real connection' (5.75), which may be a 'direct physical connection' (1.372, 2.281, 2.299), in which case an index is like 'a fragment torn away from the object' (2.231). Unlike an icon (the object of which may be fictional) an index stands 'unequivocally for this or that existing thing' (4.531).

The relationship is *not* based on 'mere resemblance' (2.248): 'indices . . . have no significant resemblance to their objects' (2.306). Shakespeare's signature is an indexical sign but it does not resemble him. 'Similarity or analogy' are not what define the index (2.305). Whereas iconicity is characterized by *similarity*, indexicality is characterized by *contiguity*. 'Psychologically, the action of indices depends upon association by contiguity, and not upon association by resemblance or upon intellectual operations' (2.306). Elizabeth Bruss (1978, 88) notes that indexicality is 'a relationship rather than a quality. Hence the sign vehicle need have no particular properties of its own, only a demonstrable connection to something else. The most important of these connections are spatial co-occurrence, temporal sequence, and cause and effect'.

Indexicality comes in many forms: for instance, road signs exhibit indexical dimensions when they signify appropriately only in the intended location (e.g. a crossroads sign at an intersection), when they point directly to what they refer (directional signposts), or when they depict something closely connected with what they stand for (an image of a knife and fork indicating nearby dining facilities) – though it should be apparent by now that none of these examples is purely indexical. Anything that 'reflects' an individual's personality is also indexical. This includes handwriting, or a distinctive individual style (e.g. of an artist or photographer). Jackson Pollock's paintings are indexical records of the painter's performance. In the art business, indexicality is a matter of considerable consequence in attribution and establishing provenance.

While photographs are also perceived as visually resembling their subjects, Peirce notes that they are not only iconic but also *indexical* (leading some to refer to them as iconic indexes or indices).

> Photographs, especially instantaneous photographs, are very instructive, because we know that in certain respects they are exactly like the objects they represent. But this resemblance is due to the photographs having been produced under such circumstances that they were physically forced to correspond point

by point to nature. In that aspect, then, they belong to the . . .
class of signs . . . by physical connection [the indexical class].

(CP 2.281)

The British philosopher Roger Scruton (1983, 122) argues that, strictly
speaking, 'photography is not representation', since 'the camera is . . .
not being used to represent something but to point to it' (ibid., 113).
Since the photographic image is an index of the effect of light, all
unedited photographic and filmic images are indexical (although we
should remember that conventional practices are always involved in
composition, focusing, developing, and so on). Such images do of
course 'resemble' visual features of their subject, and some commentators suggest that the power of the photographic and filmic image
derives from the iconic character of the medium (though a snapshot
doesn't necessarily guarantee 'a good likeness'). However, while
digital imaging techniques have eroded the indexicality of photographic images, it is the indexicality still routinely attributed to the
medium that is primarily responsible for interpreters treating them
as objective records of reality. Although a photograph generally
resembles its referent, it no longer does so when the image is
dramatically over- or under-exposed.

As the sociologist Pierre Bourdieu (1990, 164) puts it,
'Photography is ordinarily seen as the most perfectly faithful
reproduction of the real'. Photographic media seem to involve a
transparent relationship between the sign vehicle and its referent. A
photograph is based on a direct *causal* relationship to an external object.
The Pencil of Nature was the title that Henry Fox gave to his book on
photography in 1844, and subsequent writers on the subject have
referred to a photograph as a 'trace' of its subject (e.g. Sontag 1979,
154; Berger 1980, 50). Of the three types of relationship on which
signs are based, only indexicality can serve as evidence of an object's
existence. Peirce (CP 4.447) observes that 'a photograph . . . owing
to its optical connection with its object, is evidence that that appearance
corresponds to a reality'. In many contexts, photographs are regarded
as evidence of events having happened at the time they were taken,
not least in legal contexts: video surveillance cameras and speed
cameras are of course widely used in this way. However, in one of his

essays on photographic history, John Tagg, wary of 'the realist position', cautions that 'the existence of a photograph is no guarantee of a corresponding pre-photographic existent . . . The indexical nature of the photograph – the causative link between the pre-photographic referent and the sign . . . can guarantee nothing at the level of meaning'. Even prior to digital photography, both 'correction' and montage were practised, but Tagg argues that *every* photograph involves 'significant distortions' (1988, 1–3). Just as pictures resemble what they represent only in some respects, in photography whatever is shown is unavoidably transformed into a flat, decontextualized fragment which is typically much smaller in scale, and (except in film), stationary, and silent. This is an issue to which we will return in Chapter 5 when we discuss whether photography is 'a message without a code'.

As a medium, photography is primarily indexical; as a 'message' (which is dependent on how a photograph is used or interpreted), this sign relation may not be dominant. In discussing symbolicity, we noted that photographs have this potential function. Like all 'photographs that changed the world', Joe Rosenthal's famous 1945 photograph, *Raising the Flag on Iwo Jima* ('iconic' in the popular sense) is in semiotic terms primarily symbolic (see Hariman and Lucaites 2007). Peirce argues that all indexes refer to single instances (e.g. 'this man'), whereas symbolic representation can refer to general classes of instances (e.g. 'men'). Despite their literal specificity (making them unsuitable for road signs), it is possible for photographs to be used to refer to general classes. Within the genre of advertising, the potency of the famous photographic 'cowboy' ads for Marlboro cigarettes does not derive primarily from their indexicality as images of particular individuals, but rather from their symbolization of a stereotypical concept of masculinity (even to the extent that we may need to remind ourselves that this is *not* 'masculinity', because the form functions to suggest otherwise).

MIXED MODES

It is easy to slip into referring to Peirce's three forms as 'types of signs', but they are not necessarily mutually exclusive: a sign can be an icon, a symbol and an index, or any combination. For instance, a map is indexical in pointing to the locations of things, iconic in representing the directional relations and distances between landmarks, and symbolic in using conventional symbols (the significance of which must be learned).

As we have noted, we are dealing with symbolic, iconic, and indexical sign relations rather than with types of signs. Thus, Jakobson (1963c, 335) observes that 'strictly speaking, the main difference . . . is rather in the hierarchy of their properties than in the properties themselves'. Peirce was fully aware of this: for instance, we have already noted that he did not regard a portrait as a pure icon. A 'stylized' image might be more appropriately regarded as a 'symbolic icon' (ibid.). Jakobson refers to such combined terms as 'transitional varieties' (1968a, 700), though arguably these hybrid forms actually represent the norm (see Figure 1.11). Peirce insists that 'it would be difficult if not impossible to instance an absolutely pure index, or to find any sign absolutely devoid of the indexical quality' (CP 2.306). All signs could be regarded as having an indexical dimension insofar

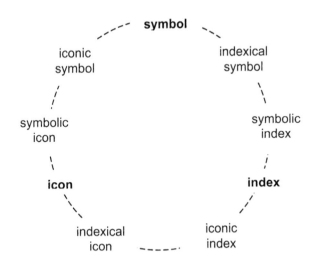

FIGURE 1.11 Hybridity in sign relations

Source: © 2016 Daniel Chandler

as they give rise to inferences about connections to the referent. The indexicality of a thermometer needs a conventional label in order to function as a sign. Jakobson (1968a, 700–1) points out that many deliberate indexes also have a symbolic or indexical quality, instancing traffic lights as being both indexical and symbolic, and noting that even the pointing gesture is not always interpreted purely indexically in different cultural contexts. Nor are words always purely symbolic – they can be 'iconic symbols' (such as onomatopoeic words) or 'indexical symbols' (as with deictic words such as 'that', 'this', 'here', 'there') (see Jakobson 1966 on iconicity and indexicality in language).

Jakobson (1966, 411) notes that Peirce's three forms of sign relations co-exist in a 'relative hierarchy' in which one form is dominant, with dominance determined by context. Thomas Sebeok suggests that 'the sign is legitimately, if loosely, labelled after the aspect that ranks predominant' (1994a, 22). Whether a sign is symbolic, iconic, or indexical depends primarily on the way in which the sign is used, so textbook examples chosen to illustrate the various sign relations can be misleading. The same sign may be used iconically in one context and symbolically in another: a photograph of a woman may stand for some broad category such as 'women' or may more specifically represent only the particular woman who is depicted. Signs cannot be classified in terms of the three forms of relations without reference to the purposes of their users within particular contexts. A sign may consequently be treated as symbolic by one person, as iconic by another and as indexical by a third. Signs may also shift in mode over time. For instance, a Rolex watch is an *index* of wealth because one must be wealthy to own one, but social usage has led to its becoming a conventional *symbol* of wealth.

Consistently with his advocacy of binary relations, Jakobson (1968a, 700) boldly asserts that Peirce's three forms of sign relations are 'actually based on two substantial dichotomies' – an assertion which understandably irritates a Peircean scholar (Bruss 1978, 92). Combining four terms used by Peirce, Jakobson proposes a matrix of his own with *contiguity* and *similarity* on one axis and the qualities of being either 'imputed' or 'factual' on the other (Table 1.12). Within this scheme, the index is based on 'factual contiguity', the icon on 'factual similarity' and the symbol on 'imputed contiguity' – leaving an initially

	contiguity	*similarity*
imputed	symbols	connotative signs
factual	indexes (or indices)	icons

TABLE 1.12 Jakobson's matrix
Source: © 2016 Daniel Chandler, based on Jakobson 1968a, 700–5

empty category of 'imputed similarity' to which Jakobson (1968a, 700–5) assigns ostensibly non-referential signs which nevertheless generate emotional connotations – such as music and non-representational visual art.

TYPES AND TOKENS

Peirce (CP 4.537) made a distinction between *tokens* and *types* which has subsequently been generally adopted within linguistics. In relation to words in a spoken utterance or written text, a count of the tokens would be a count of the total number of words used (regardless of type), while a count of the types would be a count of the *different* words used, ignoring repetitions. In the language of semantics, tokens instantiate (are instances of) their type. Eco notes that 'grouping manifold tokens under a single type is the way in which language . . . works' (1999, 146).

John Lyons notes that whether something is counted as a token of a type is relative to one's purposes – for instance:

- Are tokens to include words with different meanings which happen to be spelt or pronounced in the same way?
- Does a capital letter instantiate the same type as the corresponding lower-case letter?
- Does a word printed in italics instantiate the same type as a word printed in Roman?
- Is a word handwritten by X ever the same as a word handwritten by Y?

(Lyons 1977, 13–15)

From a semiotic point of view, such questions could only be answered by considering in each case whether the different forms signified something of any consequence to the relevant sign-users in the context of the specific signifying practice being studied.

Eco (1976, 178ff.) lists three kinds of sign vehicles, and it is notable that the distinction relates in part at least to material form:

- signs in which there may be any number of tokens (replicas) of the same type (e.g. a printed word, or exactly the same model of car in the same colour);
- 'signs whose tokens, even though produced according to a type, possess a certain quality of material uniqueness' (e.g. a word which someone speaks or which is handwritten);
- 'signs whose token is their type, or signs in which type and token are identical' (e.g. a unique original oil-painting or Princess Diana's wedding dress).

The type–token distinction may influence the way in which a text (in any medium) is interpreted. In his influential essay on 'The work of art in the age of mechanical reproduction', written in 1935, the literary–philosophical theorist Walter Benjamin (1992, 211–44) notes that technological society is dominated by reproductions of original works – tokens of the original type. Even if we do see, for instance, 'the original' of a famous oil-painting, we are highly likely to have seen it first in the form of innumerable reproductions (books, postcards, posters – sometimes even in the form of pastiches or variations on the theme) and we may only be able to 'see' the original in the light of the judgements shaped by the copies or versions which we have encountered. In the postmodern era, the bulk of our texts are 'copies without originals'.

The type–token distinction in relation to signs is important in social semiotic terms not as an absolute property of the sign vehicle but only insofar as it matters on any given occasion (for particular purposes) to those involved in using the sign. Minute differences in a pattern could be a matter of life and death for gamblers in relation to variations in the pattern on the backs of playing-cards within the same pack, but stylistic differences in the design of each type of card (such as the ace of spades), are much appreciated by collectors as a distinctive feature of different packs of playing cards.

REMATERIALIZING THE SIGN

As already indicated, Saussure sees both the signifier and the signified as non-material 'psychological' forms; language itself is a *form*, not a *substance* (*CLG* 157; 113). He uses several examples to reinforce his point. For instance, in one of several chess analogies, he notes that using ivory chessmen instead of wooden ones has no effect on the system (ibid. 43; 22). Pursuing this functional approach, he notes elsewhere that the 8.25 p.m. Geneva–Paris train is referred to as 'the same train' even though the combinations of locomotive, carriages, and personnel may change. Similarly, he asks why a street that is completely rebuilt can still be 'the same street'. He suggests that this is because it is not a purely material thing, though he insists that this is not to say that such entities are 'abstract' since we cannot conceive of a street or train outside of their material realization (ibid. 151–2; 108–9). Since Saussure sees language in terms of formal function rather than material substance, whatever performs the same function within the system can be regarded as just another token of the same type. Saussure observes that sound is not part of language but merely a substance which language puts to use. Linguistic signifiers are constituted not by their material substance but by the differences that distinguish them from each other. He adopts the perspective that the means by which the sign is produced is irrelevant because it does not affect the system (ibid. 164–6, 32; 118–20, 15). One can understand how a linguist would tend to focus on form and function within language and to regard the material manifestations of language as of peripheral interest: 'the linguist . . . is interested in types, not tokens' (Lyons 1977, 28). Indeed, Hjelmslev notes that viewing linguistic form without regard for substance enables linguistic principles to be applied to non-linguistic sign systems with forms which are analogous to those of language (1961, 102). However, social semioticians have subsequently distanced themselves from Saussure's instrumental stance, criticizing his neglect of the potential contribution of material substance to signification.

Along related lines, the philosopher Peirce (CP 4.447) declares that: 'The word "*man*" . . . does not consist of three films of ink. If the word "man" occurs hundreds of times in a book of which myriads of copies are printed, all those millions of triplets of patches of ink are embodiments of one and the same word. I call each of those embodiments a *replica* of the symbol. This shows that the word is not a thing'. However, Peirce did acknowledge the materiality of the sign: 'since a sign is not identical with the thing signified, but differs from the latter in some respects, it must plainly have some characters which belong to it in itself . . . These I call the *material* qualities of the sign'. He grants that materiality is a property of the sign which is 'of great importance in the theory of cognition'. Nevertheless, materiality had 'nothing to do with its representative function' and it did not feature in his classificatory schemes (5.287).

While Saussure did not regard the materiality of the linguistic sign as relevant to his system, most subsequent theorists who have adopted (or adapted) his model have chosen to reclaim the materiality of the sign. Semioticians must take seriously any factors to which sign-users ascribe significance, and the material form of a sign does sometimes make a difference. Contemporary theorists of 'social semiotics' generally argue that the material form of the sign may generate meanings of its own. As early as 1929 Valentin Voloshinov published *Marxism and the Philosophy of Language*, which included a materialist critique of Saussure's psychological and implicitly idealist model of the sign. Voloshinov (1973, 58) describes Saussure's ideas as 'the most striking expression' of 'abstract objectivism'. He insists that 'a sign is a phenomenon of the external world' and that 'signs . . . are particular, material things'. Every sign 'has some kind of material embodiment, whether in sound, physical mass, colour, movements of the body, or the like' (ibid., 10–11). For Voloshinov, all signs, including language, have 'concrete material reality' and the physical properties of the sign matter (ibid., 65). Roman Jakobson (1949b, 423) also rejects Saussure's notion of the immateriality of language, declaring that 'since the sound matter of language is a matter organized and formed to serve as a semiotic instrument, not only the significative function of the distinctive features but even their phonic essence is a cultural artifact'. Furthermore, although he accepts the traditional view that 'writing

... is – both ontologically and phylogenetically a secondary and optional acquisition' (1970, 455–6) and that the written word 'as a rule' functions as a signifier for the spoken word, he regards it as not only 'the most important transposition' of speech into another medium (1968a, 706) but also as characterized by 'autonomous properties' (1971c, 718). He expresses his concern that 'written language [is] often underrated by linguists' and refers the reader to Derrida's reversal of this tradition (1970, 455–6).

Structuralist theorists transformed the Saussurean model of the sign, establishing a clearcut distinction between form and meaning, signifier and signified, which Saussure had resolutely rejected. Structuralism embraced the 'primacy of the signifier'. Psychoanalytic theory contributed to the revaluation of the signifier – in Freudian dream theory the sound of the signifier could be regarded as a better guide to its possible signified than any conventional 'decoding' might have suggested (Freud 1938, 319). For instance, Freud reports that the dream of a young woman engaged to be married featured flowers – including lilies-of-the-valley and violets. Popular symbolism suggested that the lilies were a symbol of chastity and the woman agreed that she associated them with purity. However, Freud was surprised to discover that she associated the word 'violet' phonetically with the English word 'violate', suggesting her fear of the violence of 'defloration' (another word alluding to flowers) (ibid., 382–3). As the psychoanalytical theorist Jacques Lacan emphasizes (originally in 1957), the Freudian concepts of *condensation* and *displacement* illustrate the determination of the signified by the signifier in dreams (Lacan 1977, 159ff.). In *condensation*, several thoughts are condensed into one symbol, while in *displacement* unconscious desire is displaced into an apparently trivial symbol (to avoid dream censorship).

Although widely criticized as idealists and relativists, poststructuralist theorists have sought to revalorize the signifier. What Saussure's critics see as his disregard for the materiality of the linguistic sign was challenged in 1967, when the French poststructuralist Jacques Derrida, in his book *Of Grammatology*, accused him (and many other previous and subsequent theorists) of 'phonocentrism' – the privileging of speech over writing (Derrida 1967a). From Plato to Lévi-Strauss, the spoken word had held a privileged position in the

Western worldview, generating an illusion of absolute presence and transparency of meaning. Speech had become so thoroughly naturalized that 'not only do the signifier and the signified seem to unite, but also, in this confusion, the signifier seems to erase itself or to become transparent' (Derrida 1981, 22). Writing had traditionally been relegated to a secondary position. The deconstructive enterprise marked 'the return of the repressed' (Derrida 1967b, 197). In seeking to establish 'grammatology' or the study of textuality, Derrida champions the primacy of the material word. He notes that the specificity of words is itself a material dimension. 'The materiality of a word cannot be translated or carried over into another language. Materiality is precisely that which translation relinquishes' (ibid., 210). Some readers may note a degree of (characteristically postmodern) irony in such a stance being adopted by a theorist whom many regard as an extreme idealist. Derrida's ideas have nevertheless informed the perspectives of some theorists who have sought to 'rematerialize' the linguistic sign, stressing that words and texts are *things* (e.g. Coward and Ellis 1977, Silverman and Torode 1980). However, it should be noted that Derrida's accusation of phonocentrism levelled against Saussure fails to take account of Saussure's motivation to react against the existing prioritization of the written language, and that in this historical context his radical goal was to establish the spoken language as not simply as a debased form of the written language but as worthy of study in its own right.

Roland Barthes also sought to revalorize the role of the signifier in the act of writing. Once again, it should be noted that this does not reflect Saussure's own conception of the signifier–signified relationship, in which neither can precede the other. Barthes argues that in 'classic' literary writing, the writer 'is always supposed to go from signified to signifier, from content to form, from idea to text, from passion to expression' (1974, 174). However, this is directly opposite to the way in which Barthes characterizes the act of writing. For him, writing is a matter of working with the signifiers and letting the signifieds take care of themselves – a paradoxical phenomenon which other writers have often reported (Chandler 1995a, 60ff.).

Even the materialization of thoughts in different ways by different writing tools can have subtle but significant implications for the ways in which writers (particularly 'discoverers' such as Barthes) think and write, suggesting that 'to talk simply in terms of "using" tools may be as extreme a position as to talk solely of "being used" by them' (Chandler 1992, 73). Theoretical attention has thus been increasingly drawn to the material dimension of language since Voloshinov's critique of the Saussurean stance (dating from only thirteen years after the first edition of the *Cours*) and this perspective became widely accepted from around the 1970s. More recently, studies have shown that material objects can themselves function directly as signs, not only in the form of 'status symbols' (such as expensive cars) but also (in the case of particular objects which individuals regard as having some special importance for them) as part of the repertoire of signs upon which people draw in developing and maintaining their sense of personal and social identity (Csikszentmihalyi and Rochberg-Halton 1981, Chalfen 1987). People attach 'symbolic values' to television sets, furniture, and photograph albums, which are not determined by the utilitarian functions of such mundane objects. The groundwork for such thinking had already been laid within structuralism. Lévi-Strauss (1962) had explored 'the logic of the concrete' – observing, for instance, that animals are 'good to think [with]' and that identity can be expressed through the manipulation of existing things. Elsewhere, I have explored the notion that online personal profiles function as manipulable objects with which their authors can think about identity (Chandler 2006).

The *sign* as such may not be a material entity, but it has a material dimension – the signifier (or sign vehicle). Bob Hodge and David Tripp (1986, 17) insist that, 'fundamental to all semiotic analysis is the fact that any system of signs (semiotic code) is carried by a material medium *which has its own principles of structure*'. Further- more, some media draw on several interacting sign systems: television and film, for example, utilize verbal, visual, auditory, and locomotive signs. The medium is not 'neutral'; each medium has its own afford- ances and constraints and, as Umberto Eco (1976, 267) notes, each is already 'charged with cultural signification'. For instance, photographic and audio-visual media are almost invariably regarded as more real than other forms of representation. Gunther Kress and Theo van Leeuwen (1996, 231) argue that 'the material expression of the text is always significant; it is a separately variable semiotic feature'.

HJELMSLEV'S MODEL

The distinction between signifier and signified has sometimes been equated to the familiar dualism of 'form and content' (though not by Saussure). Within such a framework, the signifier is seen as the *form* of the sign and the signified as the *content*. However, the metaphor of form as a 'container' is problematic, tending to support the equation of content with *meaning*, implying that meaning can be 'extracted' without an active process of interpretation and that form is not in itself meaningful (Chandler 1995a, 104–6). The container metaphor is so deeply embedded in our discourse about communication and representation that it is almost impossible to avoid (Reddy 1979, Lakoff and Johnson 1980). While not rejecting the concept of content (in Danish *indhold*), the linguist Louis Hjelmslev sought to undermine the dualistic reduction of the sign to form–content. He declares that 'there can be no content without an expression, or expressionless content; neither can there be an expression without a content, or content-less expression' (1961, 49). He offers a framework which facilitated analytical distinctions (ibid., 47ff.). While he refers to

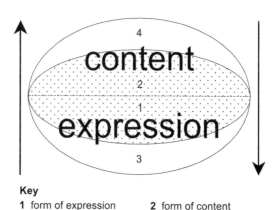

Key

1 form of expression   **2** form of content
3 substance of expression   **4** substance of content

FIGURE 1.13 Hjelmslev's stratified model of a sign (1943)

'planes' of expression and content (Saussure's *signifier* and *signified*), he enriches this dyadic model (ibid., 60). His contribution is to suggest that both *expression* and *content* have *substance* and *form* (see Figure 1.13).

Within Hjelmslev's stratified framework there are four categories in two pairs: form of expression and form of content, together with substance of expression and substance of content. Whereas Saussure had insisted that language is a non-material form and not a material substance, Hjelmslev's model allows us to analyse texts according to their various dimensions and to grant to each of these the potential for signification (see Table 1.14 for examples). Such a matrix provides a useful framework for the systematic analysis of texts, broadens the notion of what constitutes a sign, and reminds us that the materiality of the sign may in itself signify. Although Hjelmslev's 'glossematics' theory reduces reference to internal relations between the form

plane	substance	form
content [signifieds]	*substance of content:* the realm of thought, human realities, sociocultural worlds, social contexts, textual worlds, subject matter	*form of content:* specific ideas, concepts, values, ideologies, codes, cultural categories, oppositions, narratives, genres, semantic structures, thematic structures
expression [signifiers]	*substance of expression:* material culture, objects, physical materials of a medium such as images, printed words, or sounds	*form of expression:* language, lexicon, syntactic, phonological, and morphological structure, design elements, stylistic features, techniques

TABLE 1.14 Substance and form of expression and content

Source: © 2016 Daniel Chandler

of content and its substance and does not address the pragmatics of semiosis, its acknowledgement of the material dimension of the sign was important for the development of 'socio-semiotics' (see Gottdiener 1995). Hjelmslev's model was adopted by Umberto Eco (1973, 62) and Christian Metz (1971, 208ff.), and influenced the thinking of Algirdas Greimas, Gilles Deleuze (1925–95), and Félix Guattari (1930–92); even Jacques Derrida praises its revaluation of the written word.

Hjelmslev notes that according to the 'traditional' linguistic point of view, 'it seems to be true that a sign is a sign for something, and that this something in a certain sense lies outside the sign itself' (1961,57), whereas in 'modern linguistics' the sign is seen as ordering the 'content purport', which lies 'behind language' by classifying it in terms of linguistic entities, which are related to each other within the language system (ibid., 58, 74, 111–21, 127). Such a challenge to common-sense notions of the relations between signs and things will be further explored in the following chapter.

REFLECTIONS

1 Gather a range of definitions of the sign by semioticians, noting their key similarities and differences.

2 Consider several brands of chocolate or alcohol aimed at different target consumers and position each of them on a brand positioning grid (see Figure 1.6), noting how visual features such as the fonts, colours, logos, and packaging reflect this positioning.

3 What is the problem with trying to apply the three forms of sign relations (symbolic, iconic, indexical) within the Saussurean dyadic model?

4 Using a selection of official pictographic road signs, identify examples of symbolic, iconic, and indexical relations.

5 Referring to the hybrid sign forms listed in Figure 1.11, find an example of each of them.

6 Gombrich insists that 'pictures cannot assert', and Peirce says much the same. Find a minimally verbal advertisement, which seems to you to make an implicit statement through

visual cues and consider whether this example offers evidence to the contrary (and if so, how it does so). Gombrich's argument in *The Image and the Eye* is worth reading. For a discussion of this issue in relation to Peirce, see Chandler 2014.

FURTHER READING

Benveniste 1939; Bouissac 1998, entries for 'arbitrariness', 'icon', 'iconicity, 'indexicality', 'Peirce', 'Saussure', 'sign', 'value'; Bruss 1978; Culler 1985; Deledalle 2000; Harris 1987; Holdcroft 1991; Merrell 2001; Ogden and Richards 1923; Peirce 1991; Saussure 1916/2011; Sebeok 1994b, entries for 'icon', 'index', 'Peirce', 'Saussure', 'semiosis', 'sign', 'symbol'; Short 2007; Thellefsen and Sørensen 2014; Zeman 1997.

SIGNS AND THINGS

While cultural semiotics is often encountered in the form of textual analysis, there is far more to semiotics than this. One cannot engage in the semiotic study of how meanings are made in texts and cultural practices without adopting a philosophical stance in relation to the nature of signs, representation, and reality. We have already seen how models of the sign vary in their philosophical implications. For those who adopt the stance that reality always involves representation and that signs are involved in the construction of reality, semiotics is unavoidably a form of philosophy. Nothing can be known outside semiosis. One of the most famous aphorisms of the philosopher Ludwig Wittgenstein is that 'the limits of my language are the limits of my world' (1922, 68), and for 'language' we could substitute 'sign system'. No semiotician or philosopher would be so naïve as to treat signs such as words as if they were the things for which they stand but, as we shall see, this occurs at least sometimes in the psychological phenomenology of everyday life and in the uncritical framework of casual discourse.

NAMING THINGS

To semioticians, a defining feature of signs is that they are treated by their users as 'standing for' or representing other things (real or imaginary). Jonathan Swift's satirical account of the fictional academicians of Lagado outlines their proposal to abolish words altogether, and to carry around bundles of objects whenever they want to communicate. This highlights problems with the simplistic notion of signs being direct substitutes for physical things in the world around us. The academicians adopt the philosophical stance of naïve verbal realism in assuming that words simply mirror objects in an external world. They believe that 'words are only names for things', a stance involving the assumption that 'things' necessarily exist independently of language prior to them being 'labelled' with words. According to this referential theory of language there is a one-to-one correspondence between word and referent (sometimes called language–world *isomorphism*), and language is simply a *nomenclature* – an item-by-item naming of things in the world. Saussure (*CLG* 34; 16, 65) felt that this nominalism was the 'superficial view' taken by the general public (a stance he sought to undermine).

Within the lexicon of a language, it is true that most of the words are lexical words (or 'content words') and that this includes nouns that refer to 'things'; however, most of these things are abstract concepts rather than physical objects in the world. Only 'proper nouns' have specific referents in the everyday world, and only some of these refer to a unique entity (e.g. *Llanfairpwllgwyngyllgogerychwyrndrobwll-llantysiliogogogoch* – the name of a Welsh village). Even proper names are not specific as they are imagined to be: for instance, a reference to 'Charles Sanders Peirce' begs questions such as 'Peirce at what date?', 'Peirce as a philosopher or in some other role?' or even 'whose Peirce?' (e.g. 'Jakobson's Peirce'?). The communicative function of a fully functioning language requires the scope of reference to move beyond the particularity of the individual instance. While each leaf, cloud, or smile is different from all others, effective communication requires general categories or 'universals'. Anyone who has attempted to communicate with people who do not share their language will be familiar with the limitations of simply pointing to things. You can't point to 'mind', 'culture', or 'history'; these are not 'things' at all. The vast majority of lexical words in a language exist on a high level of abstraction and refer to classes of things (such as *buildings*) or to concepts (such as *construction*). Language and thought depend on categorization. Without categories, things would be unthinkable. Language, we are told in the *Cours*, is 'a principle of classification' (ibid. 25; 9). John Ellis, a literary theorist, makes a powerful case for categorization as the primary function of language. 'We know something only by relating it to other things in the way that our language alone makes possible through its hierarchy of categories' (1993, 93–4). Being able to treat even the most *dissimilar* phenomena as *functionally equivalent* (as in the case of *weeds* or *pests*) has multiple advantages. Categorization supports systematization, makes complexity manageable, speeds up recognition, reduces effort and learning, makes the most of past experience, enables the inference of further attributes, makes events predictable, guides appropriate behaviour, bonds social behaviour (through shared frameworks), and tailors the world to our purposes. Categorizing, in short, makes sense of experience. As the sociologist Eviatar Zerubavel notes, 'Things become meaningful only when placed in some category' (1993, 5). Without categorization, there can be no information or knowledge. It is in this sense that Goethe (1982, vol. 12, 432) remarks that 'everything that is factual is already theory' (*da alles Faktische schon Theorie ist*). Other than lexical words, the remaining elements of the lexicon of a language, which are also the most frequently used words, consist of grammatical words (or 'function words'), such as 'only' and 'under', which do not refer to objects in the world at all. The lexicon of a language consists of many kinds of signs other than nouns. In any case, meaning arises primarily not from isolated words but from our use of words in combination. Clearly, language cannot be reduced to the naming of objects.

The less naïve realists might note at this point that words do not necessarily name only physical things that exist in an objective material world but may also label imaginary things and also *concepts*. However, as Saussure notes, the notion of words as labels for concepts assumes that ready-made ideas exist before words, whereas he argues that there are no pre-existing ideas, and nothing is distinct without language

(*CLG* 97, 155; 65, 112). It is a rationalist and 'nomenclaturist' stance on language when words are seen as 'labels' for pre-given objects or ideas. It is reductionist: reducing language to the referential function of naming things. The variety of ways in which we use language (including for expressing social meanings) makes nonsense of its reduction to a nomenclature.

Among the key functions of language, modelling the world is fundamental. Clearly, our mental representation of the world draws on sensory data but it is inseparable from linguistic mediation. Language creates a symbolic world, and as the Austrian biologist Ludwig von Bertalanffy put it, beyond 'the immediate satisfaction of biological needs' this is the world in which we live (1968, 215). A radical response to naïve realists is that nothing exists independently of the sign systems that we use; realities are constructed by our systems of representation. The most radical ('nominalist') claims are made by the French deconstructionists, for whom reality is an 'effect' of (produced by) language. Famously, Jacques Lacan declared that 'It is the world of words that creates the world of things' (1977, 65). Since Saussure is often cited in support of such extreme linguistic idealism, we should note that such claims lack any warrant in the *Cours*. While very few would go so far in the direction of idealism as to argue that there is no reality beyond language, social constructionists argue that language does not simply name pre-existing 'natural kinds'. Categories do not exist in 'the world' – they are not facts of nature but human constructs. Language imposes patterns on our perception of the world. As Zerubavel observes, categorization is how 'we transform the natural world into a social one' (1993, 5). Our intersubjective 'virtual reality' is dependent on symbolic representation. Categories construct the social worlds in which we dwell: all experience is filtered through them. Our abstractions exist only in words, but 'abstract representations have physical efficacy. They can and do change the world. They are as real and concrete as the force of gravity or the impact of a projectile' (Deacon, 1997, 453). 'God words', which are prominent in cultural rhetoric, such as freedom, motherhood, and justice, reflect core sociohistorical values in a culture or subculture in a particular period (Wierzbicka 1997). However, no categories are 'neutral'. Since categories are functional rather than natural they are, to varying degrees, evaluative (Ellis 1993, 75). Kenneth Gergen, a psychologist, notes that '"problems" don't exist in the world as independent facts; rather we construct worlds of good and bad, and define anything standing in the way of achieving what we value as "a problem"' (2009a, 4).

We have no way of experiencing reality without categorization, but language fabricates discrete entities: where are the boundaries of a cloud or when does a smile begin? Where does the East meet the West? The external world is not tidily divided into separate 'things'. The linguist John Lyons cautions that an emphasis on reality as invariably perceptually seamless may be an exaggeration, speculating that 'most of the phenomenal world, as we perceive it, is *not* an undifferentiated continuum'; and our referential categories do seem to bear some relationship to certain features which seem to be inherently salient (1977, 247; *my emphasis*). However, since perception is shaped by linguistic categories, this is a somewhat circular argument.

The Gestalt psychologists, writing in the 1920s, reported a universal human tendency to separate a salient *figure* from what is relegated to the background, and that in visual perception such figures are experienced as distinct shapes bounded by contours. Constantly bombarded with far more sensory data than we can attend to, we need to distinguish what is significant from what is not, and identifying patterns as objects is a first step in doing so. The art historian James Elkins notes that 'it is very hard to see something that has no shape or name' (Elkins 1996, 101). However, 'there are no lines in nature' (Balzac 1831, 99), and no clear boundaries in retinal images (Gregory 1970, 15). We read objects into sensory data (categorizing them and attributing qualities to them). Language makes experience orderly by creating discrete and stable objects out of a relatively undifferentiated sensory flux; these objects are internalized as concepts. Objects and their properties have no existence independently of such linguistic mediation, although we routinely act on the basis that they do (a routine which reinforces the illusion). Walter Lippmann declares that 'for the most part, we do not first see, and then define, we define first and then see' (1922, 54–5). With the exception of intense stimuli, what 'stands out' is not inherent in external reality but rather that which seems most relevant to our current concerns and that which reflects distinctions that are important in our culture. Such distinctions are reflected in the socially meaningful categories provided by our language.

Objections such as that of Lyons clearly do not demonstrate that the lexical structure of language 'reflects' or 'corresponds to' the structure of external reality. While realists contend that basic 'natural kinds' do objectively exist in the world, to social constructionists, rather than 'carving nature at its joints' (Plato's metaphor for the reality of 'Forms' in his *Phaedrus*), our linguistic categories reflect relevance to our social purposes. As Saussure notes, if words were simply a nomenclature for a pre-existing set of things in the world, translation from one language to another would be easy (*CLG* 161; 116) whereas in fact languages differ in how they categorize the world – the signifieds in one language do not neatly correspond to those in another. Within a language, many words may refer to 'the same thing' but reflect different evaluations of it (one person's 'hovel' is another person's 'home'). Furthermore, what is signified by a word is subject to historical change.

In this sense, reality or the world is created by the language we use. As the philosopher Susanne Langer (1957, 280) put it, 'Out of signs and symbols we weave our tissue of "reality"'. It can be disturbing to recognize that in the taken-for-granted realities in which we live, 'very few bricks touch the ground' (Sapir 1934, 495). However, as the sociologist Burkart Holzner (1968, 35) notes, 'The very conception of "the world" as a stable entity is only possible because of the existence of symbols'. From the perspective of social constructionism, we create and maintain our identities, facts, social realities, relationships, and institutions through our use of the signs with which we agree to communicate. A language provides its users with a shared interpretive frame of reference which is independent of individual idiosyncrasies and the contingencies of particular communicative acts.

Saussure asserts that 'to know to just what extent a thing is a reality, it is necessary and sufficient to determine to what extent it exists in the minds of speakers' (*CLG* 128; 90). Referential realists would be quick to interpret this as linguistic relativism: the notion that different worlds are constructed in different cultures, societies, and languages. According to the so-called Whorfian hypothesis, or

Sapir–Whorf theory, named after the American linguists Edward Sapir (1884–1939) and Benjamin Lee Whorf (1897–1941), language determines reality (*linguistic determinism*) and different languages determine different worldviews (*linguistic relativism*). However, this formulation is an oft-repeated distortion. Famously, Whorf declared that

> We dissect nature along lines laid down by our native languages … We cut nature up, organize it into concepts, and ascribe significances as we do, largely because we are parties to an agreement to organize it in this way – an agreement that holds throughout our speech community and is codified in the patterns of our language.
>
> (Whorf 1940, 213–14)

Based on comparative analysis, Whorf observes that the system of categorization inherent in the grammar and lexicon of a language reflects a cultural worldview. John Ellis argues (1993, 57) that the Whorfian stance is not deterministic – it is not a causal 'hypothesis' because using language *is* thought (Whorf 1940, 207). However, it has been argued (e.g. by Tallis 1995, 52 ff.) that he did take a step too far when he insisted that the implicit agreement is 'absolutely obligatory' (Whorf 1940, 213–14), making language an inescapable prison (which it is not). If languages wholly 'determined' our thinking we would never be conscious of any 'lack of fit' (when 'words fail'). How can we 'know' that colour is a continuum if perception is wholly confined to the discrete categories provided by our language? Edward Sapir argues that 'language is a guide to social reality' (1929, 68), echoing Saussure's observation that what is real to a community can be established on the basis of its linguistic distinctions. Our experience of the world is inseparable from the language we use.

> The fact of the matter is that the 'real world' is to a large extent unconsciously built upon the language habits of the group. No two languages are ever sufficiently similar to be considered as representing the same social reality. The worlds in which different societies live are distinct worlds, not merely the same

world with different labels attached . . . We see and hear and
otherwise experience very largely as we do because the language
habits of our community predispose certain choices of
interpretation.

(Sapir 1929, 69)

This is consistent with a structuralist perspective. Edmund Leach
asserts that 'the world is a representation of our language categories,
not vice versa. Because my mother tongue is English, it seems self-
evident that *bushes* and *trees* are different kinds of things' (1964, 34).
We are rarely conscious of the role of language in our thinking,
routinely experiencing linguistic categories as if they were part of
nature. Language comes to acquire the illusion of transparency: this
feature of the medium (a key factor in its efficiency) tends to blind its
users to the part it plays in constructing their experiential worlds.

Critics argue that making inferences about differences in
worldview solely on the basis of differences in linguistic structure is
a form of linguistic idealism. On the other hand, it is naïve realism to
assume that different languages simply 'filter' the same reality.
'Languages differ not in what they can express but in what they can
express *easily* . . . It is the kind of small difference that makes a world
of difference and helps construct and maintain different worlds'
(Schudson 1984, 233). The role of metaphors in framing phenomena
will be discussed in Chapter 4.

Even if we reject the stance that our realities are inseparable
from our sign systems, we must still acknowledge that there are many
things in the experiential world for which we have no words and that
most words do not correspond to objects in the known world at all.
Thus, all words are abstractions, and there is no direct correspondence
between words and things in the world.

REFERENTIALITY

Saussure's formal model of the linguistic sign involves no direct
reference to reality outside the sign. This is not a denial of extralinguistic reality but a reflection of his understanding of his own task
as a linguist. Saussure accepts that in most scientific disciplines the

'objects of study' are 'given in advance' and exist independently of the observer's 'point of view'. However, he stresses that in linguistics, by contrast, 'it is the point of view that creates the object' (*CLG* 23; 8). It is easy to see how this might be criticized as an idealist stance. In the Saussurean model, linguistic signs are mental constructs and as part of sign systems they are socially constructed. According to the social constructionist stance, linguistic categories and signs reflect not the world but our culture's 'way of seeing'. In contrast to nomenclaturists, for whom things in the world are pre-given and simply labelled by language, Saussurean principles assert the non-essential nature of objects.

In contrast to the Saussurean model, Peirce's model of the sign explicitly features the *referent* – something beyond the sign to which the sign vehicle refers (though not necessarily a material thing). However, it also features the *interpretant*, which leads to an 'infinite series' of signs, so it has been provocatively suggested that Peirce's model could also be taken to suggest the relative independence of signs from referents (Silverman 1983, 15). In any event, for Peirce, reality can only be known via signs. If representations are our only access to reality, determining their accuracy is a critical issue. Peirce adopted from logic the notion of 'modality' to refer to the truth value of a sign, acknowledging three kinds: actuality, (logical) necessity, and (hypothetical) possibility (CP 2.454). Furthermore, his classification of signs in terms of the relationship of the sign vehicle to its referent, reflects their modality – their apparent transparency in relation to reality (symbolic relations, for instance, having low modality). Peirce asserts that, logically, signification could only ever be partial; otherwise the sign would destroy itself by becoming identical with its object (Peirce 1982–, 1.79–80).

> We actually made a map of the country, on the scale of a mile to the mile.' 'Have you used it much?' I enquired. 'It has never been spread out, yet,' said Mein Herr: 'the farmers objected: they said it would cover the whole country, and shut out the sunlight! So we now use the country itself, as its own map, and I assure you it does nearly as well.
>
> (Lewis Carroll, *Sylvie and Bruno Concluded*, Chapter 11)

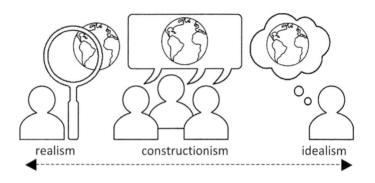

realism   constructionism   idealism

FIGURE 2.1 Realism vs. idealism

Source: © 2016 Daniel Chandler

The spectrum in Figure 2.1 is a simplified schematization of philosophical stances on what is 'real', which may serve as a reminder that
we are not always talking about the same thing when we refer to 'the
world'. The three positions illustrated foreground respectively (left to
right) the physical, social, and psychological dimensions of reality,
although these are not tidily separable. Opposing positions are often
the rhetorical constructs of critics; hard-headed realists often dismiss
those who focus on the social as cultural relativists, while the Italian
philosopher Ferruccio Rossi-Landi (1921–85) wryly observes that
'idealists tend to call mental what they find inconvenient to accept as
social' (Chatman *et al.* 1979, 358). For those who veer towards
the extreme position of philosophical *idealism*, reality is purely subjective and is constructed in our use of signs. For those drawn towards
the naïve version of ontological *realism*, objective reality exists
independently of our interpretive systems, having its own intrinsic
properties. Naïve realists reject the notion that processes of mediation
play a part in the *construction* of reality. The constructionist (or
constructivist) position is that language and other semiotic systems
do play a major part in 'the social construction of reality'. We dwell
primarily within a symbolic, intersubjective reality. Social constructionists would not suggest that *physical* reality is socially constructed

but would contend that our conception even of this is a product of shared ways of describing and classifying (Esland 1973, 78). While many cite Saussure in support of constructionism, others object to an apparent indifference towards social reality in Saussure's model (however inappropriate this is to his linguistic goals). Those on the political left in particular challenge its sidelining of the importance of the material conditions of lived existence. A non-referential sign system presents problems for those drawn to the stance of Umberto Eco (1976, 7) that 'semiotics is in principle the discipline studying everything which can be used in order to lie'.

MODALITY

Whatever our philosophical positions, in our daily behaviour we routinely act on the basis that some representations of reality are more reliable than others. We do so in part with reference to cues within texts, which semioticians (following linguists) call 'modality markers'. Such cues refer to what are variously described as the plausibility, reliability, credibility, truth, accuracy, or facticity of texts within a given genre as representations of some recognizable reality. Gunther Kress and Theo van Leeuwen acknowledge that:

> A social semiotic theory of truth cannot claim to establish the absolute truth or untruth of representations. It can only show whether a given 'proposition' (visual, verbal or otherwise) is represented as true or not. From the point of view of social semiotics, truth is a construct of semiosis, and as such the truth of a particular social group, arising from the values and beliefs of that group.
>
> (Kress and van Leeuwen 1996, 159)

From such a perspective, reality has authors; thus there are many *realities* rather than the single reality posited by objectivists. Constructionists insist that realities are not limitless and unique to the individual as extreme subjectivists would argue; rather, they are the product of social definitions and as such far from equal in status. Realities are contested, and textual representations are thus 'sites of struggle'.

Modality refers to the reality status accorded to or claimed by a sign, message, text, or genre. More formally, Bob Hodge and Gunther Kress (1988, 124) declare that 'modality refers to the status, authority, and reliability of a message, to its ontological status, or to its value as truth or fact'. In making sense of a text, its interpreters make modality judgements about it, drawing on their knowledge of the world and of the medium. For instance, they assign it to fact or fiction, actuality or acting, live or recorded, and they assess the possibility or plausibility of the events depicted or the claims made in it. This is particularly pertinent in social media, where 'fake news' proliferates. Modality judgements involve comparisons of textual representations with models drawn from the everyday world and with models based on the genre; they are therefore obviously dependent on relevant experience of both the world and the medium (Hodge and Tripp 1986; Chandler 1997b).

Clearly, the extent to which a text may be perceived as real depends in part on the medium employed. Writing, for instance, generally has a lower modality than film and television. However, no rigid ranking of media modalities is possible. John Kennedy (1974) showed children a simple line drawing featuring a group of children sitting in a circle with a gap in their midst. He asked them to add to this gap a drawing of their own, and when they concentrated on the central region of the drawing, many of them tried to pick up the pencil that was depicted in the same style in the top right-hand corner of the drawing! Being absorbed in the task led them to accept unconsciously the terms in which reality was constructed within the medium. This is not likely to be a phenomenon confined to children, since when absorbed in narrative (in many media) we frequently fall into a 'suspension of disbelief' without compromising our ability to distinguish representations from reality. Charles Peirce (CP 3.362) reflects that 'in contemplating a painting, there is a moment when we lose the consciousness that it is not the thing, the distinction of the real and the copy disappears'.

While in a conscious comparison of a photographic image with a cartoon image of the same thing, the photograph is likely to be judged as more realistic, the mental schemata involved in visual recognition may be closer to the stereotypical simplicity of cartoon images than to photographs. People can identify an image as a hand when it is drawn as a cartoon more quickly than when they are shown a photograph of a hand (Ryan and Schwartz 1956). This underlines the importance of perceptual codes in constructing reality (a topic to which we return in Chapter 5). Umberto Eco (1976, 204–5) argues that through familiarity an iconic signifier can acquire primacy over its signified. Such a sign becomes conventional 'step by step, the more its addressee becomes acquainted with it. At a certain point, the iconic representation, however stylized it may be, appears to be more true than the real experience, and people begin to look at things through the glasses of iconic convention'. Modality cues within texts include both formal features of the medium (such as flatness or motion) and content features (such as plausibility or familiarity), though it is their interaction and interpretation that are most important. The media that are typically judged to be the most realistic are photographic – especially film and television. Being less reliant than verbal language on symbolic signs, film, television, and photography involve an apparent transparency of reference, seeming to offer 'reflections of reality' (even in that which is imaginary). This is an important part of what the film theorist and semiotician Christian Metz (1931–93) is referring to when he describes the cinematic signifier as 'the imaginary signifier' (1977). But photography does not *reproduce* its object: it mediates it. While we do not mistake one for the other, we do need to remind ourselves that a photograph or a film does not simply record an event, but is only one of an infinite number of possible representations. All media texts, however 'realistic', are representations rather than recordings or reproductions of reality.

The film theorist André Bazin describes what he calls the 'reproductive fallacy' according to which the only kind of representation that can show things 'as they really are' would be one which is (or appears to be) exactly like that which it represents in every respect. Texts are almost always constructed from different materials from that which they represent, and representations cannot be replicas. For Bazin, aesthetic realism depends on a broader 'truth to reality' (1974, 64). Ien Ang (1985) argues that watching television soap operas can involve a kind of *psychological* or *emotional realism* for viewers, which exists at the connotative rather than the denotative level. Viewers find some representations emotionally or psychologically 'true-to-life' (even if at the denotative level the treatment may seem 'unrealistic'). I would argue that especially with long-running soaps (which may become more real to their fans over time) what we could call *generic realism* is another factor. Viewers familiar with the characters and conventions of a particular soap opera may often judge the programme largely in its own generic terms rather than with reference to some external reality. For instance, is a character's current behaviour consistent with what we have learned over time about that character? The soap may be accepted to some extent as a world in its own right, in which slightly different rules may sometimes apply. For J. R. R. Tolkien (1939) such 'inner consistency' accounts better for audience engagement than Coleridge's oft-invoked concept of the 'willing suspension of disbelief', according to which readers excuse narrative implausibilities when they detect a sufficient 'semblance of truth' (he was referring to poetry but the notion is widely applied to audiences in general).

What are recognized as realistic styles of representation reflect aesthetic conventions or 'codes' (see Chapter 5). Over time, certain methods of production within a medium and a genre become naturalized. The content comes to be accepted as a reflection of reality. In the case of popular television and film, for instance, the use of 'invisible editing' represents a widespread set of conventions, which has come to seem natural to most viewers (as we shall see later). In realistic texts, what is foregrounded is the content rather than the form or style of production. As in the dominant mode of scientific discourse, the medium and codes are discounted as neutral and transparent and the makers of the text retreat to invisibility. Consequently, reality seems to pre-exist its representation and to 'speak for itself'; what is said thus has the deceptive aura of objective truth.

THE WORD IS NOT THE THING

The Belgian surrealist René Magritte painted *La trahison des images* ('The Treachery of Images') in 1928/9. That it has become one of Magritte's most famous and widely reproduced works suggests the enduring fascination of its theme. At first glance, its subject is banal. We are offered a realistic depiction of an object, which we easily recognize: a smoker's pipe (in side-on view). However, the painting also includes the text 'Ceci n'est pas une pipe' ('This is not a pipe'). The inclusion of text *within* the painting is remarkable enough, but the wording gives us cause to pause. If this were part of a language lesson or a child's 'reading book' (the style reminds me of old-fashioned *Ladybird* books for children), we might expect to see the words 'This is a pipe.' To depict a pipe and then provide a 'label' which insists that 'this is not a pipe' initially seems perverse. Is it purely irrational or is there something that we can learn from this apparent paradox? As our minds struggle to find a stable, meaningful interpretation of 'this' we may not be too happy that there is no single, 'correct' answer to this question – although those of us who are 'tolerant of ambiguity' may accept that it offers a great deal of food for thought about levels (or modes) of reality. The indexical word 'this' can be seen as a key to the interpretation of this painting: what exactly does the word 'this' refer to? Anthony Wilden suggests several alternative interpretations:

- this [pipe] is not a pipe;
- this [image of a pipe] is not a pipe;
- this [painting] is not a pipe;
- this [sentence] is not a pipe;
- [this] this is not a pipe;
- [this] is not a pipe.

(Wilden 1987, 245)

Although we habitually relate the meaning of texts to the stated or inferred purposes of their makers, Magritte's own purposes are not essential to our current concerns. It suits our purposes here to suggest that the painting could be taken as meaning that this representation (or any representation) is not that which it represents. That this image of a pipe is 'only an image' and that we can't smoke it seems obvious – nobody 'in their right mind' would be so foolish as to try to pick it up and use it as a functional pipe. However, we do habitually refer to such realistic depictions in terms that suggest that they are nothing more nor less than what they depict. Any representation is more than merely a reproduction of that which it represents: it also contributes to the *construction* of reality. Even 'photorealism' does not depict unmediated reality. The most realistic representation may also symbolically or metaphorically 'stand for' something else entirely. Furthermore, the depiction of a pipe is no guarantee of the existence of a specific pipe in the world of which this is an accurate depiction. It seems a fairly generic pipe and could therefore be seen (as is frequently true of language lessons, children's encyclopaedia entries and so on) as an illustration of the 'concept' of a pipe rather than of a specific pipe. The label seeks to anchor our interpretation – a concept to which we will return later – and yet, at the same time, the label is part of the painting itself rather than a title attached to the frame. Magritte's painting could be seen as a kind of defamiliarization: we are so used to seeing things and attaching labels to them that we seldom look deeper and do not see things in their specificity. One function of art (and of surrealistic art in particular) is 'to make the familiar strange' (as the Russian formalists put it).

Alfred Korzybski (1879–1950), the founder of a movement known as 'general semantics', declares that 'the map is not the territory' and that 'the word is not the thing' (1933). The non-identity of sign and thing is, of course, a very basic Saussurean (and social constructionist) principle (Watzlawick 1984, 215). As in the anecdote about the giant map, point-to-point correspondence lacks the utility of generality offered most notably by linguistic categories. While Saussure's linguistic model is not based on referentiality, the general semanticists adopted the realist stance that language comes 'between' us and the objective world and they sought to reform our verbal behaviour to counteract the linguistic 'distortion' of reality. They felt that one reason for the confusion of signs and referents is that we sometimes allow language to take us further up the 'ladder of abstraction' than we think we are. The ladder metaphor is consistent with how we routinely refer to levels of abstraction (we talk of thinkers with 'their heads in the clouds' and of 'realists' with their 'feet on the ground'). As we move up the ladder, we move from the particular to the general, from concrete reality to abstract generalization. The general semanticists were of course hard-headed realists and what they wanted was for people to keep their feet firmly planted on the ground.

In alerting language-users to levels of abstraction, the general semanticists sought to avoid the confusion of *higher logical types* with *lower logical types*. 'A map' is of a higher (more general) logical type than 'the territory', and linguistic representation in particular lends itself to this process of abstraction. Clearly, we can learn more about a place by visiting it than by simply looking at a map of it, and we can tell more about a person by meeting that person than by merely looking at a photograph of that person. Translation from lower levels to higher levels involves an inevitable loss of specificity – as with earth being filtered through a series of increasingly fine sieves or photocopies being repeatedly made of the 'copies' that they produce. We have already noted that categorization can liberate us from being 'slaves to the particular' (Bruner *et al.* 1956, 1), but it remains important to be alert for significant losses, absences, or exclusions. While the logician may be able to keep such levels separate, in most acts of communication some 'slippage' occurs routinely, although we are normally capable of identifying what kind of messages we are dealing with, assigning them to appropriate levels of abstraction. Semioticians observe that some kind of 'translation' is unavoidable in human communication. Claude Lévi-Strauss (1961, 61) declares that 'understanding consists in the reduction of one type of reality to another' (cf. Leach 1976, 27; Greimas 1970, 13).

While it can be useful to consider abstraction in terms of levels and logical typing, the implicit filter metaphor in the general semanticists' 'ladder of abstraction' is too uni-dimensional. Any given object of perception could be categorized in a variety of ways rather than in terms of a single objective hierarchy. The categories applied depend on such factors as experience, roles, and purposes. This reminds us of the 'observer' being part of the 'observed', and raises issues of interpretation. For instance, looking at an advertisement featuring a woman's face, some viewers might assume that the image stood for women in general, others that she represented a particular type, role, or group, and yet others might recognize her as a particular individual. Knowing the appropriate level of abstraction in relation to interpreting such an image would depend primarily on familiarity with the relevant cultural conventions (or codes).

The general semanticists set themselves the therapeutic goal of 'purifying' language in order to make its relationship to reality more transparent, and from such roots sprang projects such as the development of 'Basic English' (Ogden 1930). Whatever reservations we may have about such goals, Korzybski's popularization of the principle of arbitrariness could be seen as a useful corrective to some of our habits of mind. As a caveat, Korzybski's aphorism seems unnecessary: we all know that the word 'dog' cannot bark or bite, but in some circumstances 'common sense' still leads us routinely to identify sign and thing, representation with what it represents. Readers who find this strange should consider how they would feel about 'mutilating' a photograph of someone for whom they care deeply.

In his massively influential book *The Interpretation of Dreams* (first published in 1900), Sigmund Freud (1938, 319) argues that 'dream-content is, as it were, presented in hieroglyphics, whose symbols must be translated . . . It would of course be incorrect to read these symbols in accordance with their values as pictures, instead of in accordance with their meaning as symbols'. He also observes that 'words are often treated in dreams as things' (ibid., 330). Magritte plays with our habit of identifying the sign vehicle with the referent in a series of drawings and paintings in which objects are depicted with verbal labels that 'don't belong to them'. In an oil-painting entitled *La clef des songes* (1936, usually rendered as 'The Interpretation of Dreams', in allusion to Freud) we are confronted with images of six familiar objects together with verbal labels. Such arrangements are familiar, particularly in the language-learning context suggested by the blackboard-like background. However, we quickly realize that the words do not match the images under which they appear. If we then rearrange them in our minds, we find that the labels do not correspond to *any* of the images. The relation between the image of an object and the verbal label attached to it is thus presented as arbitrary.

The confusion of the representation with the represented is a feature of schizophrenia and psychosis (Wilden 1987, 201). 'In order to be able to operate with symbols it is necessary first of all to be able to distinguish between the sign and the thing it signifies' (Leach 1970, 43). However, the confusion of 'levels of reality' is also a normal feature of an early phase of cognitive development in childhood. Jerome Bruner (1966) observes that, for pre-school children, thought and the object of thought seem to be the same thing, but that during schooling one comes to separate word and thing. The substitution of a sign for its referent (initially in the form of gestures and imitative sounds) constitutes a crucial phase in the infant's acquisition of language. The child quickly discovers the apparently magical power of words (and images) for referring to things in their absence – this property of displacement being a key 'design feature' of language (Piaget 1971, 64; Hockett 1958). It is hardly surprising that, even in mid-childhood, children sometimes appear to have difficulty in separating words from what they represent. Piaget illustrates the 'nominal realism' of young children in an interview with a child aged 9½:

> 'Could the sun have been called "moon" and the moon "sun"?'
> – 'No.' 'Why not?' – 'Because the sun shines brighter than the moon
> . . .' 'But if everyone had called the sun "moon", and the moon
> "sun", would we have known it was wrong?' – 'Yes, because the
> sun is always bigger, it always stays like it is and so does the moon.'
> 'Yes, but the sun isn't changed, only its name. Could it have been
> called . . . etc.?' – 'No . . . Because the moon rises in the evening,
> and the sun in the day.'
>
> (Piaget 1929, 81–2)

Thus for the child, words do not seem at all arbitrary. Similarly, Sylvia Scribner and Michael Cole found that unschooled Vai people in Liberia felt that the names of sun and moon could not be changed, one of them expressing the view that these were God-given names (Scribner and Cole 1981, 141).

The anthropologist Lucien Lévy-Bruhl (1857–1939) claimed that people in 'primitive' cultures had difficulty in distinguishing between names and the things to which they referred, regarding these as intrinsically connected. The fear of 'graven images' within the Judeo-Christian tradition and also magical practices and beliefs such as Voodoo are clearly related to such a phenomenon. The Canadian psychologist David Olson (1994) emphasizes the epistemological significance of writing. He refers to a proto-cuneiform clay tablet now in the British Museum, dating from 3100–3000 BCE and originating from the ancient Mesopotamian city of Ur (British Museum #140855, reg. #1989,0130.4; see MacGregor 2010, 90). The surface is divided into cells, each of which features signs representing products (schematic beer-jars with pointed bases) and corresponding quantities (symbolized by stylus marks). Olson sees this inventory as an elementary example of an early form of syntax. He argues that such 'syntactic scripts', which superseded the use of clay tokens for similar purposes, marked the end of 'word magic'. They enabled signs to be seen as representing words rather than things, language to be seen as more than purely referential, and words to be seen as (linguistic) entities in their own right. By the seventeenth century, scholars saw representations as conventionalized constructions which were relatively independent both of what they represented and of their authors; knowledge involved manipulating such signs. Olson notes that once such distinctions are made, the way is open to making modality judgements about the status of representations – such as their perceived truth or accuracy. While the seventeenth-century shift in attitudes towards signs was part of a search for 'neutrality', 'objectivity', and 'truth' (see also Chapter 4), in more recent times, of course, we have come to recognize that 'there is no representation without intention and interpretation' (1994, 197).

A Russian peasant supposedly once asked how astronomers discover the names of previously unknown stars (Vygotsky 1939)! Sophisticated literates are able to joke about the notion that names belong to things. In Aldous Huxley's novel *Chrome Yellow*, an old farmworker points out his pigs: 'Look at them, sir,' he said, with a motion of his hand towards the wallowing swine. 'Rightly is they called pigs'. Literate adults may not often seem to be prey to this sort of nominal realism. However, certain signs become regarded by some as far from arbitrary, acquiring almost magical power – as in relation to 'graphic' swearing and issues of prejudice – highlighting the point that signs are not *socially* arbitrary. Children are just as aware of this: many are far from convinced by adult advice that 'sticks and stones may break my bones, but names can never hurt me'. We may all still need some convincing that 'the word is not the thing'. In some countries there are dire consequences for burning the national flag. As an anonymous twenty-first century internet meme puts it, 'We live in a culture where people are more offended by "swear" words and middle fingers than they are by famine, warfare, and the destruction of our environment'.

Shakespeare's Hamlet refers to 'the purpose of playing, whose end, both at the first and now, was and is, to hold, as 'twere, the mirror up to nature' (*Hamlet* III, ii), and being 'true to life' is probably still a key criterion in judgements of literary worth. Realistic texts reflect a mimetic purpose in representation – seeking to imitate so closely that which they depict that they may be experienced as virtually identical (and thus unmediated). While some purely verbal signs can occasionally generate the same emotional reactions as what they represent, as conventional symbols with a low modality they cannot actually be mistaken for them. It is generally more difficult to recognize the conventionality of images that are perceived as resembling what they depict. Yet even an image is not what it represents – the presence of an image marks the absence of its referent. The difference between the sign vehicle and what it signifies is fundamental. Nevertheless, when the former is experienced as highly realistic – as in the case of photography and film – it is particularly easy to slip into regarding it as identical with what it depicts. In contrast even to realistic painting and drawing, photographs seem far less obviously authored by a human being. Just as 'the word is not the thing' and 'the map is not the territory' nor is a photograph or television news footage that which it depicts. Yet in the common-sense attitude of everyday life we routinely treat high modality signs in this way. Many realistic filmic narratives and documentaries seem to invite this confusion of representation with reality (Nichols 1981, 21). Thus television is frequently described as a 'window on the world' and we usually assume that 'the camera never lies'. We know of course that in a film a dog can bark but it cannot bite (though, when 'absorbed', we may 'suspend disbelief' in the context of what we know to be enacted drama). However, we are frequently inclined to accept 'the evidence of our own eyes' even when events are mediated by the cameras of journalists.

However realistic (in any medium) representations are experienced as being, they always involve a point of view. Representations that claim to be real deny the unavoidable difference between map and territory. In the sense that there is always a difference between the represented and its representation, 'the camera always lies'. We do not need to adopt the 'scientific' realism of the so-called general semanticists concerning the 'distortion of reality' by our signifying systems, but may acknowledge instead that reality does not exist independently of signs, turning our critical attention to the issue of *whose* realities are privileged in particular representations – a perspective which, avoiding a retreat to subjectivism, pays due tribute to the unequal distribution of power in the social world.

EMPTY SIGNIFIERS

While Saussure insists on the interdependence of the signifier and the signified and on neither preceding, or taking priority over, the other, both structuralist and poststructuralist theorists have dismissed or disregarded his stance, or have adopted his terms but not his model, arguing instead for 'the primacy of the signifier'. Many postulate a complete disconnection of the signifier and the signified (which makes no sense in the Saussurean framework). In deconstructionist discourse, an 'empty' or 'floating signifier' is variously defined as a signifier with a vague, highly variable, unspecifiable, or non-existent signified. Such signifiers mean different things to different people: they may signify many or even *any* signifieds; they may mean whatever their interpreters want them to mean. In such an unSaussurean state of radical disconnection between signifier and signified, a 'sign' only means that it means. Jonathan Culler (1985, 115) suggests that to refer to an 'empty signifier' is an implicit acceptance of its status as a signifier and is thus 'to correlate it with a signified' even if this is not known. The 'floating signifier' is referred to in the year 1950 in Lévi-Strauss's *Introduction to the Work of Marcel Mauss*. For Lévi-Strauss such a signifier is like an algebraic symbol that has no imminent symbolic value but which can represent anything. The first explicit reference to an 'empty signifier' of which I am aware is that of Roland Barthes in his essay 'Myth Today' (1957). Barthes defines an empty signifier as one with no definite signified. He also refers to non-linguistic signs specifically as being so open to interpretation that they constitute a 'floating chain of signifieds' (1964, 39).

Whereas Saussure sees the signifier and the signified (however arbitrary their relationship) as being as inseparable as the two sides of a piece of paper, poststructuralists have rejected what they have (mistakenly) seen as the wholly stable relationships embedded in his model. The French psychoanalyst Jacques Lacan (1977, 154) wrote of 'the incessant sliding of the signified under the signifier', arguing that there could be no anchoring of particular signifiers to particular signifieds. This particular claim is not as radical as it may seem, even in relation to linguistic signs, where both the phonetic and conceptual bases are inherently variable. Jacques Derrida refers (originally in the 1960s) to the 'play' or 'freeplay' of signifiers: they are not fixed to their signifieds but point beyond themselves to other signifiers in an 'indefinite referral of signifier to signified' (Derrida 1967b, 25; 'freeplay' has become the dominant English rendering of Derrida's use of the term *jeu* – see, for instance, Derrida 1967a, xix). Derrida sought to 'deconstruct' Western metaphysical systems, denying that there were any ultimate determinable meanings. Derrida coined the term *différance* to allude also to the way in which meaning is endlessly *deferred*. He argues that signs thus always 'refer to' other signs, and there is no final 'transcendental signified', independent of language, offering an illusory closure of meaning and 'a reassuring end to the reference from sign to sign' (ibid., 20). Since this is often used as a 'knock-down argument' against Saussure, we should note that 'deferral' is implicit in his concept of negative differentiation and, in his system, there is a radical indeterminacy in both concepts and sounds, and it is certainly not grounded on some 'transcendental signified'. Endless deferral is similar to Peirce's 'unlimited semiosis', although Peirce emphasizes that in practice this is inevitably cut short by the practical constraints of everyday life (Gallie 1952, 126), and that the object is ultimately graspable, whereas postmodernist theories grant no access to any reality outside signification. Whereas the structuralist rhetoric of 'decoding' and 'underlying structures' implies that stripping away layers will reveal an inner core of 'naked reality' or fundamental truth, deconstructionists insist that no solid underlying structural foundation, 'ultimate' meaning, or 'transcendental signified' can ever be located. Social constructionists agree that no matter how many layers of signification we strip away, we can never get down to unmediated reality: we are dealing with representations all the way down. Derrida (1967a, 158, 163) famously declared that *il n'y a pas de hors-texte*, which is widely translated as an idealist declaration that 'there is nothing outside the text' (more literally and less provocatively, 'there is no outside-text'). For materialist Marxists and realists, semiotic idealism is intolerable: 'signs cannot be permitted to swallow up their referents in a never-ending chain of signification, in which one sign always points on to another, and the circle is never broken by the intrusion of that to which the sign refers' (Lovell 1983, 16). However, an emphasis on the unavoidability of signification need not necessitate denying any external reality. Richard Dyer (1993, 3) asserts that 'because one can see reality only through representation, it does not follow that one does not see reality at all'. Reality can exhibit a certain recalcitrance when we seek to subordinate it to our purposes.

Romantic mythology reflects a yearning for a primal state of unmediatedness (referring to children before language or human beings before The Fall) (Chandler 1995a, 31–2). In the modern world, advertisers work hard to sell us 'authenticity' in one form or another. In his book *The Image*, Daniel Boorstin (1961) charts the rise of what he calls 'pseudo-events' – events which are staged for the mass media to report. However, any 'event' is a social construction – bounded 'events' have no objective existence, and all news items are 'stories' (Galtung and Ruge 1981). A famous study by Hastorf and Cantril (1954) of fans' perceptions of an American football match showed that the perception and recall of what might seem to be 'the same event' involved a very active *construction* of differing realities, to the extent that:

> The data here indicate that there is no such 'thing' as a "game" existing "out there" in its own right which people merely "observe". The game "exists" for a person and is experienced by him only insofar as certain happenings have significances in terms of his purpose.
>
> (Hastorf and Cantril 1954, 133)

Such purposes, of course, are not so much those of individuals but of different social groups – in this case, rival groups of football fans.

In the spirit of the romantic yearning for an unmediated world, the postmodernist Jean Baudrillard interprets many representations as a means of concealing the absence of reality; he calls such representations 'simulacra' (or copies without originals) (Baudrillard 1984). He sees a degenerative evolution in modes of representation in which signs are increasingly empty of meaning:

> These would be the successive phases of the image:
>
> It is the reflection of a basic reality.
> It masks and perverts a basic reality.
> It masks the absence of a basic reality.
> It bears no relation to any reality whatever: it is its own pure simulacrum.
>
> (Baudrillard 1988, 170)

From a semiotic point of view, those who have read this far will be aware of the problematic nature of such a formulation. Baudrillard argues against 'semio-linguistics' that 'the separation of the sign and the world is a fiction' (ibid., 84). Although he employs the terms *signifier* and *signified*, for him the latter is the referent, in contrast to Saussure's usage (so I have changed these here to *sign* (vehicle) and *referent*). He suggests that when speech and writing were created, signs were invented to point to material or social reality, a referential bond which has since been increasingly eroded. With industrialization, as advertising, propaganda, and commodification set in, the sign began to hide 'basic reality'. In the postmodern age of 'hyper-reality' in which what are only illusions in the media of communication seem very real, signs hide the 'absence of reality' and only appear to mean something. For Baudrillard, *simulacra*, the signs that characterize late capitalism, come in three forms: *counterfeit* (imitation), when there is still a direct link between signs and referents; *production* (illusion), when there is an indirect link; and *simulation* (fake), when signs stand in relation only to other signs and not in relation to any fixed external reality. Baudrillard's (1995) claim that the Gulf War never happened is certainly provocative, and it is hardly surprising that the dismissive label of semiological 'idealist' which he applies to Saussure has also been applied to him.

Such perspectives, of course, beg the fundamental question, 'What is "real"?' Just because the world we live in is a social construction doesn't make it any less real to us. Subjective (or intersubjective) realities can be just as potent as physical realities. The products of social construction *matter*. As the American sociologist William I. Thomas famously observed, 'if . . . [we] define situations as real, they are real in their consequences' (Thomas and Thomas 1928, 573). Reality and truth can thus be seen as a construction of perspective. It is not a denial of external reality to argue that much of our knowledge of the world is indirect; we experience many things primarily (or even solely) as they are represented to us within our media and communication technologies. Even photographic and filmic representations can never be neutral and transparent but are instead constitutive of reality. As Judith Butler (1999, xix) puts it, we need to ask, 'What does transparency keep obscure?'. Above all, it conceals the signs of construction.

Semiotics helps us to not to take representations for granted as reflections of reality, enabling us to take them apart and consider whose realities they represent. As the linguist Edward Sapir (1921, 38) famously remarked, 'all grammars leak'. Those who would learn from semiotics should search for structural leaks, seams, and scaffolding as signs of the making of any representation, and also for what has been excluded so that the text may seem to tell 'the whole truth'.

REFLECTIONS

1   What is the problem with the proposal by the academicians of Lagado to communicate using objects instead of words?
2   In what sense does communication create reality?
3   What does Magritte's painting *La trahison des images* teach us about representation?
4   What examples have you experienced which show people treating a sign as the thing it represents?
5   What 'empty signifiers' can you identify in recent political debates?
6   What might Derrida have meant when he declared that *il n'y a pas de hors-texte*? Google critical commentaries to identify plausible alternative interpretations.

7 In your own experience, what examples have you encountered of events that are significantly different for those involved?

8 If you have not explored an 'online world' (such as Second Life or InWorldz), try doing so (it takes some patience, so give it a fair trial). Does this experience have any influence on what you define as 'real'?

FURTHER READING

Baudrillard 1988; Berger and Luckmann 1967; Gergen 2009a; Hastorf and Cantril 1954; Holzner 1968; Korzybski 1933; Nöth 1990, Chapter 2 ('Signs and Meaning'); Pearce 1989; Tallis 1995; Watzlawick 1976 and 1984; Whorf 1940.

ANALYSING STRUCTURES

Although it is highly reductive to view semiotics as a method of textual analysis, it is in this structuralist form that it is probably most widely known in cultural studies and allied fields of study. It was developed into an influential methodology (or at least a set of methodological tools) by structuralist theorists. Although the paternity of their movement is disputed, many claimed Saussure as its founding father (though he was long dead when the term first appeared) and they selectively adopted and adapted concepts from the *Cours*. Broadly, structuralism can be seen as a search for regularities which help to explain how semiotic systems (such as the language system, genres, or cultural codes) work, through the structural analysis of texts or cultural practices reflecting their use (such as advertisements, films, or greeting rituals) – which involves identifying basic signifying units within such structures and the relationships between these elements.

HORIZONTAL AND VERTICAL AXES

For Saussure, there are two kinds of relations between signs: *syntagmatic* relations, or structural combinations, and *associative* relations (*rapports associatifs*), or systemic alternatives (*CLG* 170; 122–3). For him, syntagmatic relations in language are those between a linguistic unit and others preceding or following it in the context of a chain (such as in a sentence). Associative relations are those between a particular word and others, which are brought to mind in its current context because they have something in common with it (in form or meaning). Linguistic units are related to each other both syntagmatically and associatively and linguistic units have no significance apart from these relations (ibid. 179–80; 130). Syntagmatic and associative relations are interdependent and complementary (ibid. 177; 128).

In structuralist theory the term *paradigmatic*, introduced by Hjelmslev, subsequently replaced the term *associative*. The structuralist method of describing a language involves identifying sets of interchangeable systemic units (*paradigms*) and specifying how such units can be combined (on various levels) in textual structures (*syntagms*).

The distinction is a key one in structuralist semiotic analysis in which these two structural 'axes' (horizontal as syntagmatic and vertical as paradigmatic) are seen as applicable to all sign systems. Syntagms are the slots and paradigms are the slot fillers (see Figure 3.1). The plane of the syntagm is that of the combination of 'this-*and*-this-*and*-this' (as in the sentence, 'the man cried') while the plane of the paradigm is that of the selection of 'this-*or*-this-*or*-this' (e.g. the replacement of the last word in the same sentence with 'died' or 'sang'). Syntagms are not limited to linear sequences but can also exist as hierarchies (with different structural layers and part–whole relationships). Syntagmatic relations refer intratextually to other signifiers co-present within the text, while paradigmatic relations refer intertextually to signifiers which are absent from the text. Following Saussure, paradigms are thus referred to as relations *in absentia*, while syntagms are referred to as relations *in praesentia*. The 'value' of a sign is determined by both its paradigmatic and its syntagmatic relations.

Paradigmatic relationships operate on the level of the signifier and on the level of the signified. A paradigm is a set of associated

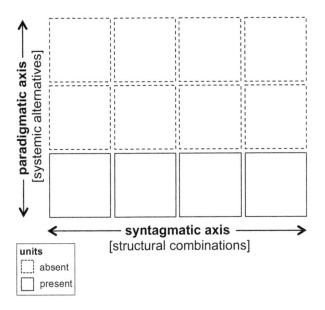

FIGURE 3.1 Syntagmatic and paradigmatic axes

Source: © 2016 Daniel Chandler

signifiers or signifieds which are all members of some defining category, but in which each is significantly different. In natural language there are grammatical paradigms such as verbs or nouns. In a given context, one member of the paradigm set is structurally replaceable with another; the choice of one excludes the choice of another. The use of one sign (e.g. a particular word) rather than another from the same paradigm set (e.g. adjectives) shapes the preferred meaning of a text. Paradigmatic relations can thus be seen as 'contrastive'. Saussure's notion of 'associative' relations is broader and less formal than what is normally meant by 'paradigmatic' relations. He refers to 'mental association' (ibid. 171; 123) and includes perceived similarities in form (e.g. homophones) or meaning (e.g. synonyms). Such similarities are diverse and range from strong to slight, and might refer to only part of a word (such as a shared prefix or suffix). He notes that there is no end (or commonly agreed order) to such associations (ibid. 174–5; 126–7). Jakobson (1962, 599) rejects this conception, insisting that there is a 'hierarchical order within the paradigmatic set'. Paradigms are not confined to the verbal mode. In film and television, paradigms include ways of changing shot (such as cut, fade, dissolve, and wipe). The medium and genre are also paradigms, and particular media texts derive meaning from the ways in which the medium and genre used differ from the alternatives.

A *syntagm* is a combination of interacting signifiers which forms a meaningful whole within a text – sometimes, following Saussure, called a 'chain'. Such combinations are made within a framework of syntactic rules. In language, a sentence, for instance, is a syntagm of words; so too are paragraphs and chapters. Syntagms are not limited to sequences. A printed advertisement is a syntagm of visual signifiers. Syntagms can contain other syntagms (in hierarchical structures). In dramatic structure, both acts and the scenes within them are syntagms. Syntagmatic relations highlight the importance of part–whole relationships (*CLG* 177; 128). Syntagmatic relations are the various ways in which elements within the same text may be related to each other. There can be whole 'networks of structured relationships' (Hockett 1958, 249).

For structuralists, any system of signification has both syntagmatic and paradigmatic axes, which organize meaning through relational differences. 'Relations are important for what they can explain: meaningful contrasts and permitted or forbidden combinations' (Culler 1975, 14). Cultural systems of signification include meals and dress codes. For a dinner menu, the syntagmatic axis would be the sequence of courses (e.g. starters, main course, and dessert), and the paradigmatic axis would be the various options for each course. Roland Barthes outlined the paradigmatic and syntagmatic elements of the 'garment system' (1967a, 26–7). The paradigmatic elements are the items that cannot be worn at the same time on the same part of the body (such as hats, trousers, shoes). The syntagmatic dimension is the juxtaposition of different elements at the same time in a complete ensemble from hat to shoes.

In the case of film, our interpretation of an individual shot depends on both paradigmatic analysis (comparing it, not necessarily consciously, with the use of alternative kinds of shot) and syntagmatic analysis (comparing it with preceding and following shots). The same shot used within another sequence of shots could have quite a different preferred reading. Actually, filmic syntagms are not confined to such temporal syntagms (which are manifested in *montage*: the sequencing of shots) but include the spatial syntagms found also in still photography (in *mise-en-scène*: the composition of individual frames). The determination of meaning in a narrative may seem to be primarily dependent on the syntagmatic dimension, but an example of a film in which the paradigmatic dimension is foregrounded is *Crash* (Dir. Paul Haggis 2004). This is a thematic film dealing with racial prejudice, and making sense of it (at least initially) requires the audience to make comparative inferences about a series of separate (and heavily cross-cut) events – only as we move towards closure does the syntagmatic dimension resume its conventional dominance.

Both syntagmatic and paradigmatic analysis treat signs as part of a system – exploring their functions within codes and subcodes – a topic to which we will return. Although we will discuss paradigmatic and syntagmatic relations separately, it should be emphasized that the semiotic analysis of a text or corpus has to tackle the system as a whole, and that the two dimensions cannot be considered in isolation. The 'grammar' of a language involves both syntagmatic (structural) regularities and paradigmatic (systemic) contrasts. The description of any semiotic system involves specifying both the relevant paradigms and also the possible combinations of one with another in syntagms. In textual analysis, we need to remember that syntagmatic differences unavoidably involve paradigmatic differences. Analytically, according to Saussure (who was, of course, focusing on the language system), one must start with the whole system and identify its elements through analysis (*CLG* 157; 113); one cannot try to construct the system by working upwards from the constituent elements. However, Roland Barthes argues that 'an important part of the semiological undertaking' is to divide the material for analysis 'into minimal significant units,. . . then to group these units into paradigmatic classes, and finally to classify the syntagmatic relations which link these units' (1967a, 48; cf. Leymore 1975, 21 and Lévi-Strauss 1972, 211). In practice, analysts are likely to need to move back and forth between these two approaches as they seek to identify the rules of the system.

THE PARADIGMATIC DIMENSION

Whereas syntagmatic analysis studies the manifest structure of a text, paradigmatic analysis seeks to identify latent elements – significant absences on which its meaning depends (which structuralists tend to interpret in terms of binary oppositions such as public–private) and to assess positive or negative connotations (revealed through the use of one sign rather than another).

As we have seen, Saussure notes that a characteristic of what he called 'associative' relations (now called paradigmatic relations) – is that (in contrast to syntagmatic relations) such relations are held *in absentia* – in the absence from a specific text of alternative signifiers from the same paradigm. Signs take their value within the linguistic system from what they are *not* (*CLG* 162; 117). The psychologist William James (1890, 584) observes that 'the *absence of an item* is a determinant of our representations quite as positive as its presence can ever be'. We have popular sayings in English concerning two kinds of absences: we refer to 'what goes without saying' and 'what is conspicuous by its absence'. What 'goes without saying' reflects what it is assumed that you take for granted as obvious. In relation to the coverage of an issue (such as in factual genres) this is a profoundly ideological absence which helps to position the text's readers, the implication being that 'people like us already agree what we think about issues like that'. As for the second kind of absence, an item that is present in the text may flout conventional expectations, making the conventional item 'conspicuous by its absence' and the unexpected item 'a statement'. This applies no less to cultural practices. If a man routinely wears a suit at his office it says very little other than that he is conforming to a norm. But if one day he arrives in jeans and a t-shirt, this will be interpreted as 'making a statement'.

Paradigmatic analysis involves comparing and contrasting each of the signs present in the text with absent signs which in similar circumstances might have been chosen, and considering the significance of the choices made. It can be applied at any semiotic level, from the choice of a particular word, image, or sound to the level of the choice of style, genre, or medium. A basic paradigm set for *shot size* in photography and film would include the type of shot actually employed (e.g. a close-up) and the possible alternatives: a mid-shot (the default) and a long shot. The use of one sign rather than another from the same paradigm is based on factors such as technical constraints, code (e.g. genre), convention, connotation, style, rhetorical purpose, and the limitations of the individual's own repertoire. Considering the alternatives within a paradigm illustrates that meaning depends on what isn't there, so for instance, the meaning of the words we use to 'express' ourselves is dependent on those we do not choose (undermining the notion of 'intention').

THE COMMUTATION TEST

Structuralist semioticians refer to the 'commutation test', which can be used in order to determine the significance of signs. This is one of the most important tools in the semiotic toolkit. Its origins lie in a linguistic test of substitution applied by the Prague school structuralists. In order to identify basic 'distinctive features' within a language (functional differences serving communicative purposes), linguists experimented with the substitution of phonemes (speech sounds), such as /b/ for /p/ (*pet*/*bet*). The Danish linguist Hjelmslev formulated his 'glossematics' version in 1938.

The original linguistic commutation test evolved into a rather more subjective form of textual analysis in a journal article by Roland Barthes in 1964, which was published in English in 1967 as a short book, *Elements of Semiology*. Barthes (1967a, 48) refers to using the commutation test to divide texts into minimal significant units, before grouping these units into paradigmatic classes. To apply this test, a particular sign in a text is selected (such as one word within a sentence), then alternatives to this sign are considered. The effects of each substitution are evaluated in terms of how this might affect the sense made of the sign. This might involve imagining the use of a close-up rather than a mid-shot, a substitution in age, sex, class, or ethnicity, substituting objects, a different caption for a photograph, etc. In short, typical uses of the commutation test involve making (or imagining) a substitution of one sign for another within a paradigm to establish the change of meaning. The test is intended to identify what information theorists refer to as 'differences that make a difference' (Bateson 1979, 99). Its use is not confined to semioticians: casting directors, for instance, are experts in imagining such substitutions in relation to alternative candidates for particular roles.

The commutation test can be used to identify the paradigms and codes to which the signs used belong. For instance, if changing the setting used in an advertisement contributes to changing the meaning, then 'setting' is one of the paradigms; the paradigm set for the setting would consist of all of those alternative signs that could have been used and that would have shifted the meaning. The test can also involve transposition – swapping over two of the existing signs, changing their original relationship (which can be very revealing in cases such as representations of gender). The influence of the substitution on the meaning can help to suggest the contribution of the original sign and also to identify syntagmatic units (Barthes 1967a, 65–7; 1967b, 19–20).

From the point of view of traditional structuralist analysis, self-presentational performances of being and doing something could be seen as analogous with the sentence in language by virtue of producing meaning through the articulation of parts on the basis of rules of combination and contrast. The relevant parts would include verbal expression, facial expressions, body movements, setting, and so on (Pettit 1977, 61–2). The meaning of each part is paradigmatically determined by contrast with a range of alternatives (limited to those which are appropriate). Just as there are only certain meaningful paradigmatic contrasts, there are also only certain possible syntagmatic combinations. The meaning of the whole changes if the meaning of any part of it changes. Structuralist analysis seeks to account for the distinctive meaning produced by particular patterns. In relation to self-presentation, this can be shown using the commutation test in a particular version ('breaching experiments') employed by the sociologist Harold Garfinkel, which involves varying one element in a normal situation in order to see what effect this has on an audience. Alternatively, in the manner of the sociologist Erving Goffman (1959), systematic analysis could be based on the significance of each element in self-presentation in terms of categories generated by the metaphor of the stage, such as role, setting, script, cue, and so on.

Logically, commutation may involve any of four basic transformations: addition, deletion, substitution, and transposition. These four basic transformational processes have been noted as features of perception and recall (Allport and Postman 1945; Newcomb 1952, 88–96). They correspond to the four general categories to which Quintilian (*c.*35–100 AD) assigns the rhetorical figures (or tropes) as 'deviations' from 'literal' language: *adjectio*, *detractio*, *immutatio*, and *transmutatio* (*Institutes of Oratory* Book I, Chapter 5, 38–41). Writing each new edition of this book has involved all of these transformations.

OPPOSITIONS

Opposites are attractive. In word association tests, 'opposites' are the most frequent responses to stimulus words (Clark 1970, 275): for instance, more often than not, 'good' evokes 'bad', 'hot' evokes 'cold', 'male' evokes 'female', 'new' evokes 'old', 'black' evokes 'white', and 'alive' evokes 'dead'. Such prototypical opposites seem fundamental but in some cases the poles can contextually 'flip': there's 'a thin line' between love and hate, madness and genius, and so on. The conventionality of opposites is evident from the fact that children are taught them at an early age. Philosophers have regarded binary oppositions as interpretively fundamental since pre-Socratic times. Plato and Aristotle's belief that human conceptions of beauty derive from the symmetry of the human body offered a natural basis for binarism – since we have two eyes, two ears, two arms, two legs, and so on. Others have sought to naturalize binarism on the basis of the two sexes (a move that has deep ideological implications). Theorists differ over whether oppositions reflect structures in language, in the mind, or in nature – or whether binarism is a particularly Western obsession. However, relational thinking enables conventional dichotomies (such as subject–object or mind–world) to be productively reconceptualised as mutually constitutive relationships (as in *yin* and *yang*). Indeed, conflict resolution often involves seeking to convert oppositions based on mutual exclusion to relations of mutual dependency.

Relational differences are not limited to opposites, and distinctions can also be made between various types of oppositions, the most important being the following:

- *ungradable antonyms* (*contradictories* or *complementaries*): mutually exclusive terms (e.g. alive–dead, on–off);
- *contraries*, which (depending on the theorist) may refer to:
  - *gradable antonyms*: polar terms on a spectrum, differing in degree (e.g. hot–cold, young–old); *or*
  - *converse terms*: presupposing a reciprocal (mutually dependent) relationship (e.g. before–after, sender–receiver).

Gradable terms clearly allow for intermediate positions. Even the apparently categorical 'black' and 'white' can of course be reconfigured as shades of grey. Whether opposites are ungradable (either/or) or gradable (more-or-less) depends in part on the context of use and the particular perspectives of users. In principle, apparently either/or binary oppositions can also be represented on a graduated scale, and much can be gained from adopting this perspective (Leach 1964, 62).

As we have seen, Saussure established the principle that linguistic signs make sense within a relational system of differences. Structuralist analysis extends this principle to texts and myths as systems of differences and oppositions. However, the structuralist emphasis on binary oppositions is more dichotomous. Binarism is particularly associated with Roman Jakobson, who argues that 'without it the structure of language would be lost' (1973, 321). The structuralist conception of binary opposition draws upon the principle of phonemic opposition in phonology formulated by Jakobson and Nicholai Trubetzkoy in the 1930s, according to which a relatively small number of oppositions between distinctive phonetic (or phonological) features forms the acoustic basis for any language (Jakobson 1941). By analogy, the primary analytical method employed by many structuralists involves the identification of binary or polar semantic oppositions (e.g. us–them, public–private) in texts or cultural practices. Most notably, the anthropologist Claude Lévi-Strauss applies this principle to kinship systems and myths, regarding all structural relations as reducible to fundamental binary oppositions such as nature–culture, raw–cooked, male–female, left–right, sacred–profane, and life–death. It is through such oppositions that we conceptualize reality. One might expect anthropologists to focus on distinctive differences in human cultures, but Lévi-Strauss sees certain basic binary oppositions as a universal feature of the human mind, and he identifies cross-cultural evidence for them in social structure, marriage rules, and myths. In his early work, 'duality, alternation, opposition and symmetry' are seen as the 'basic and immediate data of mental and social reality' (1949, 136). Such structuralist binarism is a primary target of Jacques Derrida's project of 'deconstruction' (to be discussed shortly).

As Jonathan Culler notes, 'The advantage of binarism, but also its principal danger, lies in the fact that it permits one to classify anything' (1975, 15). Binarism is rightly criticized when it leads to negative stereotyping and when it is uncritically accepted as 'the real' – as in common sense assumptions that supposedly either/or oppositions, such as male and female, or heterosexual and homosexual, exhaust the possibilities of the domains they purport to encompass (Gergen 2009a, 36). Conceptual binaries have been prominent throughout history in political rhetoric and propaganda – and have indeed been used to instigate countless wars. However, the oppositions (of whatever kind) which we employ in our cultural practices help to generate order out of the dynamic complexity of experience. Our entire system of values is built upon oppositions, which exist within sign systems rather than in the world. At the most basic level of individual survival, Leach (1970, 39) argues that humans share with other animals the need to distinguish between our own species and others, dominance and submission, sexual availability or non-availability, and the edible and the inedible. Lévi-Strauss, who sees the opposition between nature and culture as of fundamental importance, suggests that the primary reason that human beings have employed fire since prehistoric times to transform raw into cooked food is not simply because this is necessary for their survival but in order to signify their otherness from beasts – symbolically establishing an essential difference (Lévi-Strauss 1969). As the sociologist Eviatar Zerubavel puts it (1993, 2), 'Our entire social order is a product of the ways in which we separate kin from non-kin, moral from immoral, serious from merely playful, and what is ours from what is not'. We live within a world constructed from such oppositions, so they have very real social consequences. For instance, 'social practices that are not coded as conventionally masculine – such as flower-arranging or dancing – are quickly and unreflective coded by our societies and by ourselves as feminine' (Halperin 2012, 313–14).

Although nature is not tidily divided into opposites, it is a feature of culture that oppositions come to seem natural, and real, to its members. Many pairings of concepts (such as masculine–feminine and mind–body) are familiar within a culture and may seem common-sensical distinctions for everyday communicational purposes, even if some of them may be regarded as 'false dichotomies' in critical contexts. If masculinity and femininity make any sense, it is only in relation to each other. The two sexes are of course biologically *complementary*, but when we routinely refer to 'the opposite sex', it is not surprising that we slip into treating this as a symbolic dichotomy. In our constructions of social reality, such symbolism is fundamental. Our 'sense of identity' is founded upon a distinction between us and the rest of the world. Constructing an identity requires you to know who you are *not*. The opposition of self–other (or subject–object) may be illusory (and, critics say, masculinist), but it has been widely argued to be psychologically fundamental, enabling the mind to impose some degree of constancy on the dynamic flux of experience.

A common explanation of the opposition self–other derives from the account of the 'mirror stage' offered by the neo-Freudian psychoanalyst Jacques Lacan (1977). He argues that initially, in the primal realm of 'the real' (where there is no absence, loss, or lack), the infant has no centre of identity and experiences no clear boundaries between itself and the external world. The child emerges from the real and enters 'the imaginary' at the age of about 6 to 18 months, before the acquisition of speech. This is a private psychic realm in which the construction of the self as subject is initiated. In the realm of visual images, we find our sense of self reflected back by an other with whom we identify. Lacan describes a defining moment in the imaginary which he calls 'the mirror phase', when seeing one's mirror image (and being told by one's mother, 'That's *you*!') induces a strongly defined illusion of a coherent and self-governing personal identity. This helps to foster the individual's sense of a conscious self residing in an 'internal world', which is distinct from 'the world outside'.

There is a delightfully ironic quip (variously attributed) that 'The world is divided into those who divide people into two types, and those who don't'. The interpretive usefulness of simple dichotomies is often challenged on the basis that life and texts are 'seamless webs' and thus better described in terms of continua. Poststructuralists and feminist theorists have argued that binary oppositions reproduce a 'masculine' ontology (Thibault 1998a, 81). The apparently fundamental opposition of self–other has been seen as reflecting a hegemonic masculine myth based on hard male ego boundaries. The supposed universality of the conceptual opposition of nature–culture has also been questioned by some critics (Horigan 1988, 40–1). Analysts need to be wary of imposing their own cultural frameworks, assumptions, and values as opposed to identifying categories based on the frames of reference of insiders within a culture. However, interpretation always involves categorization and no categories are neutral. Nor does it seem to be a projection to suggest that cultures invariably construct orderly and manageable realities by slicing experience into categories (although there is always scope for debate about what these categories might be or how fuzzy they are). There is no shortage of examples of such categories articulated as oppositions which are regularly invoked as interpretive frameworks within a culture. Youth cultures have often been seen as binary inversions of mainstream parental or official practices or values. Binary oppositions (such as structure–agency, macro–micro levels, culture–nature, sex–gender, and public–private) are widespread in sociological theory (Jenks 1998). Meaning is not dichotomously confined to the poles of oppositions; nor does it arise from binary oppositions operating in isolated pairs, but rather operating dynamically and in interplay at more than one level within conceptual systems of opposition. The ambiguous boundary zones between interrelated oppositions (areas of 'cultural contradiction') can be sacred or taboo in various cultures, and their exploration can be very revealing (Leach 1976, 33–6). Cultural practices maintaining the conventional borders of what seem to be fundamental natural distinctions mask the permeability and fragility of the fabric of social reality. All systems leak, and it is part of the mission of the cultural semiotician to locate the leaks in order to facilitate an exploration of the role of pervasive categories and oppositions in reproducing power relations.

MARKEDNESS

Roman Jakobson generalized Nicholai Trubetzkoy's phonemic theory of *markedness*: 'Every single constituent of any linguistic system is built on an opposition of two logical contradictories: the presence of an attribute ("markedness") in contraposition to its absence ("unmarkedness")' (Jakobson 1972, 42). The concept of markedness can be applied to the poles of a paradigmatic opposition: paired signs consist of an 'unmarked' and a 'marked' form. This applies, as we shall see, both at the level of the signifier and at the level of the signified. In morphologically related oppositions, marking may be based on the presence or absence of some distinctive semiotic feature: for instance, in English, the prefix *un-*. In English, linguistically *unmarked* forms include the present tense of verbs and the singular form of nouns (Jakobson's 'zero-sign'). Markedness in language is not confined to individual words. For instance, the active voice is normally unmarked, but this is contextually variable – in the restricted genre of traditional academic writing, the passive voice is still often the unmarked form.

The markedness of linguistic signs includes semantic marking. Jakobson (1980a, 138) reports that 'the general meaning of the marked is characterized by the conveyance of more precise, specific, and additional information than the unmarked term provides'. The unmarked term is often used as a generic term, while the marked term is used in a more specific sense. General references to humanity used to use the term 'man' (which in this sense was not intended to be sex specific), and of course the word 'he' has long been used generically. In English, the female category is generally marked in relation to the male, a point not lost on feminist theorists. This extends even to visual signage, where a generic male figure is still used almost universally to represent 'people' (as well as males specifically), while a female figure is used only when females are being singled out.

Where terms are paired, the pairing is rarely symmetrical but rather hierarchical. For Jakobson (ibid., 137), hierarchy is a fundamental structural principle. Whereas Saussure had asserted that the elements of a paradigm set have no fixed order, Jakobson argues that markedness created hierarchical relations within paradigms (1962, 599; 1971c, 719–20). Oppositions are rarely equally weighted. With apologies to

George Orwell, we might coin the phrase that 'all signs are equal, but some are more equal than others'. With many of the familiarly paired forms, the two signifiers (and what they signify) are accorded different values. The unmarked term is primary, being given precedence and priority, while the marked term is treated as secondary. While linguistic markedness may not of itself imply negativity (e.g. the unmarked term *cow* versus the marked term *bull*), morphological markers (such as *un-* or *-in*) can generate negative connotations. When morphological cues are lacking, the 'preferred sequence' or most common order of paired terms usually distinguishes the first as a semantically positive term and the second as a negative one (Lyons 1977, 276).

'Term B' (the marked term in a pairing) is referred to by some theorists as being produced as an effect of 'term A' (Sedgwick 1990, 10). The unmarked term is presented as fundamental and originative while the marked term is conceived in relation to it as derivative, dependent, subordinate, supplemental, or ancillary (Culler 1985, 112). This framing ignores the fact that the unmarked term is logically and structurally dependent on the marked term to lend it substance. Derrida (1967a) demonstrates that within the oppositional logic of binarism, neither of the terms (or concepts) makes sense without the other. This is what he calls 'the logic of supplementarity': the 'secondary' term, which is represented as 'marginal' and external, is in fact constitutive of the 'primary' term and essential to it. The unmarked term is defined by what it seeks to suppress. In the pairing of oppositions or contraries, term B is defined relationally rather than substantively. The linguistic marking of signifiers in many of these pairings is referred to as 'privative' – consisting of suffixes or prefixes signifying lack or absence – e.g. *non-*, *un-*, or *-less*. In such cases, term B is defined by negation – being everything that term A is *not*. For example, when we refer to 'nonverbal communication', the very label defines such a mode of communication only in negative relation to 'verbal communication'. The unmarked term is not merely neutral but implicitly positive in contrast to the negative connotations of the marked term. The association of the marked term with absence and lack is of course problematized by those who have noted the irony that the dependence of term A on term B can be seen as reflecting a lack on the part of the unmarked term (Fuss 1991, 3).

The unmarked form is typically dominant (e.g. statistically within a text or corpus) and therefore seems to be neutral, normal, and natural. It is thus transparent – drawing no attention to its invisibly privileged status, while the deviance of the marked form is salient. Where it is not simply subsumed, the marked form is foregrounded – presented as 'different'; it is 'out of the ordinary' – an extraordinary deviational 'special case' which is something other than the standard or default form of the unmarked term. Unmarked–marked may thus be read as norm–deviation. It is notable that empirical studies have demonstrated that cognitive processing is more difficult with marked terms than with unmarked terms (Clark and Clark 1977). Marked forms take longer to recognize and process, and more errors are made with these forms.

On the limited evidence from frequency counts of explicit verbal pairings in written text (online texts retrieved using the former Infoseek search engine, September 2000), while it is very common for one term in such pairings to be marked, in some instances there is not a clearly marked term (see Figure 3.2). For instance, in general usage there seemed to be no inbuilt preference for one term in a pairing such as old–young (one is just as likely to encounter young–old). Furthermore, the extent to which a term is marked is variable. Some terms seemed to be far more clearly marked than others: in the pairing public–private, for instance, *private* is very clearly the marked term (accorded secondary status). How strongly a term is marked also depends on contextual frameworks such as genres and sociolects (the language usage of different social groups), and in some contexts a pairing may be very deliberately and explicitly reversed when an interest group seeks to challenge the ideological priorities which the markedness may be taken to reflect. Not all of the pairs listed will seem to be 'the right way round' to everyone – you may find it interesting to identify which ones seem counterintuitive to you and to speculate as to why this seems so.

The concept of markedness can be applied more broadly than simply to paradigmatic pairings of words or concepts. The informational (or referential) function of communication is itself generally unmarked insofar as it has been traditionally assumed to be the primary

high	90%+*	80%+*	70%+*	60%+*	50%+*
	indoor/outdoor				
	up/down				
	yes/no				
	East/West				
	open/closed				
	wet/dry				
	question/answer				
	true/false				
	major/minor	on/off			
	hot/cold	public/private			
	reader/writer	male/female			
	before/after	high/low			
	love/hate	parent/child	70%+*		
I	top/bottom	internal/external	black/white		
	good/bad	gain/loss	mind/body	60%+*	
N	cause/effect	human/animal	left/right	adult/child	
	front/back	past/present	positive/negative	urban/rural	
C	primary/secondary	gay/straight	art/science	product/process	
	birth/death	more/less	active/passive	horizontal/vertical	
I	presence/absence	above/below	light/dark	physical/mental	
	problem/solution	inner/outer	product/system	hard/soft	
D	win/lose	thought/feeling	sex/gender	fast/slow	
	acceptance/rejection	life/death	static/dynamic	quantity/quality	
E	inclusion/exclusion	subject/object	liberal/conservative	foreground/background	
	success/failure	producer/consumer	higher/lower	similarity/difference	
N	human/machine	work/play	teacher/learner	temporary/permanent	
	right/wrong	good/evil	war/peace	nature/culture	
C	nature/nurture	masculine/feminine	body/soul	poetry/prose	
	theory/practice	health/illness	fact/fiction	part/whole	50%+*
E	near/far	comedy/tragedy	form/content	married/single	new/old
	self/other	insider/outsider	form/function	strong/weak	large/small
	figure/ground	happy/sad	simple/complex	subjective/objective	local/global
	rich/poor	superior/inferior	original/copy	dead/alive	them/us
	fact/opinion	present/absent	means/end	shallow/deep	system/process
	system/use	clean/dirty	appearance/reality	competition/cooperation	young/old
	hero/villain	natural/artificial	competence/performance	live/recorded	majority/minority
	fact/value	speaker/listener	one/many	head/heart	foreign/domestic
	text/context	classical/romantic	speech/writing	formal/casual	structure/process
	raw/cooked	type/token	straight/curved	structure/agency	order/chaos
	substance/style	nature/technology	signifier/signified	message/medium	concrete/abstract
	base/superstructure	rights/obligations	central/peripheral	form/meaning	words/actions
	knowledge/ignorance	reason/emotion	wild/domestic	words/deeds	beautiful/ugly
	fact/fantasy	sacred/profane	stability/change	fact/theory	individual/society
low	knower/known	maker/user	realism/idealism	words/things	strange/familiar
	literal/metaphorical				
	more marked		**MARKEDNESS**		**less marked**

*Dominant order as percentage of total occurrences of both forms

FIGURE 3.2 Markedness of explicit oppositions in online texts

Source: © 2016 Daniel Chandler

function of communication. Whether in textual or social practices, the choice of a marked form 'makes a statement'. Where a text deviates from conventional expectations, it is 'marked'. Conventional, or 'over-coded' text (which follows a fairly predictable formula) is unmarked, whereas unconventional or 'under-coded' text is marked. Marked or under-coded text requires the interpreter to do more interpretive work. Nor is the existence of marked forms simply a structural feature of semiotic systems. The distinction between norm and deviation is fundamental in socialization (Bruner 1990). Social differentiation is constructed and maintained through the marking of differences. Unmarked forms reflect representational dominance and the natural-ization of dominant cultural values. Frequently, in direct relation to socio-economic status, the category of adult, white, heterosexual male is unmarked, while child/youth and/or non-white and/or non-heterosexual and/or female is marked. In such contexts, the treat-ment of women, children, non-whites, and homosexuals tends to be similar.

As one commentator puts it, 'Because the semantic opposition of unmarkedness and markedness influences our perceptions of naturalness and deviance, it forms part of the tacit system through which ideology is inscribed in language' (Groves 1998, 386). Roland Barthes (1957, 138) identifies the phenomenon of 'exnomination' in which dominant groups within a culture treat themselves as the unmarked norm (are ex-nominated) in contrast to which others are the marked categories. They define themselves as who they are *not* rather than as who they are. Where whiteness is the 'norm', white people take their own (naturalized) culture for granted and find it very difficult to define, as if they were cultureless (Perry 2001). The values of the dominant group are taken for granted as normal and natural, in contrast to those of others. Antony Easthope argues that exnomination is the basis for 'the masculine myth', in which male power has been perpetuated 'by feigning invisibility' (1990, 167). 'Power operates most effectively when it is invisible' (Colapietro 1993, 140). Identifying markedness thus helps to highlight privilege and prejudice.

Jakobson observed in 1930 that markedness 'has a signifi-cance not only for linguistics but also for ethnology and the history of culture, and that such historico-cultural correlations as life–death, liberty–nonliberty, sin–virtue, holidays–working days, and so on are always confined to relations *a*–non-*a*, and that it is important to find out for any epoch, group, nation etc. what the marked element is' (1980a, 136). Binary oppositions are frequently weighted in favour of the male, silently signifying that the norm is to be male and to be female is to be different. However, it is not always the female form that is marked: it is instructive to note which particular retail products are explicitly labelled as 'for men' or alternatively 'for women' (especially where there is a parallel unmarked, implicitly normative version).

However natural familiar dichotomies and their markedness may seem, their historical origins or phases of dominance can often be traced. For instance, perhaps the most influential dualism in the history of Western civilization can be attributed primarily to the philosopher René Descartes (1596–1650) who divides reality into two distinct ontological substances – mind and body. This distinction insists on the separation of an external or real world from an internal or mental one, the first being material and the second non-material. It created the poles of objectivity and subjectivity, and fostered the illusion that 'I' can be distinguished from my body. Furthermore, Descartes's rationalist declaration that 'I think, therefore I am' encouraged the privileging of mind over body. He presents the subject as an autonomous individual with an ontological status *prior to* social structures (a notion rejected by structuralist and poststructural theorists). He established the enduring assumption of the independence of the knower from the known. Cartesian dualism also underpins a host of associated and aligned dichotomies: reason–emotion, male–female, true–false, fact–fiction, public–private, self–other, and human–animal. Many feminist theorists lay a great deal of blame at Descartes's door for the orchestration of the ontological framework of patriarchal discourse. One of the most influential of theorists who have sought to study the ways in which reality is constructed and maintained within discourse by such dominant frameworks is the French historian of ideas, Michel Foucault, who focuses on the analysis of 'discursive formations' in specific historical and socio-cultural contexts (1970, 1974).

DECONSTRUCTION

Roman Jakobson (1984) highlights what seem to be tensions and contradictions within Saussure's *Cours*. He had already identified the terms that he saw as foregrounded by Saussure within his oppositions, such as *langue* (the language system) rather than *parole* (its use), synchrony (the language state in a particular period) rather than diachrony (language change), the paradigmatic rather than the syntagmatic, linear temporality rather than spatial concurrence and the immateriality of form rather than the substance of the signifier (1949a, 54; 1949b, 423; 1956, 74–5; 1966). Saussurean oppositions are productively regarded as complementary (Jakobson 1971c, Harris 1987), but binary thinking is deeply embedded in Western ways of thinking and tends to be adversarial (and thus self-perpetuating). Bob Hodge and Gunther Kress outline an explicitly social and materialist framework for semiotics based on reclaiming what they see as 'the contents of Saussure's rubbish bin' (1988, 17) – but Jakobson, Voloshinov, and Derrida had already ransacked it.

While other critical theorists have been content to 'valorize term B' in the semiotic analysis of textual representations, the work of the poststructuralist philosopher Jacques Derrida, includes a radical 'deconstruction' of Saussure's *Course in General Linguistics*, not only revalorizing terms that he chose to regard as devalorized in the *Cours*, but more radically seeking to destabilize all oppositional frameworks (1967a and 1967b). This is part of a quest to expose what he sees as the 'phonocentric' privileging of speech over writing in Western culture. If phonocentrism is taken to be an unconscious bias, this is an unwarranted claim. 'What is natural to mankind is not oral speech, but the faculty of constructing . . . a system of . . . signs' (*CLG* 26; 10). Nevertheless, Saussure does note that writing is semiologically dependent on (and therefore secondary to) the linguistic sign system (ibid. 45; 23–4). The 'primacy of speech' was a linguistic orthodoxy in the nineteenth century, and linguists after Saussure have continued to subscribe to it. It was part of a defence of the oral tradition in reaction to what was seen as a widespread over-privileging of the written form. Saussure thus made a conventional distinction between speech and writing but he also acknowledges that they are comparable sign systems of 'signs that express ideas' (ibid. 33; 16). Written signs are signs in their own right.

Although Saussure had clearly stressed the inseparability of the signifier and the signified, and that neither had priority in his model of the linguistic sign, Derrida attacks what he sees as the privileging of the signified over the signifier, subordinating material form to less material forms, and thus perpetuating the traditional opposition of matter and spirit, or substance and thought. Derrida's argument suggests that his primary target is not the *Cours* itself, but its various reinterpretations by structuralists such as Jakobson, Lévi-Strauss, Hjelmslev, Barthes, Lacan, and Benveniste (Daylight 2011).

ALIGNMENT

Oppositions are seen by structuralist theorists as part of what they often refer to as the 'deep [or 'hidden'] structure' of texts, shaping the preferred reading (note that this 'deep structure' metaphor owes nothing to Saussure). Such oppositions may appear to be resolved in favour of dominant ideologies but poststructuralists argue that tensions between them *always* remain unresolved. It is not in isolation that the rhetorical power of oppositions resides, but in their articulation in relation to other oppositions. Some of these linkages (such as masculine–feminine, mind–body) are regularly aligned in cultural practices and texts so that 'vertical' relationships develop (such as masculine–mind, feminine–body) – as feminists and queer theorists have noted (e.g. Grosz 1993, 195; Butler 1999, 17). As Kaja Silverman (1983, 36) observes, 'a cultural code is a conceptual system which is organized around key oppositions and equations, in which a term like "woman" is defined in opposition to a term like "man", and in which each term is aligned with a cluster of symbolic attributes'. Within such a system, for instance, 'the distinction between style and content, or style and substance, is a crucial one for separating appearance from reality: style counts as feminine and substance as masculine, since masculinity is fundamentally concerned with the true content of things, whereas femininity is concerned with frivolous matters such as appearance' (Halperin 2012, 326). When such conceptual alignments are made explicit like this, we may recoil from the disturbing implications, but, in the course of everyday life, such connotations are generated unconsciously and accepted uncritically as part of the fabric of social reality.

Applying the concept of marked forms to mass media genres, Merris Griffiths examined the production and editing styles of television advertisements for toys. Her findings showed that the style of advertisements aimed primarily at boys had far more in common with those aimed at a mixed audience than with those aimed at girls, making 'girls' advertisements' the marked category in commercials for toys (Chandler and Griffiths 2000). Notably, the girls' ads had significantly longer shots, significantly more dissolves (fade out/fade in of shot over shot), fewer long shots and more close-ups, fewer low shots, more level shots, and fewer overhead shots. The gender-differentiated use of production features that characterized these children's commercials reflected a series of binary oppositions – fast–slow, abrupt–gradual, excited–calm, active–passive, detached–involved. Their close association in such ads led them to line up consistently together as stereotypically masculine vs. feminine qualities. The 'relative autonomy' of formal features in commercials seems likely to function as a constant symbolic reaffirmation of the broader cultural stereotypes that associate such qualities with gender – especially when accompanied by gender-stereotyped content. Readers may care to reflect on the way in which 'brown goods' and 'white goods' have traditionally been sold in high-street electrical shops (Cockburn and Ormrod 1993, Chapter 4). Brown goods such as televisions, video-recorders, camcorders, and sound-systems were primarily targeted at men and the sales staff focused on technical specifications. White goods such as refrigerators, washing-machines, and cookers were targeted at women and the sales staff focused on appearance. The extent to which this particular pattern still survives in your own locality may be checked by some investigative 'window-shopping'.

The notion of conceptual alignment can be traced to Claude Lévi-Strauss's discussion of analogical relationships which generate systems of meaning within cultures. Influenced by Jakobson, Lévi-Strauss (1972, 21) sees certain key binary oppositions as the invariants or universals of the human mind, cutting across cultural distinctions. His studies of cultural practices identify underlying semantic oppositions in relation to such phenomena as myths, totemism, and kinship rules. Individual myths and cultural practices defy interpretation, making sense only as a part of a system of differences and oppositions expressing fundamental reflections on the relationship of nature and culture. Lévi-Strauss argues that binary oppositions form the basis of underlying 'classificatory systems', while myths represent a dreamlike working over of a fundamental dilemma or contradiction within a culture, expressed in the form of paired opposites. Apparently fundamental oppositions such as male–female and left–right become transformed into 'the prototype symbols of the good and the bad, the permitted and the forbidden' (Leach 1970, 44; cf. Needham 1973). Such conceptual alignments are a key part of the process through which social realities are constructed and maintained.

Pierre Bourdieu (1997, 194) argues that gender is a 'master binary' that 'appears founded in the nature of things because it is echoed virtually everywhere'. This is not because it maps tidily onto biological sex differences (as gender essentialists assume). Gender is constructed differently in different cultures, and in different historical periods. The polarization of masculine–feminine is deeply naturalized through its close symbolic association with various mutually-reinforcing dualisms, such as: active–passive, mind–body, reason–emotion, hard–soft, vision–sound, straight–curved, culture–nature, public–private, plain–fancy, instrumental–expressive, rational–intuitive (see also Figure 3.5). There is nothing 'natural' about such associations; it is the cultural familiarity of particular associations that makes them seem so. Gender does not explain differences: it results from the creation of differences. Conceptual alignments are part of the social construction of gender roles.

How do such conceptual alignments arise? Foucault suggests that 'to look for the meaning of something is to discover what it resembles' (cited in Culler 1973, 36). More specifically, Lévi-Strauss (1962) argues that within a culture 'analogical thought' leads to some oppositions (such as edible–inedible) being perceived as metaphorically resembling the 'similar differences' of other oppositions (such as native–foreign). This resemblance is not between the apparent referents, but '*between . . . two systems of differences*' (1964, 77). This yields a series of homologous oppositions, such as *raw is to cooked as nature is to culture* (in structuralist shorthand 'raw : cooked :: nature : culture') (1969), or – in the Cartesian dualism of the modern Western world – culture : nature :: people : animals :: male : female :: reason : passion (Tapper 1994, 50). The classification systems of a culture are a way of encoding differences within society by analogy with perceived differences in the natural world (somewhat as in Aesop's *Fables*) (Lévi-Strauss 1969, 90–1). They transform what are perceived as natural categories into cultural categories and serve to naturalize cultural practices. The social opposition of us–other is frequently metaphorically mapped onto spatial segmentations of the environment such as earth–sky, land–sea, or town–country (Leach 1973, 48). 'The mythical system and the modes of representation it employs serve to establish homologies between natural and social conditions or, more accurately, it makes it possible to equate significant contrasts found in different planes: the geographical, meteorological, zoological, botanical, technical, economic, social, ritual, religious and philosophical' (Lévi-Strauss 1969, 93). Such homologies function as mechanisms for translating between different levels of social reality (Lévi-Strauss 1962, 76). The aggregation of fourfold distinctions associated with Aristotle's 'four elements' and sustained in various combinations over two millennia are of this kind (Chandler 2002, 102–3). The alignments that develop within such systems are not without contradictions, and Lévi-Strauss argues that the contradictions within them generate explanatory myths – such codes must 'make sense' (1962, 228).

In his critique of Saussure, Jakobson warns that in our interpretive strategies we should beware of allowing separate oppositions to slip into unquestioned alignments, as in the treatment of synchrony (or dyadic models) as always static and of diachrony (or triadic models) as always dynamic. Some alignments are stronger and more durable than others, resisting polar reversal or disassociation. Rather than treating Saussure's oppositions as strict dichotomies, Jakobson (1981, 64) proposes (in a quasi-poststructuralist vein) apparently oxymoronic alternative formulations such as 'permanently dynamic synchrony'. Although Lévi-Strauss's analytical approach remains formally 'synchronic', involving no study of the historical dimension, he does incorporate the possibility of change: oppositions are not fixed and structures are transformable (as indeed they are for Saussure). Lévi-Strauss notes that we need not regard such frameworks from a purely synchronic perspective. 'Starting from a binary opposition, which affords the simplest possible example of a system, this construction proceeds by the aggregation, at each of the two poles, of new terms, chosen because they stand in relations of opposition, correlation, or analogy to it'. In this way, structures may undergo transformation (1962, 161). Indeed, the ultimately arbitrary character of alignments makes them inherently unstable.

Aesthetic 'movements' can also be interpreted in terms of paradigms of characteristic oppositions. Each movement can be loosely identified in terms of a primary focus of interest: for instance, realism tends to be primarily oriented towards the world, neo-classicism towards the text, and romanticism towards the author. Such broad goals generate and reflect associated values. Within a particular movement, various oppositions constitute a palette of possibilities for critical theorists within the movement. For instance, the codes of romanticism can be seen as built upon various implicit or explicit articulations of such oppositions as: expressive–instrumental, feeling–thought, emotion–reason, spontaneity–deliberation, passion–calculation, inspiration–effort, genius–method, intensity–reflection, intuition–judgement, impulse–intention, unconsciousness–design, creativity–construction, originality–conventionality, creation–imitation, imagination–learning, dynamism–order, sincerity–facticity, natural–artificial, and organic–mechanical. The alignment of some of these pairs generates further associations: for instance, an alignment of spontaneity–deliberation with sincerity–facticity equates spontaneity with sincerity. More indirectly, it may also associate their opposites, so that deliberation reflects insincerity or untruthfulness. Romantic literary theorists often proclaimed spontaneity in expressive writing to be a mark of sincerity, of truth to feeling – even when this ran counter to their own compositional practices (Chandler 1995a, 49ff.). Even within 'the same' aesthetic movement, various theorists construct their own frameworks, as is illustrated in Abrams's (1971) study of romantic literary theory. Each opposition (or combination of oppositions) involves an implicit contrast with the priorities and values of another aesthetic movement: thus (in accord with the Saussurean principle of negative differentiation) an aesthetic movement is defined by what it is *not*. The evolution of aesthetic movements can be seen as the working-out of tensions between such oppositions.

Turning from the aesthetic to the commercial sphere, the strategic manipulation of conceptual alignments has been a common feature of the application of semiotics to marketing since British Telecom's famous advertising campaign of the 1990s – 'It's Good to Talk'. That campaign sought to increase men's willingness to use the (landline) telephone at home – avoided by many men partly because of the feminine connotations of its domestic location and its association with 'small-talk'. The traditional gender stereotypes also led men to favour 'instrumental' (and therefore short) calls rather than 'expressive' (and more expensive) uses of the medium – a state of affairs that was eventually undermined by the mobile phone's colonization of the (traditionally masculine) public sphere. Part of the research involved mapping alignments in this universe of discourse. This technique involves representing two associated pairs of oppositions as horizontal and vertical axes dividing the semantic space into four quadrants of dominant cultural norms and contradictions (Figure 3.3 is an example of this kind of semantic grid). In the case of the BT research, one axis related to gender (masculine–feminine) and the other related to importance (important–trivial). The quadrants generated by their intersection highlight a 'cultural norm', which is an alignment of feminine usage with emotional, trivial, [domestic] small-talk and of masculine usage with rational, important, [public] 'big talk' (a term so unmarked that a label had to be invented) (Alexander 1995). Innovative brands are deliberately positioned or repositioned 'against the grain', and challenging this stereotypical alignment included using gruff-voiced, 'no-nonsense' actor Bob Hoskins – a 'man's man' – to front the campaign.

The attention-grabbing slogan for a campaign launched in 2005 for the washing powder Persil™ in the UK was 'dirt is good'. This provocative inversion of the Christian folklore that 'cleanliness is next to godliness' can be seen as part of a deliberate strategy of conceptual realignment which has a distinctly Lévi-Straussean flavour (see in particular Lévi-Strauss 1968). For many years, the core concept had been that 'Persil washes whiter' (alluded to even by Barthes 1957,

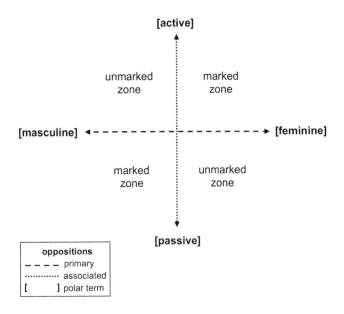

FIGURE 3.3 Zones of markedness in a conceptual alignment

Source: © 2016 Daniel Chandler

40–2). Soap powder and detergent advertising (distinguished by Barthes in their rhetorical appeals) had long reflected conceptual frameworks in which cleanliness–dirt and godliness–evil were vertically aligned with science–nature. In other words, the vertical alignments had been of dirt with evil and with nature. This went back to the days when the advertising for many domestic products regularly featured white-coated 'scientists' – often in laboratories – 'testing' the product and representing it as a technological advance. In the new campaign, 'dirt is good' was the slogan for print ads and television commercials in which we were shown people enjoying themselves outdoors and getting dirty in the process. The company literature also refers to one of their goals being to do 'the least possible harm to the environment'. The new campaign thus challenged the traditional alignment of cleanliness, godliness, and science. Within this modified mythological framework not only had dirt become explicitly good (rather than godly) but (inexplicitly) nature rather than science had become the hero. Viewers might also infer that 'dirt is fun'. This implication generates a new pairing – namely, fun–boredom (aligning boredom with evil as in the proverbial wisdom that 'the devil makes work for idle hands'). This mythological revolution was accomplished in the simplest and yet most 'theologically' radical switch – no less than the moral inversion of good and evil. In addition to the need to position (or reposition) the product in relation to rival brands, part of the thinking was presumably that consumers no longer had the faith in science (or indeed God) that they were once assumed to have. Of course, whether this revolution in conceptual alignment, generated by semiotically-inspired marketing, actually 'caught the public imagination', would require empirical testing, but it wasn't long afterwards that Persil ran its 'small is mighty' campaign for its washing-machine liquid.

THE SEMIOTIC SQUARE

For the structuralist Algirdas Greimas, it is through conceptual oppositions that meaning is created, so identifying such oppositions is the key task of a textual analyst. Consequently, he developed 'the semiotic square' (*le carré sémiotique*) – an influential tool for the semantic mapping of conceptual frameworks (1987, xiv, 49). It goes beyond the simple either/or of binary oppositions. Greimas drew upon the 'logical square' of scholastic philosophy and Saussure's notion that meaning is based on a system of relations in which concepts are defined negatively by their relations with the other terms within the system (*CLG* 162; 117).

The semiotic square (Figure 3.4) is a map of the semantic space within the particular universe of discourse that is under investigation. It represents an implicit conceptual framework. The four corners (S1, S2, Not S2, and Not S1) are positions within the system, which may be occupied by concrete or abstract notions (sometimes referred to as term A, term B, term not-B, and term not-A). The double-headed arrows represent bilateral relationships. Greimas refers to the logical relations between the four positions as *contrariety* or opposition, *complementarity* or implication, and *contradiction*.

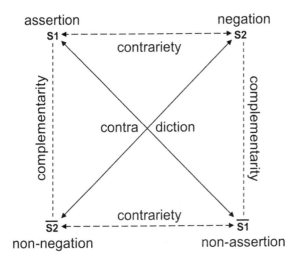

FIGURE 3.4 The semiotic square

Source: Adapted from Nöth 1990, 319 (with corrections)

In the diagram the positions of the square's founding terms are labelled S1 and S2 on the upper horizontal axis. These top corners of the Greimasian square represent a dialectical opposition between terms A and B – *contraries*, or strongly-opposed concepts that are closely linked within the same semantic domain (e.g. beautiful–ugly). Logically, for there to be semantic space available for the two derivative terms, the square's primary terms need to be gradable antonyms – concepts that are comparatively graded on the same implicit dimension. However, deconstructionists have also used the square to problematize binary oppositions, which are conventionally treated as being based on mutually exclusive terms (e.g. alive–dead).

The initial contraries on the upper horizontal axis determine those on the lower one, which are their simple negations, labelled Not S2 and Not S1 (e.g. not-ugly and not-beautiful). Unlike contraries (e.g. beautiful–ugly), the *contradictories* (e.g. beautiful–not-beautiful and ugly–not-ugly) are of course mutually exclusive (either/or) categories. The negations represent untidy categories which are not accounted for by simple binary oppositions: unlike the square's founding terms, they often lack exact lexical equivalents in everyday language. The use of the semiotic square can thus help to reveal 'absences' or semantic spaces that are frequently neglected. Not S2 and Not S1 together constitute a challenge to the conceptual adequacy of the initial pairing, highlighting the deconstructional potential of this tool. Not S1 consists of more than simply S2 (e.g. something that is not beautiful is not necessarily ugly and something that is not ugly is not necessarily beautiful). The vertical relationships of *complementarity* offer us an alternative conceptual synthesis of S1 with Not S2 and of S2 with Not S1 (e.g. beautiful with not ugly or of ugly with not beautiful). A fully labelled square represents a conceptual map of the whole of the relevant universe of discourse to which the analyst relates the subject matter.

While this suggests that the possibilities for signification in a semiotic system are richer than the simple either/or of binary logic, they are nevertheless subject to 'semiotic constraints' – 'deep structures' providing basic axes of signification. The semiotic square highlights 'hidden' underlying concepts in a text or practice and examples have been built around contraries such as: masculine–feminine, active–passive, good–bad, rich–poor, natural–cultural, traditional–modern, thin–fat, illness–health, allies–enemies, reason–emotion, for–against, work–play, fact–fiction. In the spirit of structuralists such as Lévi-Strauss and Leach, Fredric Jameson (1981) uses the square for ideological analysis by mapping the conceptual frameworks within which texts (like cultural myths) seek to resolve fundamental contradictions or dilemmas in order to achieve ideological (as well as structural) closure. While this approach is widely used to serve the academic function of deconstruction, it has also been employed commercially in brand-building to construct myths that offer consumers a way of resolving a problem or situation that previously involved some kind of contradiction (as in the case of the Persil 'Dirt is Good' campaign).

Identifying the primary concepts in relation to the thematic or narrative structure of the material being examined and selecting the particular words to be used to refer to them is the initial analytical task. In the choice of the two basic terms, analysts usually favour familiar words where possible. For the process to be productive in meeting analytical objectives, it is likely to involve recursive reframing and refinement, so this crucial task can be demanding. In his foreword to an English translation of a book by Greimas, Jameson reflects on his own 'unorthodox' use of the technique. He suggests that the analyst should begin by provisionally listing all of the concepts to be coordinated, including even apparently marginal ones. He argues that the order of the terms in the primary opposition is crucial: we have already seen how the first (unmarked) term in such pairings is typically privileged. After four terms have been established, analysts tend to move on to finding adequate lexical labels for the semantic scope of each pairing (so for beautiful–ugly this might be 'aesthetic evaluation'). Jameson notes that 'each of the four primary terms threatens to yawn open into its own fourfold system' (in Greimas 1987, xv–xvi), adding that 'the entire mechanism . . . is capable of generating at least ten conceivable positions out of a rudimentary binary opposition' (ibid., xiv). Many analysts situate one square within another (tilted like a lozenge), representing semantic interaction between two related frames of reference and opening up further semantic spaces. Figure 3.5 is my own attempt to represent the general visual form of such expansions of Greimas's original semiotic square, though the details of particular versions vary. Although this is another grid representing conceptual alignments, it should be noted that it is a different approach to that discussed earlier (Figure 3.3), leading in some instances to confusion. At the risk of adding to the confusion, I feel obliged to mention that (according to Barthes) Jakobson notes that binary oppositions (*a/b*) can also be extended by considering them alongside the 'neutral' form (neither *a* nor *b*) and the 'mixed' form (both *a* and *b*) (Barthes 1994, 170).

The semiotic square has been used to serve diverse analytical purposes in various contexts. Jameson has applied it to novels and films (1972, 167–8; 1981; 1991). Dan Fleming offers an accessible application to children's toys (Fleming 1996, 147ff.). Gilles Marion (1994) has used it to suggest four purposes in communicating through clothing: wanting to be seen; not wanting to be seen; wanting not to be seen; and not wanting not to be seen. Jean-Marie Floch (2000, 116–44) has used it to illustrate an interesting exploration of the

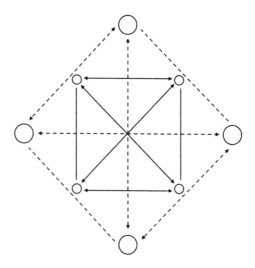

FIGURE 3.5 The semiotic square expanded

Source: © 2016 Daniel Chandler

'consumption values' represented by Habitat and Ikea furniture. That the use of the semiotic square can lead different interpreters to identify different oppositional values in the same text or cultural practice is not a criticism (many texts invite alternative interpretations). However, critics have argued that sometimes its use leads to reductionist and programmatic 'decodings', or offers an illusion of objectivity and coherence that disguises loose argument and highly subjective opinions. I have already alluded to the confusion generated by the use of idiosyncratic forms of the grid. Nevertheless, Jameson insists that the square can be invaluable as a heuristic 'discovery principle' and for the pedagogical function of clarifying and communicating potential patterns in complex material (in Greimas 1987, xv).

THE SYNTAGMATIC DIMENSION

Saussure, of course, emphasizes the systemic relationship of signs to each other. His primary examples of signs are individual words, though he recognizes that we usually communicate through *groups* of signs, which are composite signs (*CLG* 177; 128). Thinking and communication depend on *discourse* rather than isolated signs. The focus in the *Cours* on the language *system* rather than on its *use* means that discourse is neglected. The linking together of signs is conceived solely in terms of the grammatical possibilities that the system offers. Most linguists did not venture higher than the analytical level of the sentence until the 1970s. This led some theorists to abandon semiotics altogether in favour of a focus on discourse while others sought to reformulate a more socially oriented semiotics (e.g. Hodge and Kress 1988). However, this is not to suggest that Saussurean principles, or structuralist techniques inspired by them, are worthless. Analysts still engage in textual studies based on structuralist principles. It remains important for anyone interested in the analysis of texts to be aware of what these principles are. Structuralists study texts as *syntagmatic* structures correlated with paradigmatic distinctions. The syntagmatic analysis of a text (whether it is verbal or nonverbal) involves studying its structure and the relationships between its parts. Structuralist semioticians seek to identify elementary constituent structural units (not necessarily linear sequences) within the text – its syntagms. The use of one syntagmatic structure rather than another within a text is meaningful. The study of syntagmatic relations reveals the conventions or 'rules of combination' underlying the production and interpretation of texts.

SPATIAL RELATIONS

As a result of Saussure's influence, syntagms are often defined only as 'sequential' (and thus temporal – as in speech and music). Saussure emphasizes 'auditory signifiers', which 'are presented one after another' and 'form a chain'. The aural medium unfolds in time. However, even in auditory signs sequential relations are not the only dimension: in music, while sequence may seem the most obvious feature, chords, polyphony, and orchestration are manifestations of *simultaneity*. Furthermore, we may grant that temporal relations tend to be dominant in auditory signs, but in visual signs it is *spatial* relations that are dominant. 'Linearity' is the second of Saussure's two 'general principles' (*CLG* 103; 70). He is concerned with the verbal medium, and unidirectional flow is a feature of speech and also the basic order of writing (regardless of readers – or indeed writers – being able to jump backwards and forwards). Nonverbal visual signs are not tied to unidirectionality (ibid. 103; 70). As Jakobson notes, we need to recognize the importance of spatial as well as temporal syntagmatic relations (1956, 74–5; 1963a, 59; 1963c, 336). Spatial syntagms are important not only in the whole range of what we usually think of as visual media (such as drawing, painting, and photography) but also in the graphic medium of writing – in circumstances where specific layout contributes to the meaning (not only in relatively unusual genres such as 'shape poems' but also routinely in contexts such as notices, newspapers, and magazines). Jakobson recognizes key differences between the dimensions of sequentiality and simultaneity and suggests that one important consequence is that whereas a verbal or musical sequence 'exhibits a consistently hierarchical structure and is resolvable into ultimate, discrete, strictly patterned components', in the case of a 'primarily spatial, simultaneously visible picture' there are 'no similar components . . . and even if some hierarchical arrangement appears, it is neither compulsory nor systematic' (1963c, 336). Saussure does note that visual signifiers (he instances nautical flags) 'can exploit more than one dimension simultaneously' (*CLG* 103; 70). Of course many semiotic systems (including all audio-visual media, such as television and film) rely heavily on both spatial and temporal syntagms. In any case, what Jakobson (1963c, 336) calls Saussure's 'linearity dogma' is clearly *not* a 'general principle' of the sign (even of linguistic signs) and any adequate semiotic framework should acknowledge this.

The 'cognitive semanticists', George Lakoff and Mark Johnson (1980), have shown how fundamental 'orientational metaphors' are routinely linked to key concepts in a culture. Let us briefly consider three key spatial relations in visual images: left–right, top–bottom, and centre–margin. The horizontal and vertical axes are not neutral dimensions of pictorial representation. Since writing and reading in European cultures proceed primarily along a horizontal axis from left to right (as in English but unlike, for instance, Arabic and Hebrew), the 'default' for reading a picture within such reading/writing cultures (unless attention is diverted by some salient features) is likely to be generally in the same direction (Chan and Bergen 2004). This is especially likely where pictures are embedded in written text, as in the case of magazines and newspapers. There is a long-established tendency in European paintings and drawings for movement to enter from the left (Wölfflin 1940, Gaffron 1950, Oppé 1994). A similar pattern has been noted in the theatre, from the perspective of the audience (Arnheim 1974, 35). Even professional photographers sometimes flip an image 'for easier left-to-right viewing' (Joseph and Saunders 2000, 130). Within this tradition, right-facing action has even been perceived as enhancing speed. Such practices have generated associated symbolism and connotations. Right-facing arrows feature in media player buttons such as 'play' and 'fast forward'. In Western business magazines, it is quite common for 'facing the future' to be visually signified by images of people facing or moving to the right. Even without a caption, the left-hand and right-hand elements of a visual image can also signify 'before' and 'after' (following the relevant reading/writing direction).

This left-to-right convention in the European visual tradition (regardless of the actual visual scanning path traversed by the eyes in any particular case) has also given rise to the notion that the viewer is more likely to identify with a figure on the left (where they 'enter') than on the right (where a figure is more likely to be 'looked at'). Symbolically, within this tradition, the left is 'our side'. In Western propaganda, it is not uncommon to find an image on the left representing 'us' while an image on the right represents 'them'. In side-on images of people shaking hands, Herbert Zettl (1990, 112) argues that Westerners tend to see the person on the left shaking hands with the person on the right (rather than vice versa). The person on the left is thus the initiator and left–right is aligned with active–passive (or sender–receiver). In the old Microsoft Instant Messenger chat app (discontinued in 2013), the default emoticons included a male facing right – this (rather than the female emoticon facing left) was normally selected by whoever initiated a virtual hug. The French sociologist Robert Hertz demonstrated long ago (1909) that societies ascribe symbolic significance to the left and right sides of the body. As a deviation from a norm in contexts such as handedness, the left-hand side has 'sinister' connotations in many cultures. The right-hand side has also frequently been associated with masculinity (Rudofsky 1947) so, in terms of Lévi-Straussean analogical thinking, right is to left as male is to female. For instance, buttons on men's garments are traditionally on this side.

The vertical axis also carries connotations. Arguing for the fundamental significance of orientational metaphors in framing experience (see also Chapter 4), Lakoff and Johnson observe that (in English usage) *up* has come to be associated with *more* and *down* with *less*. They outline further associations: *up* is associated with goodness, virtue, happiness, consciousness, health, life, the future, high status, having control or power, and with rationality, while *down* is associated with badness, depravity, sickness, death, low status, being subject to control or power, and with emotion (Lakoff and Johnson 1980, Chapter 4). In pictorial composition, for one signifier to be located 'higher' than another is consequently not simply a spatial relationship but also an evaluative one in relation to their signifieds. Erving Goffman's slim volume *Gender Advertisements* (1979) explores the depictions of male and female figures in magazine advertisements. Although it is unsystematic and only some of his observations have been supported in subsequent empirical studies, it is widely celebrated as a classic of visual sociology. Probably the most relevant of his observations for our purposes here is that 'men tend to be located higher than women' in these ads, symbolically reflecting the routine subordination of women to men in society (43).

Another key spatial dimension is that of centre and margin. The composition of some visual images is based primarily not on a left–right or top–bottom structure but on a dominant centre and a periphery. This is related to the fundamental perceptual distinction between *figure* and *ground* (which applies also to auditory, taste, olfactory, and haptic perception). Selective perception involves 'foregrounding' some features and 'backgrounding' others. We owe the concept of 'figure' and 'ground' in perception to the Gestalt psychologists. In the case of visual images, we routinely distinguish a dominant shape (a 'figure' with a definite contour) from what our current concerns relegate to the background (or 'ground'). In visual images, the figure tends to be located centrally.

SEQUENTIAL RELATIONS

The most obvious example of sequential relations is narrative. Some critics claim that differences between narratives and non-narratives relate to differences among media; others claim that narrative is a 'deep structure' independent of the medium. Narrative theory (or narratology) is a major interdisciplinary field in its own right, and is not necessarily framed within a semiotic perspective, although the analysis of narrative is an important branch of semiotics. Semiotic narratology is concerned with narrative in any mode – literary or non-literary, fictional or non-fictional, verbal or visual – but tends to focus on minimal narrative units and the 'grammar of the plot'. It follows in the tradition of the Russian formalist Vladimir Propp (1895–1970) and the French anthropologist Claude Lévi-Strauss.

Christian Metz (1968, 17) observes that 'a narrative has a *beginning and an ending*, a fact that simultaneously distinguishes it from the rest of the world'. There are no 'events' in the world (Galtung and Ruge 1981). What counts as an 'event' is determined by one's purposes. Narrative form creates events. Perhaps the most basic narrative syntagm is a linear temporal model composed of three phases – equilibrium–disruption–equilibrium – a 'chain' of events corresponding to the beginning, middle, and end of a story (or, as Philip Larkin put it, describing the formula of the classic novel: 'a beginning, a *muddle* and an end'; *my emphasis*). In the orderly Aristotelian narrative form, *causation* and *goals* turn *story* (chronological events) into *plot*: events at the beginning cause those in the middle, and events in the middle cause those at the end. This is the basic formula for classic Hollywood movies in which the storyline is given priority over everything else. The film-maker Jean-Luc Godard declared that he liked a film to have a beginning, a middle, and an end, but not necessarily in that order; in 'classical' (realist) narrative, events are always in that order, providing continuity and closure.

Narratives help to make the strange familiar. They provide structure, predictability, and coherence. In this respect, they are similar to schemas for familiar events in everyday life. Turning experience into narratives seems to be a fundamental feature of the human drive to make meaning. We are 'storytellers' with 'a readiness or pre-disposition to organize experience into a narrative form' which is encouraged in our socialization as we learn to adopt our culture's ways of telling (Bruner 1990, 45, 80).

Narrative coherence is no guarantee of referential correspondence. The narrative form itself has a content of its own. Narrative is such an automatic choice for representing events that it seems unproblematic and natural. Bob Hodge and Gunther Kress (1988, 230) argue that the use of a familiar narrative structure serves 'to naturalize the content of the narrative itself'. Where narratives end in a return to predictable equilibrium this is referred to as narrative *closure*. Closure is often effected as the resolution of an opposition. Structural closure at the level of the text is regarded by many theorists as reinforcing a preferred reading, or in Hodge and Kress's terms, reinforcing the status quo. According to theorists applying the principles of Jacques Lacan, conventional narrative (in dominant forms of literature, cinema, and so on) also plays a part in 'the constitution of the subject'. While narrative appears to demonstrate unity and coherence within the text, the subject participates in the sense of closure (Nichols 1981, 78).

STRUCTURAL REDUCTION

The structuralist's inductive search for underlying patterns highlights the similarities between what may initially seem to be very different narratives. 'The magic number 7' is often used to refer to the number of basic plot formulas (e.g. Booker 2004), the term being derived from George Miller (1956), who was referring to items in working memory. Freud suggests that there are only seven basic jokes; even these can be reduced to a two-part structure of 'set-up and punchline'. We are all familiar with the structure of most popular narratives – either bad people enjoy initial successes but ultimately come to a nasty end or good people experience misfortunes but ultimately enjoy a happy ending (these are combined in the Bond movies, for instance). Roland Barthes asserts that a narrative cannot be produced 'without reference to an implicit system of units and rules' (1977a, 81). The structural analyst's first task is to identify minimal units, their functions, and the rules for their combination. As Barthes (ibid., 88) notes, 'the first task is to divide up narrative and . . . define the smallest narrative units

. . . Meaning must be the criterion of the unit: it is the functional nature of certain segments of the story that makes them units – hence the name "functions" immediately attributed to these first units'.

In a highly influential book, *The Morphology of the Folktale* (1928), the Russian narrative theorist Vladimir Propp reported that 100 fairy tales that he had analysed were all based on the same basic formula. He reduced them to around thirty 'functions'. 'Function is understood as an act of character defined from the point of view of its significance for the course of the action' (21). In other words, such functions are basic units of action. As Barthes (1977a, 106) notes, structuralists avoid defining human agents in terms of 'psychological essences', but rather define participants not in terms of 'what they are' as 'characters' but in terms of 'what they do'. Propp lists seven *roles* – the *villain*, the *donor*, the *helper*, the *sought-for person (and her father)*, the *dispatcher*, the *hero*, and the *false hero* – and schematized the various 'functions' within the story. Many commentators have sought to apply this framework beyond its original scope, but this can seem rather forced.

This form of analysis downplays the specificity of individual texts in the interests of establishing *how* texts mean rather than *what* a particular text means. It is by definition, a 'reductive' strategy, and some literary theorists fear that it threatens to make Shakespeare indistinguishable from *Star Wars*. Even Barthes (1974, 3) notes that 'the first analysts of narrative were attempting . . . to see all the world's stories . . . within a single structure' and that this is a task which is 'ultimately undesirable, for the text thereby loses its difference'. Despite this objection, Fredric Jameson suggests that the method has redeeming features. For instance, the notion of a grammar of plots allows us to see 'the work of a generation or a period in terms of a given model (or basic plot paradigm), which is then varied and articulated in as many ways as possible until it is somehow exhausted and replaced by a new one' (1972, 124).

Unlike Propp, both Lévi-Strauss and Greimas based their interpretations of narrative structure on underlying oppositions. Lévi-Strauss sees the myths of a culture as variations on a limited number of basic themes built upon oppositions related to nature versus culture (note that even the traditional distinctions between signs as natural or conventional reflect this opposition). For Lévi-Strauss any myth can be reduced to a fundamental structure. He wrote that 'a compilation of known tales and myths would fill an imposing number of volumes. But they can be reduced to a small number of simple types if we abstract from among the diversity of characters a few elementary functions' (1972, 203–4). Myths help people to make sense of the world in which they live. Lévi-Strauss sees myths as a kind of message from our ancestors about humankind and our relationship to nature; in particular, how we became separated from other animals. For instance, myths of the domestic fireside mediate our transition from nature to culture and from animality to humanity via the transition from the raw to the cooked (1969). However, the meaning is not to be found in any individual narrative but in the patterns underlying the myths of a given culture. Such myths make sense only as part of a system in which each can be reduced to the same underlying structure. Through a process of transformation by substitution Lévi-Strauss demonstrates that the structures of individual myths within a set are 'homologous' – that is, 'orderly' structural correspondences or isomorphisms can be detected between them. The search for such structural homologies is a central structuralist quest. Lévi-Strauss treats myths as a kind of language. He reports (1972, 211) that his initial method of analysing the structure of myths into 'gross constituent units' or 'mythemes' involves 'breaking down its story into the shortest possible sentences'. This approach is based on an analogy with the 'morpheme', which is the smallest meaningful unit in linguistics. In order to explain the structure of a myth, Lévi-Strauss classifies each mytheme in terms of its 'function' within the myth and finally relates the various kinds of function to each other. He sees the possible combinations of mythemes as being governed by a kind of underlying universal grammar, which is part of the deep structure of the mind itself.

A good example of the Lévi-Straussean method is provided by Victor Larrucia in his own analysis of the story of Little Red Riding-Hood (originating in the late seventeenth century in a tale by Perrault) (Larrucia 1975). According to this method the narrative is summarized in several (paradigmatic) columns within a grid, each column corresponding to some unifying function or theme (see Figure 3.6). The original sequence (indicated by numbers) is preserved when the grid

1	Grand-mother's illness causes mother to make grandmother food	2	Little Red Riding Hood (LRRH) obeys mother and goes off to wood	3	LRRH meets (wolf as) friend and talks		
4	Woodcutter's presence causes wolf to speak to LRRH	5	LRRH obeys wolf and takes long road to grandmother's	6	Grandmother admits (wolf as) LRRH	7	Wolf eats grand-mother
				8	LRRH meets (wolf as) grandmother		
		9	LRRH obeys grandmother and gets into bed	10	LRRH questions (wolf as) grandmother	11	Wolf eats LRRH

FIGURE 3.6 Little Red Riding Hood

Source: Larrucia 1975, 528

is read (syntagmatically) row by row. Rather than offering any commentators' suggestions as to what themes these columns might represent, I will avoid authorial closure and leave it to readers to speculate for themselves. Suggestions can be found in the references (Larrucia 1975; Silverman and Torode 1980, 314ff.).

The structuralist semiotician and literary theorist Algirdas Greimas (who established 'the Paris school' of semiotics) proposes a 'grammar of plot' which can generate any known narrative structure (1966 and 1987). As a result of a 'semiotic reduction' of Propp's seven roles he identifies three types of narrative syntagms: *syntagms performanciels* – tasks and struggles; *syntagms contractuels* – the establishment or breaking of contracts; *syntagms disjonctionnels* – departures and arrivals (Culler 1975, 213; Greimas 1987). Greimas claims that three basic binary oppositions underlie all narrative themes, actions, and character types (which he collectively calls 'actants'); namely, *subject–object* (Propp's *hero* and *sought-for person*), *sender–receiver* (Propp's *dispatcher* and *hero* – again) and *helper–opponent* (conflations of Propp's *helper* and *donor*, plus the *villain* and the *false hero*) – note that Greimas argues that the hero is both *subject* and *receiver*. The *subject* is the one who seeks; the *object* is that which is sought. The *sender* sends the object and the *receiver* is its destination. The *helper* assists the action and the *opponent* blocks it. He extrapolates from the *subject–verb–object* sentence structure, proposing a fundamental, underlying 'actantial model' as the basis of story structures. He argues that in traditional syntax, 'functions' are the roles played by words – the *subject* being the one performing the action and the *object* being 'the one who suffers it' – a definition of the sentence which goes back to the ancient Greeks (Jameson 1972, 124). For Greimas, stories thus share a common structure. However, critics have not always been convinced of the validity of Greimas's methodology or of the workability or usefulness of his model (e.g. Culler 1975, 213–14, 223–4).

Syntagmatic analysis can be applied not only to verbal texts but also to audio-visual ones. In film and television, a syntagmatic analysis would involve an analysis of how each *frame*, *shot*, *scene*, or *sequence* related to the others (these are the standard levels of analysis in film theory). At the lowest level is the individual *frame*. Since films are projected at a rate of twenty-four frames per second, the viewer is never conscious of individual frames. At the next level up, a *shot* is a 'single take' – an unedited sequence of frames, which may include camera movement. A shot is terminated by a cut (or other transition). A *scene* consists of more than one shot set in a single place and time. A *sequence* spans more than one place and/or time but it is a logical or thematic sequence (having 'dramatic unity'). A linguistic model leads semioticians to a search for units of analysis in audio-visual media, which are analogous to those used in linguistics. In the semiotics of film, crude equivalents with written language are sometimes postulated, such as the frame as morpheme (or word), the shot as sentence, the scene as paragraph, and the sequence as chapter (suggested equivalences vary among commentators). For members of the Glasgow University Media Group, the basic unit of analysis is the shot, delimited by cuts and with allowance made for camera movement within the shot and for the accompanying soundtrack (Davis and Walton 1983b, 43). However, if the basic unit is the shot, the analytical utility of this concept is highly restricted in the case of a film like Hitchcock's *Rope* (1948), in which each shot (or take) lasts up to ten minutes (the length of a reel of film at the time the film was made). Similarly, what is one to make of shots-within-shots in a film like Buster Keaton's *Sherlock Jr.* (1924), where we see a film within a film? Shots can be broken into smaller meaningful units (above the level of the frame), but theorists disagree about what these might be. Above the level of the sequence, other narrative units can also be posited.

Christian Metz (1968) offers elaborate syntagmatic categories for narrative film. For him, these syntagms are analogous to sentences in verbal language, and he argues that there are eight key filmic syntagms that are based on ways of ordering narrative space and time.

- the *autonomous shot* (e.g. establishing shot, insert);
- the *parallel syntagm* (montage of motifs);
- the *bracketing syntagm* (montage of brief shots);
- the *descriptive syntagm* (sequence describing one moment);
- the *alternating syntagm* (two sequences alternating);
- the *scene* (shots implying temporal continuity);
- the *episodic sequence* (organized discontinuity of shots);
- the *ordinary sequence* (temporal with some compression).

However, Metz's '*grande syntagmatique*' has not proved an easy system to apply. Beyond the fourfold distinction between frames, shots, scenes and sequences, the interpretive frameworks of film theorists differ considerably. In this sense at least, there is no cinematic 'language'.

LANGUE AND PAROLE

In seeking to establish a rigorous linguistic methodology, which he saw as lacking in the older nineteenth-century (historical) linguistics, Saussure made what is now a famous terminological distinction between different 'objects of study' – *langue* (a particular language system) and *parole* (discourse, or language in use), both being part of the broader category of *langage* (natural language). This epistemological distinction was an important contribution to linguistic theory. *Langue* is the *system*, including its values, relationships, rules, and conventions; *parole* is the discourse that instantiates that system (its use in particular instances and contexts). Language depends on the relation between its system of potentialities and their selective actualization on any given occasion. Saussure sought to untangle the language system from that which is extrinsic to it. The system (a socially-shared semiotic resource for meaning-making) must not be conflated with its use: a distinction that has escaped some of Saussure's critics. The lack of exact equivalents in English may help to account for the difficulty experienced by some English readers in appreciating it (a very Saussurean point related to linguistic values).

Langue is only part of *langage*, but for Saussure it is at the heart of linguistics (*CLG* 25; 9). The linguistic system, like a symphony, has a virtual reality, which is independent of the way in which it is performed (ibid. 36, 18). The system is of a higher logical type than its use; discourse logically presupposes a language system that makes meaningful speech acts possible. It is axiomatic for Saussure that there is no *parole* without *langue* because signs are constituted by their position in a system (cf. Bühler 1933, 111–12). The study of *langue* is an essential prerequisite for the study of language as a whole, whereas *parole* is dependent on contingent, contextual, non-linguistic factors. Thus for Saussure, the study of a language must initially focus on it as a system, identifying its conventions, its units, and their relations. The editors of the *Cours* note that Saussure had also planned to offer an account of *parole*, or 'the linguistics of speaking', but that sadly he died before doing so (*CLG* 10; lv). He was well aware of importance of the social context of signification.

Saussure's distinction between *langue* and *parole* is fundamental, but he stresses that they are interdependent (ibid. 37; 18). Without recognizing their complementary functions we cannot understand how language works. As Raymond Tallis argues, 'Meaning arises out of the interaction between system and context' (1995, 76). Meaning involves both *valeur* (in *langue*) and *signification* (in *parole*). Although 'context' as such is referred to only fleetingly in the *Cours*, this is the domain of *parole* (for an insightful interpretation of Saussurean theory to account for the complementary perspective of signs in use, see Thibault 1997). Within *langue*, there is only the general potential for meanings in the form of linguistic values, and the signifier and the signified are defined purely negatively in relation to other terms in the system; only in particular instances of *discourse* is the fusion of the linguistic sign positively realized, and specific meaning determined (*CLG* 162, 166; 117, 120–1). In *parole*, words are usually encountered within the textual context of other words and such syntagmatic contexts play a key part in determining relevant meanings. The sentences in which words make sense are uttered in speech or composed in writing: these sentences are not part of the language system itself (ibid. 30, 148, 172; 14, 106, 124). Reference (via 'referring expressions', typically in the form of chains of signs) is only possible within the context of discourse. We have established that the language system does not 'refer to reality', but language is of course used in real-world contexts by individual speakers and writers in particular discourses for many functions, including referential functions (see Chapter 6). Nowhere in the *Cours* is it claimed that *discourse* cannot be deployed contextually for the purpose of referring (however mediatedly) to entities and states of affairs in the experiential world. *Messages* have referents: we usually know what we are talking about. However, referentiality does not explain the language system. A clear distinction between *langue* and *parole* helps to avoid the confusion of a signified with a referent. Many post-Saussurean theorists (structuralists and post-structuralists) collapse these distinctions, reducing language to *langue* and treating the signified as a referent, the most extreme idealists among them claiming that reality is merely an 'effect' of language. Saussure cannot be held responsible for his misinterpreters.

Structuralist theorists adopted and adapted the distinction between *langue* and *parole*, but they did not develop a theorization of signs in use. Saussure outlined his distinction in relation only to verbal language, and it wasn't until 1928 that the Russian linguists Roman Jakobson and Yuri Tynyanov argued that the principle could be extended to other cultural forms (Jakobson 1985, 26). According to this distinction, in a secondary semiotic system such as literature (built upon what Russian semioticians refer to as the 'primary modelling system' of language), a particular literary work is an instance of *parole* within a system of literary conventions and norms, and in cinema, individual films can be seen as the *parole* of a system of cinematic 'language'. The structuralist emphasis is on the system itself.

Marxist theorists have been particularly critical of Saussure. In the late 1920s, Valentin Voloshinov (1973) rejected his emphasis on internal relations within the system of language and sought to reverse what he saw as the prioritization of *langue* over *parole*. The meaning of a sign is not in its relationship to other signs within the language system but rather in the social context of its use. 'The sign is part of organized social intercourse and cannot exist, as such, outside it, reverting to a mere physical artifact' (ibid., 21). We learn from the *Cours* that the linguistic sign system is sustained by the community of speakers and there is explicit reference to 'the social forces that influence language' (*CLG* 33, 112; 15, 77). However, Voloshinov had a more radical agenda: the sign, as he put it, is 'an arena of the class struggle' (1973, 23); 'whenever a sign is present, ideology is present too' (ibid., 10).

A key objection from Saussure's critics is that the prioritization of system over usage fails to account for changes in the system. Although Saussure's training was in historical linguistics, his approach represents a reaction against the dominant nineteenth-century tradition of comparative and historical linguistics. He regards his priority as a linguist as being to study the 'language state' (*état de langue*) 'synchronically' as if it were frozen in time (like a photograph) – rather than 'diachronically' – in terms of its evolution over time (like a film). This is another analytical distinction. Saussure's goal is not to replace a diachronic approach with a synchronic one. Indeed, Parts III–V of the *Cours* explore the historical evolution of languages – which many critics seem to overlook. Saussure acknowledges that 'the system and its history ... are so closely related that we can scarcely keep them apart' (*CLG* 24; 8). However, different methodologies are required to study language states and historical changes. If language is understood as comprising a succession of states, the synchronic perspective is logically prior to the diachronic one. Explaining the workings of an arbitrary language system requires the analysis of relations within the system, rather than causal accounts of the evolution of its elements. It would be difficult to explain the everyday decoding of language without reference to a relatively stable *langue*. Only in the synchronic state can we understand how words have meaning. A synchronic approach identifies the systemic relations which govern meanings in a speech community (ibid. 140; 99–100). Without such a grounding, diachronic approaches to changes in the system cannot be undertaken.

Saussure's critics nevertheless object to what they see as a neglect of process and historicity in comparison with historical theories like Marxism (Voloshinov 1973, 61). Jakobson and Tynyanov declared in 1927 that 'pure synchronism now proves to be an illusion', adding that 'every synchronic system has its past and its future' (ibid., 166). Jakobson stresses the dynamic relation between diachrony and synchrony. In cultural studies, a purely synchronic approach underplays the dynamic nature of sign systems (for instance, television conventions change fairly rapidly compared to conventions for written language). It can also underplay dynamic changes in cultural myths, which signification both alludes to and helps to shape.

Saussure is misrepresented by many of his critics. He does not see the language system as static, but rather as homeostatic – functioning to maintain a dynamic equilibrium within its constantly changing network (*CLG* 154; 110). His *system* is a conceptual map of relations at a given time: it is a synoptic representation (rather than a dynamic one) but it does not represent a static 'structure'. Saussure is well aware that the language system is historically constituted and that languages are always changing. He would have agreed with critics that any 'fixing' of the language system is both temporary and socially determined (Coward and Ellis 1977, 6, 8, 13). At no one time is a language system entirely stable or fixed (*CLG* 234; 171). *Langue* is inherently variable (like all semiotic systems). The *Cours* explicitly refers to 'varying degrees of shifts in the relationship between the signified and the signifier' (ibid. 113; 78). The system evolves through innovation in *parole* (ibid. 77–8; 112–13), and *langue* reflects typical patterns of use.

Despite being adopted by many as the 'father of structuralism', Saussure was not a structuralist. Structuralists claim to derive many of their principles from (their readings of) the *Cours*, while some poststructuralists criticize him for principles which he did not endorse, some of which were in fact derived from structuralists (Tallis 1995). Many of these misinterpretations have been highly influential, even when directly contrary to Saussure's own principles (Daylight 2011).

The structuralist movement (led in particular by Jakobson and Lévi-Strauss) initiated a quest to identify and describe patterns of 'structural relations' within texts and cultural practices and what they saw as 'underlying structures' transcending particular instances (a metaphor that does not derive from Saussure). In a programmatic response to the *Cours*, social semioticians have prioritized *parole* over *langue* and diachrony over synchrony.

In response to structuralist practices, sociological critics note that structural elements need not only to be related to one another and interpreted, but also to be contextualized in terms of the social systems which give rise to them, while a psychologist objects that 'the question of whether categories like sacred/profane and happiness/misery are psychologically real in any meaningful sense is not posed and the internal logic of structuralism would suggest it need not be posed' (Young 1990, 184). When analysts identify patterns within a text, not all of them demonstrate the significance of such patterns. Nor can it be claimed that oppositions are 'contained within' texts rather than generated by interpretation. None of these criticisms are unanswerable, however, and we would be foolish to forego the insights which may still be gained from exploring the structural analysis of texts and social practices, armed with a very particular set of skills.

REFLECTIONS

1 If you want to understand gender representation, deliberate reversals can be very revealing. Apply the commutation test by looking at some printed advertisements featuring either women or men and considering the semantic shift if people of the other sex had been chosen and depicted in exactly the same way.

2 As an exploration of conceptual alignment, tell people that the left side of the brain is associated with logic, and ask them to list which other functions are particularly associated with each hemisphere.

3 In your local stores, which particular retail products are explicitly labelled either as 'for women' or 'for men' with the normative version of the same product not labelled in this

way? What gender messages can be inferred for each kind of product?

4 The example of the Persil 'Dirt is Good' campaign illustrated how innovative advertisers seek to generate a non-traditional conceptual alignment. Find an example of your own of this process in action. What attempted realignment does it demonstrate?

5 What issues are raised by mapping public–private against social–antisocial in relation to social media?

6 What examples can you find of advertisements that offer evidence enabling you to infer that right-facing figures signify the future and/or that left-facing figures signify the past? Note that if you are examining advertisements in right-to-left writing systems, the frame of reference should be reversed.

7 Propp lists seven *roles*: the *villain*, the *donor*, the *helper*, the *sought-for person (and her father)*, the *dispatcher*, the *hero*, and the *false hero*. Although this framework is usually difficult to apply beyond the texts to which he refers, many people have pointed out that it can be applied fairly easily to the characters in *Star Wars*: check your own suggestions against those you can find online.

FURTHER READING

Barthes 1967a; Bouissac 1998, entries for 'actantial model', 'actants', 'binarism', 'deconstruction', 'grande syntagmatique', 'langue and parole', 'markedness', 'narrative structures', 'narratology', 'opposition', 'paradigm', 'semiotic square', 'structuralism', 'structure', 'synchronic and diachronic'; Douglas 1966, 1973b, and 1975; Floch 2000; Greimas 1987; Horigan 1988, Chapter 2; Jakobson and Lévi-Strauss 1970; Larrucia 1975; Leach 1970 and 1976; Lévi-Strauss 1969 and 1972; Leymore 1975; Mazzalovo 2012; Metz 1968; Mitry 2000; Propp 1928; Protevi 2005, entry for 'structuralism'; Robey 1973; Sebeok 1994b, entries for 'structuralism and post-structuralism', 'structure', 'synchronic/diachronic'; Sturrock 1979 and 1986; Williamson 1978.

CHALLENGING
THE LITERAL

Semiotics represents a challenge to the 'literal' insofar as it questions the possibility of meaning what we say or saying what we mean, and of perceiving or representing 'the way things are'. We always mean more than we say and sometimes even the opposite, and we can only ever selectively perceive or represent things from a particular perspective. In this chapter, we will explore the ways in which semioticians have problematized two key distinctions: between the literal and the figurative and between denotation and connotation.

Literalism involves treating the meanings of messages as limited to their explicit factual, informational, or propositional content. Literalists equate the meaning with the message: meaning is seen as 'contained' in the message rather than as dependent on its interpretation. From this perspective, a verbal message means only what it says, and an image means only what it depicts. Literalism presupposes an 'unvarnished version of the truth' and a transparent medium in which it can be represented (both illusory concepts). Utterances and texts rarely, if ever, 'say what they mean': their intended meaning involves

informational	COMMUNICATION FUNCTION	aesthetic

foregrounds

content	form/style
literal	figurative
denotation	connotation
objectivity	subjectivity
representation	signification
unambiguity	polysemy
closure	openness
seriousness	playfulness

FIGURE 4.1 Informational vs. aesthetic functions

Source: © 2016 Daniel Chandler

more than that which is explicitly expressed. Understanding even the simplest messages and representations always requires us to go 'beyond the information given' – in the famous phrase of the American psychologist Jerome Bruner (1973). The closest we get to the literal representation of objects and events is in indexical media such as photography, but even here, the 'subject' of a photograph is never free of 'the way it is taken' (in both senses). As we shall see in Chapter 6, communication and representation serve many functions, among which informational and aesthetic functions are widely represented as a fundamental pairing of polar opposites (see Figure 4.1). Literalism, which focuses on the informational function, reflects what literary theorists have referred to as the 'cloak theory' of language, in which stylistic devices are seen as merely 'the dress of thought' – in contrast to 'mould theory', in which the form of expression is seen as giving shape to thoughts and feelings (Chandler 1995a, 14–15). The cloak and the mould are of course powerful metaphors that both reflect and shape how we think about the relation between thought and language. Such polarizations ascribe causal primacy either to thought or language, but it may be more productive to think of these as interdependent.

RHETORICAL TROPES

A sea-change in academic discourse, which has been visible in many disciplines, has been dubbed 'the rhetorical turn' or 'the discursive turn'. The central proposition of this contemporary trend is that, far from being merely the dress of thought, rhetorical forms are deeply and unavoidably involved in the shaping of realities. Form and content are inseparable. Language is not a neutral medium and our choice of words matters. The North American literary theorist Stanley Fish (1980, 32) insists that 'it is impossible to mean the same thing in two (or more) different ways'. To say that a glass is 'half empty' is not the same as saying that it is 'half full'. In common usage, we refer dismissively to 'heated rhetoric', 'empty rhetoric', and 'mere rhetoric', but all discourse is unavoidably rhetorical, and as a system of expression that mediates reality, rhetoric and its devices are as much the concern of semioticians as of rhetoricians.

In communication or representation, *tropes* have been tra-ditionally classified as marked deviations from a supposed norm of literal expectations (though deconstructionists and others have challenged the hierarchy that privileges the literal). In relation to language, tropes are 'figures of speech' that change the usual meanings of words. While literal language 'means what it says', figurative language 'says one thing and means another' (or 'your mother', as a Freudian joke puts it). Similarly, pictorial 'metaphors' symbolically depict one thing but are intended to refer to another. The issue of 'how one thing can mean another' is at the heart of semiotics (Watt 1998, 675).

The conventions of figurative language constitute a rhetorical code, which is part of the reality maintenance system of a culture or sub-culture. It is a code that relates ostensibly to how things are represented rather than to what is represented. Occasionally in everyday life our attention is drawn to an unusual metaphor. However, much of the time – outside of 'poetic' contexts – figures of speech retreat to 'transparency'. Such transparency tends to anaesthetize us to the way in which the culturally available stock of tropes acts as an anchor linking us to the dominant ways of thinking within our society (Lakoff and Johnson 1980). Our repeated exposure to, and use of, such figures of speech subtly sustains our tacit agreement with the shared assumptions of our society. Tropes do not operate in isolation and are inextricably associated. For instance, when we refer metaphorically to 'putting things into words' this involves a further implicit metaphor of language as a 'container' – a view of language that has particular implications (Reddy 1979). Yet the use of tropes is unavoidable. We may think of figurative language as most obviously a feature of poetry and more generally of 'literary' writing, but there is more metaphor on the street than in Shakespeare.

In seventeenth-century England, the scientists of the Royal Society sought 'to separate knowledge of nature from the colours of rhetoric, the devices of the fancy, the delightful deceit of the fables' (Thomas Sprat, 1667: *The History of the Royal Society*). They saw the 'trick of metaphors' as distorting reality. An attempt to avoid figurative language became closely allied to the realist ideology of objectivism. Language and reality, thought and language, and form and content are regarded by realists as separate, or at least as separable. They favour the use of the 'clearest', most 'transparent' language for the accurate and truthful description of facts. However, language isn't glass (as the metaphorical references to clarity and transparency suggest), and it is unavoidably involved in the construction of the world as we know it. In everyday life, we routinely employ metaphorical language in developing our ideas, and thus 'by indirections find directions out' (*Hamlet* II, i). Banishing metaphor is an impossible task since it is central to language. Ironically, the writings of the seventeenth-century critics of rhetoric – such as Sprat, Hobbes, and Locke – are themselves richly metaphorical.

Veering towards philosophical idealism, some argue that all language is metaphor or even that reality is a product of metaphors. Others, including I. A. Richards and George Lakoff, argue that there can be no text that 'means what it says' (which is how literal language is often defined); there is no neutral form of communication or representation (and thus the literal–metaphorical dichotomy is unsustainable – a position adopted by Derrida). Since in 'non-literal' forms what is said or depicted is not what is meant, establishing the most likely intended meaning requires interpretation. Constructionists insist that metaphors are pervasive and largely unrecognized within a culture or sub-culture and that highlighting them is a useful key to identifying whose realities such metaphors privilege. Identifying figurative tropes in texts and practices can help to highlight underlying thematic frameworks; semiotic textual analysis sometimes involves the identification of a 'root metaphor' or 'dominant trope'. Michel Foucault argues that the dominant tropes within the discourse of a particular historical period determine what can be known – constituting the basic *episteme* of the age (Foucault 1970). Derrida (1974) shows how philosophers in the European tradition have historically referred to the mind and the intellect in terms of tropes, based on the presence or absence of light; everyday language is rich in examples of the association of thinking with visual metaphors (bright, brilliant, dull, enlightening, illuminating, vision, clarity, reflection, etc.).

While the most closely-related and obvious conceptual alignment of the literal–metaphorical opposition is with denotation–connotation (Figure 4.1), it is also part of a much larger system of associations, such as with plain–fancy, prose–poetry, science–art, black-and-white–colourful, truth–falsehood, objective–subjective, rational–emotional, and masculine–feminine. All of these oppositions are mutually reinforcing – generating and sustaining a web of long-lasting cultural connotations and interpretive biases.

Each figurative device involves a different form of association or connection. Here we explore four key tropes, beginning with metaphor.

METAPHOR

Metaphor is so widespread that it is often used as an umbrella term (another metaphor!) to refer broadly to any non-literal feature in communication and representation. In a more specific sense, it refers to a figure of speech based on analogy (the word 'as' or 'like' in the closely-related form of simile makes this explicit). Whereas in an analogy the connection is literal, in metaphor it is figurative. Metaphors allude to an unexpected similarity between apparently disparate things, saying that '*this* is (like) *that*'. Lakoff and Johnson argue that 'the essence of metaphor is understanding and experiencing one kind of thing in terms of another' (1980, 5). We often use more concrete analogies to make abstractions 'easier to grasp'. Metaphors may even be essential to understanding, helping to bridge the gap between the familiar and the strange, the given and the new, and linking different conceptual domains. As Claude Lévi-Strauss emphasizes, human cultures depend upon analogical thinking. We seem driven to find similarities between things. 'Everything is similar to everything else in some respect, and the relative importance of any specific relation of similarity depends on context and purpose' (Lopes 1996, 18; cf. Mitchell 1987, 56–7). The ubiquity of tropes in visual as well as verbal forms can be seen as reflecting our fundamentally *relational* understanding of reality. Reality is framed and constructed within systems of analogy.

Semiotically, a metaphor has often been envisaged as a new sign generated by the replication and combination of the signifier of one sign and the signified of another (Figure 4.2) (see Jakobson 1966, 417). This is the traditional Aristotelian 'substitution model' of metaphor where '*a* stands for *b*', though in the 'interactionist' model (Richards 1936) it is contended that many metaphors involve concepts interacting beyond the level of single words and cannot be reduced to literal forms without a significant loss of associational meaning. In contrast to the substitution model, metaphors may depend on the simultaneous presence of two signifier-signified pairs.

In literary terms, a metaphor consists of a 'literal' primary subject (or 'tenor') expressed in terms of a 'figurative' secondary subject (or 'vehicle') (ibid., where the 'ground' is introduced as a third term representing the meaning provided by an interpretant). If the metaphor takes the basic form '*term a* is *term b*', *term a* is the tenor or primary

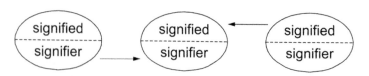

FIGURE 4.2 Metaphorical substitution

Source: © 2016 Daniel Chandler

topic and *term b* is the figurative vehicle which is 'substituted' for it. Or, in the cognitive-conceptual model of Lakoff and Johnson (1980), where metaphor is a cognitive process, *term a* is the 'target domain' and *term b* is the 'source domain'.

Typically, metaphor expresses an abstraction in terms of a more well-defined concept, as in 'all the world's a stage' (*As You Like It* II, vii). With a 'fresh metaphor', the connection is unfamiliar: we must make an imaginative leap to recognize the resemblance to which it alludes. Metaphors initially seem to disregard 'literal' or denotative resemblance but some kind of resemblance or association must become apparent if the metaphor is to make any sense at all to its interpreters. The basis in resemblance makes the relation iconic (although there is always a conventional dimension). Since the relation of similarity is not explicit in a metaphor, inference or 'cognitive elaboration' is required. Thus more interpretive effort is required in making sense of metaphors than of more obvious signs, although this interpretive effort may be experienced as pleasurable. Many metaphors become so habitually employed that much of the time we hardly notice that we are using metaphors at all, and yet one study found that, on average, an English speaker produces around 3,000 novel metaphors per week (Pollio *et al.* 1977).

Metaphors need not be verbal. In film, a pair of consecutive shots is metaphorical when there is an implied comparison of the two shots. For instance, a shot of an aeroplane followed by a shot of a bird flying would be metaphorical, implying that the aeroplane is (or is like) a bird. So too would a shot of a bird landing accompanied by the sounds of an airport control tower and of a braking plane – as in an airline commercial cited by Charles Forceville (1996, 203). In most cases, the context would cue us as to which is the primary subject. An advertisement for an airline is more likely to suggest that an aeroplane is (like) a bird than that a bird is (like) an aeroplane. As with verbal metaphors, we are left to draw our own conclusions as to the points of comparison. Advertisers frequently use visual metaphors. Despite the frequently expressed proposition that images cannot assert (or negate), metaphorical images often imply that which advertisers prefer not to make verbally explicit.

Visual metaphor can also involve a function of 'transference', transferring certain qualities from one sign to another. In relation to advertising, this has been explored by Judith Williamson in her book, *Decoding Advertisements* (1978). It is of course the role of advertisers to differentiate similar products from each other, and they do this by associating a product with a specific set of social values. Advertisers are in the business of selling signs. In contemporary society, advertising is a primary source through which we learn the dominant associations of particular signs, so we can claim that 'ads teach us to consume signs' (Goldman 1992, 39). Advertisers routinely engage in the practice of 'meaning transfer', in which a campaign seeks to associate a product with imagery already positively valued by the target market (such as a person, an object, or a setting reflecting their aspirations), creating a 'commodity sign' (ibid., 37). The implicit message is that purchasing the product associates the consumer with the same values. In such contexts, the message derives much of its power from being inexplicit, passing 'under the radar' as in so many contemporary minimalist ads. As early as the 1950s, an ad executive wrote, 'We no longer buy oranges, we buy vitality' (Packard 1957, 35).

George Lakoff and Mark Johnson (1980) illustrate several kinds of metaphor underlying most of our fundamental concepts:

- *orientational* metaphors primarily relating to spatial organization (up–down, in–out, front–back, on–off, near–far, deep–shallow, and central–peripheral);
- *ontological* metaphors which associate activities, emotions and ideas with entities and substances (most obviously, metaphors involving personification);
- *structural* metaphors: overarching metaphors (building on the other two types) which allow us to structure one concept in terms of another (e.g. rational argument is war, or time is a resource).

Lakoff and Johnson argue that although metaphors vary from culture to culture, they are not arbitrary, being derived initially from our physical, social, and cultural experience (cf. Vico 1744, 129). In all societies, symbolic significance is attributed to the body and its parts, making it what Mary Douglas calls a 'natural symbol' (1966, 1973a). Associations or analogies with the physical orientation of the body in space understandably feel more 'natural' than more abstract symbolism. Lakoff and Johnson argue that metaphors form systematic clusters such as that ideas (or meanings) are objects, linguistic expressions are containers, and communication is sending – an example derived from Michael Reddy's discussion of 'the conduit metaphor' (1979).

Metaphors matter: they are consequential. For instance, the metaphor that 'argument is war' 'structures the actions we perform in arguing' (Lakoff and Johnson 1980, 4). Within this metaphorical framework, arguments are thus battles that are 'lost' or 'won' by individuals rather than a way of deepening our shared understanding. 'Your claims are indefensible'; 'he attacked every weak point in my argument'; 'his criticisms were right on target'. Metaphors not only cluster but can cohere in the extended form of cultural myths, which Lévi-Strauss sees as founded on 'root metaphors' (see also Pepper 1942). Lakoff and Johnson (1980) argue that dominant metaphors tend both to reflect and influence values in a culture or subculture: for instance, the pervasive Western metaphors that *knowledge is power* and *science subdues nature* are involved in the maintenance of the ideology of objectivism (associated with naïve referential realism).

This echoes the Whorfian perspective that the lexical and grammatical categories of different languages structure experience differently (Whorf 1940). Certain metaphors become naturalized and we do not tend to notice the ways in which they can channel our thinking. The technologies of our time have frequently been adopted as metaphors for the mind: Freud had a steam-engine model of the brain in which urges rush through it and dreams act as a safety-valve, behaviourist psychology is dominated by a push-button interpretation of human behaviour, and the rhetoric of cognitive psychology is steeped in the imagery of the computer, thought being referred to as information processing. Ruling metaphors reorganize experience. They foreground ways of thinking that are consistent with them and background alternatives (which simply don't 'come to mind'). 'Changes in our conceptual system do change what is real for us and affect how we see the world and act upon those perceptions' (Lakoff and Johnson

1980, 145–6). As poets know, changing familiar metaphors helps to denaturalize our taken-for-granted ways of seeing and doing things. Shifting your metaphors can shift your perspective.

METONYMY

While metaphor is based on apparent unrelatedness, metonymy is a function that involves using one concept to stand for another which is directly related to it or closely associated with it in some way. Metonyms are based on various indexical relationships, notably the substitution of *effect* for *cause*. The best definition I have found is that 'metonymy is *the evocation of the whole by a connection*. It consists in using for the name of a thing or a relationship, an attribute, a suggested sense, or something closely related, such as effect for cause . . . the imputed relationship being that of *contiguity*' (Wilden 1987, 198; *my emphasis*). It can be seen as based on substitution by conjuncts (things found together) or on functional relationships. Many of these forms notably make an abstract referent more concrete, although some theorists also include substitution in the opposite direction (e.g. *cause* for *effect*). Part–whole relationships are sometimes distinguished as a special kind of metonymy or as a separate trope, as we will see shortly. Metonymy includes the substitution of:

- *effect* for *cause* ('Don't get hot under the collar!' for 'Don't get angry!');
- *object* for *user* (or associated *institution*) ('the press' for journalists);
- *substance* for *form* ('plastic' for 'credit card');
- *place* for *event*: ('Chernobyl changed attitudes to nuclear power');
- *place* for *person* ('No. 10' for the British prime minister);
- *place* for *institution* ('The Pentagon isn't saying anything');
- *institution* for *people* ('The government is not backing down').

Lakoff and Johnson argue that (as with metaphor) particular kinds of metonymic substitution may influence our thoughts, attitudes, and actions by focusing on certain aspects of a concept and suppressing other aspects that are inconsistent with the metonym. For instance, 'The ham sandwich wants his check [bill]' clearly depersonalizes the customer (1980, 39).

As with metaphors, metonyms may be visual as well as verbal. Metonymy is widely employed in advertisements in which the implicit proposition is that buying the product is a way of buying the lifestyle with which it is associated. An ad for pensions in a women's magazine asks the reader to arrange four images in order of importance: each image is metonymic, standing for related activities (such as shopping bags for material goods). Metonymy is common in cigarette advertising in countries where legislation prohibits depictions of the cigarettes themselves or of people using them. The famous ads for Benson and Hedges and for Silk Cut cigarettes are good examples of this.

Jakobson argues that whereas a metaphorical term is connected with that for which it is substituted on the basis of similarity (and contrast), metonymy is based on contiguity or proximity (1953, 232; 1956, 91, 95). As we have seen, Peirce notes that contiguity is an indexical feature (CP 2.306). Metonymy can be seen as a textual (or – as in thoughts and dreams – quasi-textual) projection of indexicality. Metonyms lack the evidential potential of indexicality unless the *medium* is indexical – as in photography and film. However, it is on the basis of perceived indexicality that metonyms may be treated as 'directly connected to' reality in contrast to the mere iconicity or symbolism of metaphor. Metonyms seem to be more obviously 'grounded in our experience' than metaphors since they usually involve direct associations (Lakoff and Johnson 1980, 39). Metonymy does not require transposition (an imaginative leap) from one domain to another as metaphor does. This difference can lead metonymy to seem more natural than metaphors – which when still 'fresh' are stylistically foregrounded. Jakobson suggests that metonymy tends to be foregrounded in prose, whereas metaphor tends to be foregrounded in poetry (1956, 95–6). He regards 'so-called realistic literature' as 'intimately tied with the metonymic principle' (1960, 375). Such literature represents actions as based on cause and effect and as contiguous in time and space. While metonymy is associated with realism, metaphor is associated with romanticism and surrealism (1956, 92).

SYNECDOCHE

The definition of synecdoche varies from theorist to theorist (sometimes markedly). The rhetorician Richard Lanham (1969, 97) represents the most common tendency to describe synecdoche as 'the substitution of part for whole, genus for species or vice versa'. Thus, one term is more comprehensive than the other, and the substitution may move from the particular to the general or from the general to the particular. Some theorists restrict the directionality of application (e.g. part for whole but *not* whole for part). Some limit synecdoche further to cases where one element is *physically* part of the other. Here are some examples:

- *part* for *whole* (e.g. 'get your butt over here!');
- *whole* for *part* (e.g. 'the market' for customers);
- *species* for *genus* (*hypernymy*) – the use of a *member of a class* (*hyponym*) for the *class* (*superordinate*) that includes it (e.g. *a* 'mother' for 'motherhood');
- *genus* for *species* (*hyponymy*) – the use of a *superordinate* for a *hyponym* (e.g. 'machine' for 'computer').

In photographic and filmic media a close-up is a simple synecdoche – a part representing the whole (Jakobson 1956, 92). The formal frame of any visual image (painting, drawing, photograph, film, or television frame) is synecdochic in that it suggests that what is being offered is a 'slice-of-life', and that the world outside the frame is carrying on in the same manner as the world depicted within it. Peirce himself drew attention to this form of indexicality: 'A painting always represents a fragment of a larger whole. It is broken at its edges' (CP 1.176). This is perhaps particularly so when the frame cuts across some of the objects depicted within it (as in the innovative practice of Edgar Degas) rather than enclosing them as wholly discrete entities. Synecdoche invites or expects the viewer to 'fill in the gaps'. Much of a film consists of the use of synecdoche: in a routine technique, familiar scenarios (such as bars or banks) are represented via successive shots of selected generic features that serve to summon up the whole scene in our minds. Advertisers frequently employ this trope. The goods displayed in shop windows synecdochically signify what one may expect to find for sale within.

Any attempt to represent reality can be seen as involving synecdoche, since it can only involve selection (and yet such selections serve to guide us in envisaging larger frameworks). While indexical relations in general reflect the closest link that a representation can be seen as having with a referent, the part–whole relations of synecdoche reflect the most direct link of all. That which is seen as forming part of a larger whole to which it refers is connected existentially to what is represented – as an integral part of its being. Jakobson notes the use of 'synecdochic details' by realist authors (1956, 92). In 'factual' genres a danger lies in what has been called 'the metonymic fallacy' (more accurately the 'synecdochic fallacy') whereby the represented part is taken as an accurate reflection of the whole of that which it is taken as standing for – for instance, a white, middle-class woman standing for all women (Barthes 1974, 162; Alcoff and Potter 1993, 14). The problem is of course that no such example can ever escape accusations of representational bias. Framing is always highly and unavoidably selective. 'Because representation is always "broken", that is always incapable of reproducing the social totality, any . . . image . . . cannot avoid signifying biases, exclusions, and denials' (Hariman and Lucaites 2007, 37).

Some theorists identify synecdoche as a separate trope, some see it as a special form of metonymy and others subsume its functions entirely within metonymy. Eco (1976, 280–1) cites a classical distinction whereby metonymy involves 'a substitution within the framework of the conceptual content' while synecdoche involves a substitution 'with other aspects of reality with which a given thing is customarily connected'. Jakobson notes that both metonymy and synecdoche are based on *contiguity* (1956, 95). Synecdoche can similarly be seen as another textual form of indexicality (though once again lacking evidential potential unless the medium used is indexical). If the distinction is made as outlined above, metonymy in its narrower sense would then be confined to functional connections such as causality. Even if synecdoche is given a separate status, general usage would suggest that metonymy would remain an umbrella term for indexical links as well as having a narrower meaning of its own.

IRONY

Irony is the most radical of the four main tropes. As with metaphor, the ironic sign seems to signify one thing but we know from a co-present sign that it actually signifies something very different. Where it means the *opposite* of what it says (as it usually does), it is based on binary opposition. Irony may thus reflect the opposite of the thoughts or feelings of the speaker or writer (as when you say 'I love it' when you hate it) or the opposite of the truth about external reality (as in 'There's a real crowd here' when it's deserted). It can also be seen as being based on substitution by *dissimilarity* or *disjunction*. While typically an ironic statement signifies the opposite of its literal signification, such variations as understatement and overstatement can also be regarded as ironic. At some point, exaggeration may slide into irony.

Irony is not usually as difficult to recognize as it might seem, partly because all communication requires us to infer the meaning most likely to have been intended. Markers of ironic status (such as a sarcastic intonation or a 'knowing' smile) are not part of the explicit verbal message. In Britain, a fashion for 'air quotes' (gestural inverted commas) in the 1980s was followed in the 1990s by a fashion for some young people to mark spoken irony – after a pause – with the word 'Not!', as in 'he is a real hunk – not!'. However, irony is often more difficult to identify. All of the tropes involve the non-literal substitution of a new signified for the usual one, and comprehension requires a distinction between what is *said* and what is *meant*. Thus they are all, in a sense, *double* signs. Irony has sometimes been referred to as a form of 'double-coding'. Whereas the other tropes involve shifts in what is being referred to, irony involves a shift in modality. The evaluation of the ironic sign requires the retrospective assessment of its modality status. Re-evaluating an apparently literal sign for ironic cues requires reference to perceived intent and to truth status. An ironic statement is not, of course, the same as a *lie* since it is not intended to be taken as 'true'. Irony thus poses particular difficulties for the literalist stance of formalists that meaning is immanent – that it lies *within* a text.

Irony is a marked form. Limited use is usually intended as a form of humour. Frequent use may be associated with reflexiveness, detachment, or scepticism. It sometimes marks a cynical stance that assumes that people never mean or do what they say. Sustained use may even reflect nihilism or relativism (nothing – or everything – is true). While irony has a long pedigree, its use has become one of the most characteristic features of postmodern texts and aesthetic practices. Where irony is used in one-to-one communication, it is of course essential that it is understood as being ironic rather than literal. However, with larger audiences it constitutes a form of 'narrowcasting', since not everyone will interpret it as irony. Dramatic irony is a form whereby the reader or viewer knows something that one or more of the depicted people do not know.

MASTER TROPES

Giambattista Vico (1668–1744) is usually credited with being the first to identify metaphor, metonymy, synecdoche, and irony as the four basic tropes (to which all others are reducible), although this distinction can be seen as having its roots in the *Rhetorica* of Peter Ramus (1515–72) (Vico 1744, 129–31). This reduction was popularized in the twentieth century by the American rhetorician Kenneth Burke (1897–1993), who referred to the four 'master tropes' (Burke 1969, 503–17). Figure 4.3 represents Frederic Jameson's 'unorthodox' use

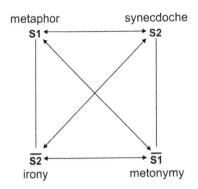

FIGURE 4.3 The four 'master tropes' as a semiotic square

Source: Adapted from Jameson in Greimas 1987, xix

of the semiotic square to map relationships between these tropes (see Jameson in Greimas 1987, xix). Note that such frameworks depend on a distinction being made between metonymy and synecdoche, but that such terms are often defined differently or not defined at all. In his book *Metahistory*, White (1973, ix) sees the four 'master tropes' as part of the 'deep structure' underlying different historiographical styles. Jonathan Culler (following Hans Kellner) even suggests that they may constitute 'a system, indeed *the* system, by which the mind comes to grasp the world conceptually in language' (1981, 65).

White argues that 'the fourfold analysis of figurative language has the added advantage of resisting the fall into an essentially *dualistic* conception of styles' (1973, 33). Roman Jakobson adopts two tropes rather than four as fundamental – metaphor and metonymy. White felt that Jakobson's approach, when applied to nineteenth-century literature, produces the reductive dichotomy of 'a romantic–poetic–Metaphorical tradition' and 'a realistic–prosaic–Metonymical tradition'. However, Jakobson's notion of two basic axes has proved massively influential. He argues that metaphor is a paradigmatic dimension (vertical, based on selection, substitution, and similarity) and metonymy a syntagmatic dimension (horizontal, based on combination, contexture, and contiguity) (1956, 90–6). Many theorists have adopted and adapted Jakobson's framework, such as Lévi-Strauss (1962) and Lacan (1977, 160).

DENOTATION AND CONNOTATION

Meaning includes both denotation and connotation. In communication and representation, denotative meaning is primarily associated with an informational function and connotative meaning with an aesthetic function (see Figure 4.1). The definitions of these terms vary, so it should be noted that they are being used in this context in the stylistic sense rather than the philosophical one. 'Denotation' tends to be described as the definitional, literal, obvious, elementary, or common-sense meaning of a sign. In the case of linguistic signs, the denotative meaning is what a dictionary attempts to provide. A picture denotes what it depicts (though in traditional philosophical usage the term denotation is restricted to that which actually exists in the world).

Beyond its literal meaning, a particular word or image may of course have connotations: for instance, sexual connotations. 'Is there any such thing as a *single entendre*?' quipped the British comic actor Kenneth Williams. There is no denotation without connotation: secondary overtones may be read into any signs regardless of intention. In literary and everyday discourse, 'connotation' often refers to personal associations for individuals, but semiotics focuses on those that are widely recognized within a culture or subculture. Signs are more 'polysemic' – more open to interpretation – in their connotations than their denotations, though context usually acts as a constraint.

Roland Barthes declares (1967a, 89ff.) that Saussure's model of the sign focuses on denotation at the expense of connotation, though one might reasonably object that this may be more true of structuralist models than of Saussure's, since *langue* as a system of differential values includes implicit relations, and his notion of associative relations is broader than the notion of paradigmatic relations. Barthes drew on Hjelmslev to offer an account of this important dimension of meaning. Connotative meanings require knowledge of social context, and since they require interpretation and may exceed any intentional meaning, they challenge a simplistic structuralist model of 'decoding'. In 'The photographic message' (1961) and 'The rhetoric of the image' (1964), Barthes argues that in photography, connotation can be (analytically) distinguished from denotation. As John Fiske, a cultural theorist, puts it, 'denotation is *what* is photographed, connotation is *how* it is photographed' (1982, 91). However, in photography, denotation is generally foregrounded at the expense of connotation. The photograph appears to be a 'natural sign' produced without the intervention of a code (an issue to which we will return). In analysing the realist literary text, Barthes (1974, 9) came to the conclusion that connotation produces the illusion of denotation, the illusion of the medium as transparent. Thus denotation is just another connotation. From such a perspective, denotation can be seen as no more of a natural meaning than is connotation but rather as a process of *naturalization*. Such a process leads to the powerful illusion that denotation is a purely literal and universal meaning, which is not at all ideological, and that those connotations which seem most obvious to individual interpreters are just as natural.

According to an Althusserian reading, when we first learn denotations, we are also being positioned within ideology by learning dominant connotations at the same time (Silverman 1983, 30). In a class-ridden culture, almost anything can connote socio-cultural status, producing and reproducing positions of dominance and submission as if these were natural. Connotations tend to support cultural stereotypes. Subtlety, restraint, and understatement are markers of upmarket 'sophistication'. 'Loudness' has social connotations: we 'know our place' in the market and in society when we are literally shouted at in a commercial such as that for a cleaning product called Cillit Bang™, which ran in the UK from 2005 to 2013 and featured the catchphrase, 'Bang and the dirt is gone!', which seemed designed to irritate those for whom it was not intended. In English, even visual 'vulgarity' is sometimes referred to as 'loud'. A visual hierarchy of taste has developed (notably in advertising) in which subtle cues such as smaller fonts, empty white space, and muted colours have come to connote quality and refinement, while attention-grabbing cues such as large bold fonts, clutter, and bright, strong, primary colours connote bad taste (Birren 1956, 17–18; Sahlins 1976, 183; Robertson 1994; Hine 1995, 218–19; Heath 2012, 150–1). Connotational frameworks are 'organized around key oppositions and equations' within cultural codes, each pole being 'aligned with a cluster of symbolic attributes' (Silverman 1983, 36). In the case of the examples of visual signifiers of 'taste' (such as in upmarket ads), it is intriguing to note that muted colours (and so on) also carry feminine connotations, while those for 'bad taste' (such as primary colours in downmarket ads) carry additional connotations of masculinity and of childhood. Table 4.4 summarizes some common connotations of design features in promotional materials (such as advertisements and websites), suggesting some interesting underlying conceptual alignments in the cultural assumptions of designers. There are of course exceptions to this pattern: these are tendencies rather than 'rules'. While such features are typically employed to engage a particular target audience, culturally dominant connotations are also widely assumed to represent their (stereotypical) 'preferences' (Moss 2014).

While theorists may find it analytically useful to distinguish connotation from denotation, in practice such meanings cannot be neatly separated. Most semioticians argue that no sign is purely denotative –

signifiers	signifieds	
	upmarket or *female* or *more educated*	*downmarket* or *male* or *less educated*
colour	paler, greyer, less contrast	brighter, primary, contrastive
font size	smaller	larger
layout	more free space	less free space

TABLE 4.4 Connotations of design features

Source: © 2016 Daniel Chandler

lacking connotation. Valentin Voloshinov (1973, 105) insists that no strict division can be made between denotation and connotation because 'referential meaning is moulded by evaluation . . . meaning is always permeated with value judgement'. There can be no neutral, literal description or depiction that is free of an evaluative element. Structural semioticians who emphasize the relative arbitrariness of the sign and social semioticians who emphasize diversity of interpretation and the importance of cultural and historical contexts are hardly likely to accept the notion of a literal meaning. Denotation simply involves a broader consensus. The denotational meaning of a sign would be broadly agreed upon by members of the same culture, whereas no inventory of the connotational meanings generated by any sign could ever be complete. Connotation is looser, more subtle, more ambiguous, and less conventional than denotation. Certain connotations are widely recognized at an unconscious level. A striking example of this was revealed in a study in which some familiar oppositions were listed and for each one subjects were asked which of the poles 'went with' a square and which with a circle (Liu and Kennedy 1993). The list of oppositions included: light–heavy, soft–hard, happy–sad, love–hate, alive–dead, mother–father, good–evil, and bright–dark. Since the reader may care to check their own responses to this task, the results of the study are summarized on a subsequent page as Table 4.7.

Connotation and denotation are often described in terms of levels of representation, meaning, or semiosis. Roland Barthes adopted

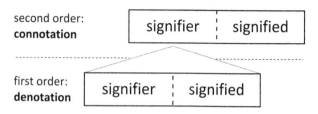

FIGURE 4.5 Barthes' stratified model of connotation

Source: © 2016 Daniel Chandler, based on Barthes 1967a, 89–90

from Louis Hjelmslev the notion that there are different 'orders of signification' (Barthes 1957, 124; 1961; 1967a, 89–94; 1967b, 27ff; Hjelmslev 1961, 114ff.). In Barthes' stratified model of connotation, denotation is the first order of signification; connotation is the second (Figure 4.5). The denotative sign becomes the signifier of a connotative sign. Barthes' greatly simplified version of Hjelmslev's 'glossematics' sign model disregarded the dimensions of substance and form (see Table 1.14). For Barthes, connotation involves the translation of a sign into other signs and denotation leads to a chain of connotations. This is the mechanism by which signs may seem to signify one thing but are loaded with multiple meanings. For instance, a cultural sign such as an item of clothing, which has a non-communicational function on the denotative level, may also have cultural connotations of social status, giving it an ideological value which implicates it in the reproduction of status differences. This reframing of the Saussurean model of the sign is analogous to the 'infinite semiosis' of the Peircean sign in which the interpretant can become the representamen of another sign. However, it can also tend to suggest that denotation is an underlying and primary meaning – a notion that many theorists have challenged.

Language is not neutral and transparent. The choice of words often involves connotations, as in references to 'strikes' vs. 'disputes', 'terrorists' vs. 'freedom fighters', and so on. In Barthes' concept of *exnomination*, when we refer to those beyond the groups to which we belong, the labels we apply are marked. However, it is often more nuanced than a simple binary of self–other or us–them. Bertrand Russell refers to the way in which we 'load' words more negatively

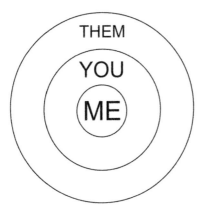

FIGURE 4.6 Concentric frames of reference

Source: © 2016 Daniel Chandler

the more distantly we position the target person or group from ourselves (see Figure 4.6). On a BBC radio programme, *The Brains Trust* (26th April 1948), he gave examples such as: 'I am firm; you are obstinate; he is a pig-headed fool' and 'I have reconsidered the matter; you have changed your mind; he has gone back on his word'. This is now usually labelled an 'emotive conjugation'. The denotation remains the same: the connotations are significantly different. Our paradigmatic choices generate connotations. Subtle changes of style or tone may involve different connotations: such as changing from sharp focus to soft focus when taking a photograph or using different fonts for exactly the same text.

Connotation is not a purely paradigmatic dimension, as Saussure's characterization of this dimension as 'associative' might suggest. While absent signifiers with which a signifier may be associated are clearly a key factor in generating connotations, so too are syntagmatic associations. Whether connotations are 'highly charged' and perceived as 'positive' or 'negative' is strongly contextual (as in the case of labels such as 'queer'). Both connotations and denotations are subject not only to socio-cultural variability but also to historical factors: they change over time. John Fiske (1982, 92) warns that 'it is often easy to read connotative values as denotative facts'. Just as dangerously seductive, however, is the tendency to accept denotation as the literal, self-evident truth. Semiotic analysis can help us to counter such habits of mind.

While the dominant methodologies in semiotic analysis are *qualitative*, semiotics is not incompatible with the use of quantitative techniques. In 1957 the American psychologist Charles Osgood (1916–91), together with some of his colleagues, published a book entitled *The Measurement of Meaning* (Osgood *et al.* 1957). In it, these communication researchers outline a technique called the *semantic differential* (SD) for the systematic mapping of *connotations* (or 'affective meanings'). The technique involves a test in which people are asked to give their impressionistic responses to a particular object, state, or event by indicating specific positions in relation to a series of bipolar adjectives (normally at least nine pairs) on a scale of one to seven. For instance, in order to explore the connotations of fonts, one might use oppositions such as: warm–cool, serious–playful, masculine–feminine, traditional–modern, casual–formal, fancy–plain. The aim is to locate a concept in 'semantic space', normally in three dimensions: *evaluation* (good–bad); *potency* (strong–weak); and *activity* (active–passive). The method has proved useful in studying attitudes and emotional reactions. Martin Krampen (1983) used the

circle	square	%
soft	hard	100
mother	father	94
happy	sad	94
good	evil	89
love	hate	89
alive	dead	87
bright	dark	87
light	heavy	85

TABLE 4.7 Connotations of circles and squares (showing percentage agreeing)

Source: Adapted from Liu and Kennedy 1993

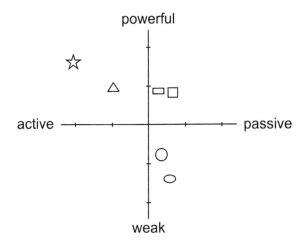

FIGURE 4.8 Subjective ratings of geometrical shapes

Source: Adapted from Krampen 1983, 151–2

SD to explore the connotations of shapes for 88 high school and trade school students. He mapped their ratings on a two-dimensional grid, which placed pointed, angular forms in the active and powerful quadrant, in contrast to rounded forms, which appeared in the weak and passive quadrant (see Figure 4.8).

In a commentary on Osgood's original investigations, Ernst Gombrich stresses the sensory cross-modality of connotation in relation to the key relational poles of friendly–hostile (Figure 4.9; see also Figure 5.1). He refers to this as a 'natural code of equivalences' (1963, 59) between emotional states and sensory cues (colours, shapes, and sounds), which he sees as reflecting a universal 'inborn disposition . . . to equate certain sensations with certain feeling tones' (ibid., 58). Roman Jakobson discusses such synaesthesia in relation to the iconicity of speech sounds (1990, 422–47).

This brief exploration of the unconscious connotations of shapes makes it particularly clear that connotations are far less a matter of individual subjectivity than of social intersubjectivity. Things do not mean whatever we want them to mean. Connotations are not purely

poles of liking	sensation	vision	sound
friendly	happy, warm, light	bright, red, curvy	fast, loud, high
hostile	sad, cold, heavy	dark, blue, angular	slow, soft, low

TABLE 4.9 Sensory connotations in relation to liking

Source: Adapted from Gombrich 1963, 58–9

personal meanings (any more than denotations are wholly 'objective'). They flow through culture. Just like denotative meanings, they are generally recognized by most members of a culture because they reflect common experiences and expectations reflected in countless representations and communicative acts. Intersubjective responses are shared to varying extents by members of a culture, and are constrained by the interpreter's cultural repertoire. On any given occasion, only a limited range of connotations would make any sense. Some cultural artefacts are more connotative than others; those with the most widely-recognized and most well-established connotations act as anchors for closely aligned associations. Such close links are very long-lasting, but connotational alignments are dynamic and contextually variable, the strength of links is far from constant, and weaker links can fall away (or even switch polarity within an alignment). Readers can explore this for themselves in the context of the history of popular cultural 'icons' (Browne *et al.* 1990, Cross 2002, Hariman and Lucaites 2007, Feldges 2008, Berger 2012, Moeschberger and Phillips DeZalia 2014; see also the photographic montage in Pakula's 1974 film *The Parallax View*). The remarkable degree of consensus about core connotations reveals significant cultural constraints on meaning-making, and the pervasiveness of these patterns of connotations leads semioticians to identify them as connotational codes.

Marcel Danesi has suggested that 'in a basic sense, the semiotic study of advertising is a study of connotation' (1999, 103). Much of the seductive power of advertising derives from drawing on associational meanings, so that we don't even realize that we are being influenced (Heath 2012). In the 'elaboration likelihood model' of persuasion, this is the power of the 'peripheral route', which operates affectively rather than cognitively through connotations, metaphors, and symbols, without any explicit message, information, or argument (Petty and Cacioppo 1986). Such an approach can be particularly effective when we are not paying much attention because our critical defences are down. People are more likely to be persuaded by messages that do not seem to be designed to influence them (Janis and Hovland 1959). We are rarely conscious of such constraints on our 'personal' judgements and of our own conformity to them. That we are 'making up our own minds' is at the core of the modern 'myth of individualism' (Callero 2013, Morris 1991).

MYTH

The discourse of individualism is among the 'explanatory' cultural frameworks, which have been interpreted by some cultural semioticians as myths or mythologies. We usually associate myths with classical fables about the exploits of gods and heroes, and popular usage of the term 'myth' suggests that it refers to beliefs that are demonstrably false, but the semiotic use of the term (Greek *mythos*, 'story') does not necessarily suggest this. Like metaphors (from which many myths arise), cultural myths help us to make sense of our experiences within a culture: they express and serve to organize shared ways of conceptualizing phenomena within a culture (Lakoff and Johnson 1980, 185–6). In the contemporary world, such myths draw upon and are generated by a 'cultural vocabulary' based on such sources as the famous photographs, filmic moments, and mp3s, which 'everyone knows'.

We have already seen that for the anthropologist Lévi-Strauss myths operate through binary oppositions, which function to naturalize the cultural. These oppositions underlie symbolic and connotational codes, and myths work as interrelated sets which are variations on a theme, with no single myth telling 'the whole story' (Leach 1973, 50–1). Lévi-Strauss argues that all cultures try to account for contradictions by creating myths. Within consumer cultures, which are a major

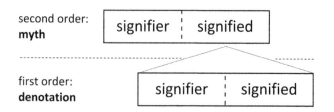

FIGURE 4.10 Barthes' stratified model of myth

Source: © 2016 Daniel Chandler, based on Barthes 1967a, 90

agency for the circulation of normative cultural myths, 'brand myths' are also generated. The founder of the agency that was involved in the 'It's Good to Talk' campaign, similarly claims that 'A *brand*'s myth is the belief by consumers that the brand offers them a way of resolving a problem or situation that hitherto represented some kind of contradiction' (Valentine nd).

In the framework of Barthesian cultural studies, myth, like connotation, can be seen as a higher order of signification (Figure 4.10). Louis Hjelmslev (1961, 125) had argued that above the connotative level there is 'a metasemiotic' to which belonged geographical, historical, political, sociological, psychological, and religious issues relating to such concepts as 'nation, ... region, ... the value forms of styles, personality ... mood, etc.' For instance, an image may denote 'a child' in a context that generates the connotation of innocence; this forms part of what Roland Barthes would call a higher level (historically modern and Romantic) 'myth' of childhood which functions ideologically to justify dominant assumptions about the status of children in society. Barthes (1957, 124–6) does not see the myths of contemporary culture as simply a patterned agglomeration of connotations but as ideological narratives, and, following Hjelmslev, he sees mythical form as a metalanguage, which he defines as 'a system whose plane of content is itself constituted by a signifying system' (1967a, 90). Whereas in the case of connotation, the denotative sign becomes the *signifier* of the connotative sign (Figure 4.5), in the case of myth, 'the language (or the modes of representation which are assimilated to it) ... which myth gets hold of in order to build its own system' becomes the *signified* of the mythical metalanguage (Barthes 1957, 124; cf. Hjelmslev 1961, 114, 119–20 and Lévi-Strauss 1969, 12).

The mythological or ideological order of signification can be seen as reflecting major (culturally variable) concepts underpinning particular worldviews. For Roland Barthes, myths are the dominant ideologies of our time. Objectivism, for instance, is a pervasive myth in Western culture. It allies itself with scientific truth, rationality, accuracy, fairness, and impartiality and is reflected in the discourse of science, law, government, journalism, morality, business, economics, and scholarship (Lakoff and Johnson 1980, 188–9). Other myths or mythical discourses include those of masculinity and femininity, freedom, individualism, Englishness, success, and so on. Barthes is probably most famous for his insightful analyses of some of the tacit myths of popular culture, notably in the essays represented in the anthology entitled *Mythologies* (1957). He addresses many types of contemporary cultural myths – most famously in his analysis of a cover photo in the magazine *Paris Match* depicting a young black soldier saluting the (unseen) French flag (1957, 125–56) and of the 'Italianicity' of an advertisement for Panzani pasta (1977a). We do not have space to discuss these much-anthologized and explicated examples here, but the general thrust of his analytical approach will be illustrated in the following chapter.

Lévi-Strauss sees myths as systems of binary alignments mediating between nature and culture. Semioticians in the Saussurean tradition treat this relationship as relatively arbitrary (Lévi-Strauss 1972, 90, 95). A focus on arbitrariness offers a lever for exposing ideological myths. Barthes (1957, 136) argues that mythical signification always emerges as 'in part motivated, and unavoidably contains some analogy' (leading it to be experienced as natural) and only 'the worn-out state of a myth can be recognized by the arbitrariness of its signification'. For him (as for Lévi-Strauss), myths serve the ideological function of *naturalization* (Barthes 1964, 45–6). Their function is to naturalize the cultural – in other words, to make dominant cultural and historical values, attitudes, and beliefs seem entirely natural, normal, self-evident, timeless, obvious common sense – and thus objective and true reflections of 'the way things are'. This is a basic function of language itself. The appeal to the natural, as in 'human nature', explains nothing (since it is a social and historical construct) and reinforces the status quo. Ideological myths serve the interests of the social groups which propagate them. Barthes was a Marxist, and he saw myth as serving the ideological interests of the bourgeoisie. 'Bourgeois ideology . . . turns culture into nature,' he declares (1974, 206). Myths can function to hide the ideological function of signs. The power of such myths is that they 'go without saying' and so appear not to need to be deciphered, interpreted, or demystified. The similarity to Lévi-Strauss is clear here: 'I . . . claim to show, not how men think in myths, but how myths operate in men's minds without their being aware of the fact' (Lévi-Strauss 1969, 12). Barthesian semiotics demonstrates that deconstructing tropes, connotations, and myths can be revealing but that they cannot be reduced to the 'literal'. Barthes excelled at this kind of analysis but the task of 'denaturalizing' the cultural assumptions embodied in such forms is problematic when the semiotician is also a product of the same culture, since membership of a culture involves taking for granted many of its dominant ideas. Barthes at his best is a hard act to follow, but those who do try to analyse their own cultures in this way must also seek to be explicitly reflexive about their 'own' values.

Rhetoric and connotation generate complex signs, and myths are complex sign systems which generate further ideological signs. Rather than characterizing myths simply as a cluster of tropes and connotations, Barthes argues that they function in a more integrated fashion both in their content (ideology) and in their form – as metalinguistic semiotic systems or *codes*, of which specific cultural connotations and tropes can be seen as fragments (1957, 119–20, 145–6). It is to codes that we now turn our attention.

REFLECTIONS

1 How do you recognize a pictorial metaphor (for instance, in an advertisement)?

2 Generate some of your own 'emotive conjugations' along the lines suggested by Bertrand Russell, beginning with 'I am friendly . . .', 'I say what I think . . .', 'I am open-minded . . .'.

3 What contrasting examples can you find which illustrate the targeted use of design features in promotional materials summarized in Table 4.4?

4 Along the lines of the dominant connotations of circles and squares listed in Table 4.7, explore which poles of a series of verbal oppositions people consider 'go with' a vertical and a horizontal line. Alternatively, you could use a similar approach to investigate the connotations of sounds (such as high, loud, or fast sounds vs. low, soft, or slow sounds).

5 Investigate the supposedly masculine and feminine connotations of a selection of type fonts by getting some friends to rank them and discuss their evaluations with you. What features seem to lead to these judgements?

6 Find some advertisements that are wordless (ignoring logos) and try to infer implicit claims. Do they involve metaphor or connotation? How do you make sense of them?

7 Which famous photographs, filmic moments, or mp3s does 'everyone know' in your circle of friends?

8 In what ways is individualism a 'myth'?

FURTHER READING

Berger 2012; Bouissac 1998, entries for 'denotation and connotation', 'metaphor', 'metonomy', 'myths'; Browne *et al.* 1990; Clifton 1983; Cross 2002; Feldges 2008; Forceville 1996; Gombrich 1963; Hariman and Lucaites 2007; Heath 2012; Lakoff and Johnson 1980; Lanham 1969; Lodge 1977; Moss 2014; Murphy 2001; Ortony 1979; Osgood *et al.* 1957; Pepper 1942; Richards 1936; Sebeok 1994b, entries for 'denotation/connotation', 'metaphor', 'myth', 'rhetoric'; Sloane 2001, entries for 'figures of speech', 'irony', 'metaphor', 'metonymy', 'synecdochē'; White 1973; Whittock 2009.

CODES

The concept of *code* is prominent in structuralist discourse. There is only a passing reference in the *Cours* to the language code (*le code de la langue*) (*CLG* 31; 14). Deriving his terms from information theory, Roman Jakobson reformulated Saussure's distinction between *langue* and *parole* as one between *code* and *message* (1952, 224). For Jakobson, any 'given utterance (message) is a combination of constituent parts (sentences, words, phonemes, etc.) selected from the repository of all possible constituent parts (code)' (1956, 61). He refers to *langue* as 'the totality of the conventions of a language', seeing this 'overall code' as a 'system of systems' which includes a hierarchy of subcodes (1985, 30–1). Thus, the structuralist concept of code can be seen as somewhat indirectly indebted to the Saussurean concept of *langue*. Usage varies, but *codes* are most often defined as sign systems or interpretive systems. In structuralist theory, the production and interpretation of messages and texts (in any medium) are seen as dependent upon codes.

Codes organize signs into meaningful systems, and in language-like systems they correlate signifiers and signifieds through the structural forms of syntagms and paradigms. Codes are thus regarded as central in communication and representation. Since the (intended) meaning of a sign depends on the code within which it is situated, codes provide a framework within which signs make sense. They embody rules or conventions of interpretation which systematically regulate the ways in which meanings are produced. This is not the same as saying that codes alone determine meaning. However, if signs are unmotivated, then it is clear that establishing their intended meaning requires familiarity with an appropriate interpretive system. If we are not familiar with the code of traffic lights we cannot understand when a red light signifies 'Stop!'. In the case of a code as basic as that for traffic lights, 'decoding' seems relatively programmatic, suggesting that codes function like dictionaries or look-up tables. However, even in the case of traffic lights, we noted in Chapter 1 that it is not quite as simple as that – the red light makes no sense on its own but only as part of a relational set (a very Saussurean notion). To regard 'decoding' as a programmatic process would be reductive – under-estimating the cognitively active role of individual interpreters. Reading any kind of text or message involves identifying appropriate frames of reference. Meaning is not 'contained' within texts: they need to be supplemented in order to be understood. Making sense of them involves going beyond their explicit content, bringing to them 'certain expectations; a prior knowledge of possibilities or probabilities' (Gombrich 1996, 153). We read meaning *into* texts, drawing upon our existing knowledge and experience of signs, referents, and codes in order to make explicit what is only implicit.

Communication and representation require codes to be (largely) shared, and in the familiar interactional routines of everyday life, codes are mostly established in advance (although not everything is precoded, and inference is important). A semiotic code is closely associated with a set of interpretive and representational practices familiar to its users, and the conventions of codes represent a social dimension in structuralist semiotics. In this sense, all codes are social. Lewis Carroll's Humpty Dumpty declares that 'when *I* use a word, it means just what I choose it to mean – neither more nor less' (*Through the Looking Glass*, 1872). Texts and situations may be 'open to inter-pretation' but Humpty Dumpty was mistaken: if we are trying to communicate, signs cannot mean whatever each individual wants them to mean. The sociologist Stuart Hall (1973, 131) insists that 'there is no intelligible discourse without the operation of a code'. Meaning requires negotiation with reference to shared, intersubjective frameworks. An adequate degree of overlap in ways of framing experience is a necessary condition for successful communication. Jakobson (1960, 353) notes that 'any act of communication . . . requires . . . a code fully, or at least partially, common to . . . the encoder and decoder of the message'. Society and social relationships depend on the existence of such signifying systems. Our ways of life are codified in our clothes, food, homes, and so on (Leach 1973, 39). Sociologists argue that each individual has a repertoire of codes and that access to codes is unevenly distributed in society but is largely shared by those within particular social groups.

Codes provide relational frameworks within which social and cultural meanings are produced. Unfamiliar experiences are interpreted analogically in relation to already codified knowledge. The dominant codes help to maintain a broad conceptual consensus and thus facilitate cultural transmission. Although the meanings attached to objects and practices derive from social rules and conventions, within a culture these are taken for granted as natural. As David Halperin (1990, 44) puts it, 'acculturation consists . . . in learning to accept as natural, normal, and inevitable what is in fact conventional and arbitrary'. Semioticians seek to identify and describe the various codes that are taken for granted in this way. The task of the analyst involves identifying and making explicit the system of distinctions, conventions, categories, operations, and relations underlying a particular social practice, which gives familiar phenomena cultural meaning and value as signs. A structural approach seeks to identify the fundamental units of a code and to identify the systematic relationships between them.

THE LANGUAGE MODEL

Structuralists treat language as 'the gold standard', often citing out of context the reference in the *Cours* to language as a potential 'master-pattern' for sign systems (*CLG* 34, 101; 16, 68). Umberto Eco (1973,

60) argues that the 'basic assertion' of a linguistic model is that 'all sign systems can be analysed in the same sense in which linguistics can, that is as a dialectic between codes and messages'. Social codes or cultural systems are seen as analogous to verbal languages in structure and/or functions (communicating or encoding meaning). The French anthropologist Claude Lévi-Strauss treats social activities such as culinary customs, modes of dress, and table manners as systems of behaviour which are structured like languages, with their own grammar. The British anthropologist Edmund Leach declares that:

> *All* the various non-verbal dimensions of culture, such as styles in cooking, village lay-out, architecture, furniture, food, cooking, music, physical gesture, postural attitudes and so on are organised in patterned sets so as to incorporate coded information in a manner analogous to the sounds and words and sentences of a natural language . . . It is just as meaningful to talk about the grammatical rules which govern the wearing of clothes as it is to talk about the grammatical rules which govern speech utterances.
> (Leach 1976, 10)

Using the same analogy, he observes that,

> All of us must eat, but under normal social conditions no human beings just eat indiscriminately. Cultural rules prescribe a classification which distinguishes between food and not-food. Other cultural rules specify how food shall be collected and prepared and how and when it shall be eaten. In every cultural system there is a 'grammar' of food behaviour which is as complex and specific as the grammar of speech.
> This is equally true of sexual behaviour. Just as there is cultural discrimination between what is food and what is not food, so also there is cultural discrimination between what is sexually permitted and what is sexually forbidden. These are distinctions of culture and not of nature; they result from rules and conventions, not from in-born animal instincts.
> (Leach 1973, 46)

It has become commonplace for cultural phenomena to be referred to metaphorically as languages but theorists need to make explicit their criteria for such an analogy. According to the French linguist André Martinet (1908–99), language has two abstract structural levels, or *double articulation* (now more commonly known as *duality of patterning*). Jakobson (1976, 230) asserts that 'language is the only system which is composed of elements which are signifiers and yet at the same time signify nothing'. In speech, these elements at the lower structural level ('second articulation') are phonemes (distinctive sound units such as /b/ or /p/); in writing, they are graphemes (written characters such as <a> or <e>). At the higher structural level ('first articulation') are meaningful combinations of these basic units (words, sentences, and so on). Charles Hockett (1958) regards double articulation as a key 'design feature' of language. It is largely responsible for the creative economy of language. As Wilhelm von Humboldt famously put it, language makes 'infinite use of finite means' (1836, 91). The English language, for instance, has only about forty or fifty phonemes but these can generate hundreds of thousands of words. Similarly, from a limited vocabulary we can generate an infinite number of sentences (subject to the constraint of syntax, which governs structurally valid combinations). It is by *combining* words in multiple ways that we can seek to render the particularity of experience. If we had individual words to represent every particularity, we would have to have an infinite number of them, which would exceed our capability of learning, recalling, and manipulating them.

Double articulation does not seem to occur in the natural communication systems of animals other than humans. A key semiotic debate used to be whether or not semiotic systems such as photography, film, or painting have double articulation. The philosopher Susanne Langer (1957, 93) argues that while visual media such as photography, painting, and drawing have lines, colours, shadings, shapes, proportions, and so on, which are 'abstractable and combinatory', and 'just as capable of *articulation*, i.e. of complex combination, as words', they have no vocabulary of units with independent meanings.

> A symbolism with so many elements, such myriad relationships, cannot be broken up into basic units. It is impossible to find the

> smallest independent symbol, and recognize its identity when the same unit is met in other contexts . . . There is, of course, a technique of picturing objects, but the laws governing this technique cannot properly be called a 'syntax', since there are no items that might be called, metaphorically, the 'words' of portraiture.
>
> (Langer 1957, 95)

Rather than dismissing 'non-discursive' media for their limitations, however, Langer suggests that they are more complex and subtle than verbal language and are 'peculiarly well-suited to the expression of ideas that defy linguistic "projection"'. We should not seek to impose linguistic models upon other media since the laws that govern their articulation 'are altogether different from the laws of syntax that govern language'. Treating them in linguistic terms leads us to 'misconceive' them: they resist 'translation' (ibid., 93–7).

Despite the limitations of the language model in relation to non-linguistic sign systems, it is fundamental in structuralist theory. Although the criterion of double articulation is now commonly regarded as inapplicable to such systems, various minimum semantic, syntactic, and pragmatic criteria have been proposed. Structuralists seek to identify discrete word-like units within such systems (collectively forming a lexicon – a vocabulary) and a basic syntax for producing sentence-like structures. There has also been philosophical debate over whether a logical subject-predicate structure can be identified in pictorial media – the *subject* identifying a referent and the *predicate* being an assertion made about it (e.g. Kjørup 1974, Novitz 1977, Eaton 1980, Wolterstorff 1980, Korsmeyer 1985, Lopes 1996). The pragmatic criterion lowers this highly restrictive bar for propositional status, allowing for cases where statements can be inferred in appropriate contexts of use: for instance, a portrait can represent a referent and an appropriate caption can function as an assertion about it (Chandler 2014).

Broadly, the more conventionalized and standardized a sign system is, the more likely some theorists are to regard it as language-like, though many such systems work only within a contextually-limited universe of discourse (as in road sign systems). The intended meaning of some signs is more open to interpretation than that of others, depending more on associational or connotational meaning. As we saw in the last chapter, distinguishing connotation from denotation is problematic. However, where associative meanings are widely shared within a culture or subculture, some theorists regard them as operating within 'connotational codes'. These less highly-coded systems, where the intended meaning is less determinate, are sometimes labelled 'weak communication'.

The structuralist obsession with the linguistic model drove a reductive quest to submit all semiotic systems to this framework. Processes of communication and representation cannot be wholly reduced to the operation of codes (a concept which we have noted owes nothing to the *Cours*). Many aspects of human activity are not formally codified and the 'decoding' of implicit communication depends on inference. Even in routine everyday interaction, not every element is precoded. There is always scope for inference, negotiation, and improvisation (including code-switching). Umberto Eco argues that although many messages conform to normative codes, transgressive messages have the potential to change them (1976, 161). Leach declares that 'new forms are being created all the time' (1973, 39).

DIGITAL AND ANALOGUE CODES

Denotation is sometimes regarded as a *digital* code, based on either/or distinctions of *kind*, and connotation as an *analogue* code, based on 'more-or-less' differences of *degree*. Communication involves both modes. Anthony Wilden, a Canadian communication theorist, declares that 'no two categories, and no two kinds of experience are more fundamental in human life and thought than continuity and discontinuity' (1987, 222). While we experience time as a continuum, we may represent it in either analogue or digital form. A watch with an analogue display (with hour, minute, and second hands) has the advantage of dividing an hour up like a cake (so that, in a lecture, for instance, we can 'see' how much time is left). A watch with a digital display (displaying the current time as a changing number) has the advantage of precision, so that we can easily see exactly what time it is 'now'.

We have a deep attachment to analogical modes and we have often tended to regard digital representations as less real or less authentic – at least initially (as in the case of the audio CD compared to the vinyl LP). The analogue–digital distinction (which generates a host of oppositional connotations) is frequently represented as natural versus artificial – a logical extension of Claude Lévi-Strauss's argument that continuous is to discrete is as nature is to culture (1969, 28). The privileging of the analogical may be linked with the defiance of rationality in romantic ideology (which still dominates our conception of ourselves as 'individuals'). In analogue codes, 'it is almost impossible . . . *not* to communicate' (Wilden 1987, 225). Beyond any conscious intention, we communicate through gesture, posture, facial expression, intonation, and so on. Analogue codes unavoidably 'give us away', revealing such things as our moods, attitudes, intentions, and truthfulness (or otherwise). Although the appearance of the 'digital watch' in 1971, and the subsequent 'digital revolution' in audio- and video-recording have led us to associate the digital mode with electronic technologies, digital codes have existed since the earliest forms of language – and writing is a digital technology. Signifying systems impose digital order on what we often experience as a dynamic and seamless flux. The very definition of something as a sign involves reducing the continuous to the discrete. Jakobson and other structuralists see binary (either/or) distinctions as a fundamental process in the creation of signifying structures. Distinctions and oppositions are digital. Digital codes involve discrete units such as words and 'whole numbers', and depend on the categorization of what is signified. Of course, the to-and-fro of discourse allows for 'shades of meaning', but there can be no communication without such shared categories.

Analogical signs (such as visual images, gestures, textures, tastes, and smells) involve graded relationships on a continuum. They can signify infinite subtleties which seem 'beyond words'. Emotions and feelings are analogical. Unlike symbolic signs, motivated signs blend into one another. There can be no comprehensive catalogue of such dynamic analogue signs as smiles or laughs. Analogue signs can of course be digitally reproduced (as is demonstrated by the digital recording of sounds and of both still and moving images) but they cannot be directly related to a standard 'dictionary' and syntax in the way that linguistic signs can. This is of course a semiotic difference, not a shortcoming based on a linguistic benchmark, and it highlights the importance of a general model of the sign. The North American film theorist Bill Nichols (1981, 47) notes that 'the graded quality of analogue codes may make them rich in meaning but it also renders them somewhat impoverished in syntactical complexity or semantic precision. By contrast, the discrete units of digital codes may be somewhat impoverished in meaning but capable of much greater complexity or semantic signification' (cf. Wilden 1972, 118, Wilden 1987, 138; Watzlawick *et al.* 1967, 66–7).

It is frequently noted that the propositional functions of assertion and negation are dependent on digital codes – as exemplified by human languages. Sol Worth (1981) argues that 'pictures can't say ain't', while Ernst Gombrich (1982, 138, 175) insists that 'statements cannot be translated into images' and that 'pictures cannot assert' – a contention foreshadowed in Peirce (CP 2.291). Such stances are adopted in relation to images unattached to verbal texts – a simple verbal caption may be sufficient to enable an image to be used in the service of an assertion (Chandler 2014). While images serving such communicative purposes may be more 'open to interpretation', contemporary visual advertisements are a powerful example of how images may be used to make implicit claims which advertisers often prefer not to make more openly in words (Messaris 1997, Heath 2012).

TYPOLOGIES

Semioticians seek to identify codes and the tacit rules and constraints, which underlie the production and interpretation of meaning within each code. They have found it convenient to divide codes themselves into groups. Different theorists favour different taxonomies, and while structuralists often follow the 'principle of parsimony' – seeking to find the smallest number of groups deemed necessary – 'necessity' is defined by *purposes*. No taxonomy is innocently neutral and devoid of ideological assumptions. One might start from a fundamental divide between analogue and digital codes, from a division according to sensory channels, from a distinction between verbal and nonverbal, and so on. The most widespread codes in any societies are their natural languages, within which (as with other codes) there are many 'sub-codes'. A fundamental sub-division of language into spoken and written forms is often regarded as representing a broad division into different codes rather than merely subcodes. One theorist's code is another's subcode and the value of the distinction needs to be demonstrated. Stylistic and personal codes are often described as subcodes (e.g. Eco 1976, 263, 272). The various kinds of codes overlap, and the semiotic analysis of any text or practice involves considering several codes and the relationships between them. A range of typologies of codes can be found in the literature of semiotics. I refer here only to those which are most widely mentioned in the context of media, communication, and cultural studies (the particular tripartite framework presented here is my own).

Interpretive codes:

- perceptual codes: e.g. of visual perception;
- ideological codes: more broadly, these include codes for 'encoding' and 'decoding' texts and the '-isms', such as individualism, liberalism, feminism, racism, materialism, capitalism, progressivism, conservatism, socialism, objectivism, and populism.

Social codes:

- verbal language (phonological, syntactical, lexical, prosodic);
- bodily codes (bodily contact, proximity, physical orientation, appearance, facial expression, gaze, head-nods, gestures, and posture);
- commodity codes (fashions, clothing, cars);
- behavioural codes (protocols, rituals, role-playing, games).

Representational codes:

- scientific codes, including mathematics;
- aesthetic codes within the various expressive arts (poetry, drama, painting, sculpture, music, etc.) including classicism, romanticism, realism;

- genre, rhetorical, and stylistic codes;
- mass media codes including photographic, televisual, filmic, radio, newspaper, and magazine codes, both technical and conventional (including format).

These three types of codes correspond broadly to three key kinds of knowledge required by interpreters of a text, namely knowledge of:

1 the world (social knowledge, including situational knowledge);
2 the medium and the genre (representational knowledge);
3 the relationship between (1) and (2) (modality judgements).

The 'tightness' of semiotic codes themselves varies from the rule-bound closure of logical codes (such as computer codes) to the interpretive looseness of poetic codes. Most codes are not explicitly formulated and are usually followed unconsciously. Some theorists question whether some of the looser systems constitute codes at all (e.g. Guiraud 1975, 24, 41, 43–4, 65; Corner 1980). 'Decoding' requires 'interpretation'.

INTERPRETIVE CODES

'There are no facts, only interpretations', declares Friedrich Nietzsche in his unpublished 1880s notebooks. Data cannot become information without being related to an existing frame of reference. As we shall see in Chapter 6, interpretation is framed not only by codes but also by context, and is not solely an act of 'decoding' but also of inference. However, our expository focus here is on codes, and we begin with their mediating role in perception.

Many semioticians argue that even our perception of the natural world depends on codes. Such an assertion may lead naïve realists to reach for their guns, but it does not entail denying that our knowledge of the external world draws upon data from our senses, or that our sensory systems ground our experiences in the context of our physical environment. Although we know that our senses can deceive us, correlating several different sensory systems helps us to confirm or refute perceptual hypotheses. It would be foolish to deny that material reality has some extralinguistic or extrasemiotic basis; our semiotic systems clearly have some basis in phenomenal reality. However, our common-sense experience of perception as providing direct, immediate knowledge of the world is a powerful illusion. For instance, although retinal images supply sensory data, this reaches the brain in encoded form, and we never see those images – however convincing 'mental images' may seem to be (Gregory 1979, 57). It is extremely difficult to shake off the common-sense assumption that the world is exactly as it appears to us in our 'mind's eye'. However, we can never see things 'as they are', but only as framed by our perceptual and semiotic systems, which predispose us to view the world in particular ways. '"Reality" is always already encoded, it is never "raw"' (Fiske 1987, 4–5). The world is not immediately given because there is no perception without interpretation: data must be selected and organized into meaningful patterns on the basis of our existing knowledge of the world (Gregory 1998). Order must be imposed on the ever-changing sensory mosaic for objects to be inferred from patterns – for the analogical to become digital. Sensation has traditionally been distinguished from perception as a lower, passive function, but we now know that order is imposed even at the sensory receptors (Blakemore 2001). The British psychologist Richard Gregory argues that 'perceiving is a kind of thinking' (1970, 59). In the 'perceptual cycle' outlined by the cognitive psychologist Ulric Neisser (1976), perception selectively draws upon sensory data in making hypotheses about the external world, but the mind's search for data is guided by 'anticipatory schemata' (conceptual frameworks).

Perception transforms the perpetual analogical flux of the sensory world into digital signs – 'percepts *are* signs' (Sebeok 1986, 4; my italics). Gombrich declares that 'to perceive is to categorize, or classify' (1982, 286). Categorization is an essential basis for perceptual selectivity. As we noted in Chapter 2, categories are not pre-given 'natural kinds' in the external physical world; nor are they universal features 'hardwired' in the mind, but rather they are culturally-variable ways of organizing and stabilizing experience. Colours, for instance, do not exist 'out there': they are human constructs. The categories within a language are a resource for making the world manageable and meaningful. Once we have categorized something as a known object, we go beyond the evidence of the current sensory data, inferring various attributes from prior experience or knowledge of objects assigned to the same type. Categorization rather than communication can indeed be seen as the primary function of language (Ellis 1993). We have already referred to the importance of linguistic categorization in human perceptual processes in relation to the Sapir–Whorf hypothesis and Lakoff and Johnson's cognitive semantics; our cultural categories and dominant metaphors shape what we experience as real. The world that we encounter in perception is 'the world as a semantic field', which is familiar to us because we are both 'products of the same culture' (Mepham 1973, 125–6).

It is sobering to reflect that 'if we had the sensory apparatus of some other of the Earth's organisms, "reality" would seem quite different' (Rock 1984, 3). The human perceptual world – our 'reality' – is not the only perceptual world there is: different species experience different worlds. Things seem 'the way they are' because perceptual systems are adapted to selectively represent the environment in ways that serve the particular needs of different organisms (Jacob 1982, 56), and, for human beings, things are also differentiated in the ways they are because of the distinctions provided by our languages. What we experience as reality are 'patterns of relations' (Leach 1968, 29–30). In this sense, perception does not passively record the real: it actively creates it.

According to the Gestalt psychologists, there are certain universal features in human visual perception. In semiotic terms, these can be seen as constituting a fundamental perceptual code. First and foremost, if we are to perceive something as an object, we must separate a dominant shape (a 'figure' with a definite contour) from what our current concerns relegate to 'background' (or 'ground'). 'Perception,' declares Richard Gregory, 'is generally a matter of deciding between alternatives' (1979, 57). An illustration of this is the famous ambiguous figure, which initially seems to be either a white vase on a black background or two human faces in silhouette facing each other against a white background. Images such as this are ambiguous concerning figure and ground. In such cases, context influences perception, leading us to favour one interpretation over the other ('perceptual set'). The relation of text to context is also that of figure and ground. James Elkins argues that 'The concept of figure and ground . . . can easily . . . be claimed as the basis of understanding and meaning itself . . . Without a contrast between one thing and another, I cannot know anything . . . Contrast creates meaning' (1998, 79–80). Perception is in this sense *relational*.

The Gestalt theorists outlined several principles of perceptual organization which they saw as fundamental and universal. In visual perception, these lead us to interpret ambiguous images in one way rather than another. They are illustrated in standard textbooks on the psychology of perception, and a brief summary must suffice here. Visual elements tend to be grouped together as a single, bounded figure (a *gestalt*) on the basis of: proximity or similarity, when they move together, when lines suggest a smooth continuity of direction, when a shape seems 'closed', symmetrical, surrounded, relatively small in relation to a background, in the lower area of a horizontally divided field, or convex. Such diverse and often competing principles serve the overarching principle of *prägnanz*, which is that the simplest and most stable interpretations are favoured. Some perceptual codes are *learned* and culturally variable rather than innate and universal (Deregowski 1980). However, the Gestalt principles can be seen as reinforcing the notion that the world is not simply and objectively 'out there', but is constructed in the process of perception.

We are rarely aware of our own habitual ways of seeing the world. We are routinely anaesthetized to a psychological mechanism called 'perceptual constancy', which stabilizes the relative shifts in the apparent shapes and sizes of people and objects in the world around us as we change our visual viewpoints in relation to them. Without mechanisms such as categorization and perceptual constancy, the world would be what William James (1890, 488) famously called a 'great blooming and buzzing confusion'. Perceptual constancy ensures that 'the variability of the everyday world becomes translated by reference to less variable codes' (Nichols 1981, 26). Adopting such a perspective does not entail positing 'a closed world of codes' (Tagg 1988, 101) or the denial of the existence of what is represented outside the processes which represent it. Reality always exceeds the grasp of representation.

All codes have ideological implications. There are no ideologically neutral sign systems: signs function to persuade as well as to represent (representation always serves purposes). Sign systems which are naturalized within a culture serve to naturalize and reinforce particular framings of 'the way things are'. Roland Barthes (1977a, 116) argues that a 'reluctance to declare its codes characterizes bourgeois society and the mass culture issuing from it: both demand signs which do not look like signs'. He undertook to expose the self-effacing codes which serve to perpetuate the power of dominant groups. Semiotic analysis always involves ideological analysis. Many cultural semioticians have followed Barthes in regarding their primary task as denaturalizing dominant codes. Semiotic denaturalization has the potential to show ideology at work and to demonstrate that taken-for-granted assumptions about 'the way things are' can be challenged.

Although Roland Barthes argues that cultural forms are codified to encourage a reading that favours the interests of the dominant class, what is encoded is not necessarily what is decoded. Some messages or texts are less open to interpretation than others (as in road signs vs. paintings) but few have a single meaning for everyone. The German-born sociologist Burkart Holzner (1968, 21) notes that 'each person . . . approaches the environment in which he moves with a limited and specific repertory of frames of reference . . . These . . . are found in a patterned distribution within a structured social system'. People read texts in different ways, deploying their own repertoires of the cultural and subcultural codes to which they have access. The British sociologist Stuart Hall outlines the role of social positioning in the interpretation of mass media texts by different social groups. Hall suggests three hypothetical interpretive codes or positions for the reader of a text (1973, 136–8):

- *dominant (or 'hegemonic') reading*: the reader fully shares the text's code and accepts and reproduces the *preferred reading* (a reading which may not have been the result of any conscious intention on the part of the author(s)) – in such a stance the code seems natural and transparent;

- *negotiated reading*: the reader partly shares the text's code and broadly accepts the preferred reading, but sometimes resists and modifies it in a way which reflects their own position, experiences, and interests (local and personal conditions may be seen as exceptions to the general rule) – this position involves contradictions;
- *oppositional ('counter-hegemonic') reading*: the reader, whose social situation places them in a directly oppositional relation to the dominant code, understands the preferred reading but does not share the text's code and rejects this reading, bringing to bear an alternative frame of reference (radical, feminist, etc.) (e.g. when watching a television broadcast produced on behalf of a political party they normally vote *against*).

As an illustrative example of these interpretive positions or codes of reception, consider an award-winning television commercial usually called *Fish on a Bicycle* (accessible via YouTube), produced in 1996 for Guinness by the agency Ogilvy & Mather. It is a very interesting example of how we infer preferred meanings even when a message is not explicit. Briefly, it is a black-and-white film (lasting one minute) showing a sequence of shots of women playing darts, laughing together in a pub, driving a truck, shooting pool, arm-wrestling, working on a dustcart, emerging from a mine shaft, and operating a pneumatic drill. We are then shown the old feminist slogan that 'a woman needs a man like a fish needs a bicycle', followed by shots of a completely empty maternity ward and the campaign catchphrase that 'Not everything in black and white makes sense'. After a shot of the product, the final scene shows a fish riding a bicycle. We can infer from such a representation whose worldview it reflects and what the preferred reading is. A dominant or hegemonic reading might involve agreeing with the implication in the ad that it doesn't make sense that women don't need men (i.e. of course women need men) and we can laugh at the way women (and/or feminist fantasies) are depicted (a chauvinist reading). A negotiated reading might be that women do need men (as the ad implies) but we can laugh at the ad without being offended because it shows how daft men and their insecurities can be. An oppositional feminist reading might be that women really don't need men and this is offensive chauvinist propaganda, which we shouldn't appear to endorse by letting sexist men see us finding it amusing.

Hall's framework is based on the assumption that the latent meaning of the text is encoded in the dominant code. This is a stance that tends to reify the medium and to downplay conflicting tendencies within texts. Also, some critics have raised the question of how a 'preferred reading' can be established. Poststructuralist social semioticians would urge us not to seek such a reading within the form and structure of the text. Just as a reductive reading of Hall's model could lead to the reification of a medium or genre, it could also encourage the essentializing of readers (e.g. as 'the resistant reader') whereas reading positions are multiple, dynamic, and contradictory. Despite the various criticisms, Hall's model has been very influential, particularly among British theorists.

The British sociologist David Morley (1980) employed this model in his studies of how different social groups interpreted a television programme. Morley demonstrated differential access to the representational codes of a programme in the 'news magazine' genre. He insists that he did *not* take a *social determinist* position in which individual 'decodings' of a text are reduced to a direct consequence of social class position. 'It is always a question of how social position, as it is articulated through particular discourses, produces specific kinds of readings or decodings. These readings can then be seen to be patterned by the way in which the structure of access to different discourses is determined by social position' (Morley 1983, 113). Different interpretive communities have access to different representational and interpretive codes (which offer them the potential to understand and sometimes also to produce texts which employ them). Morley adds that any individual or group might operate different decoding strategies in relation to different *topics* and different *contexts*. A person might make 'oppositional' readings of the same material in one context and 'dominant' readings in other contexts (Morley 1981, 9 and 1992, 135). He notes that in interpreting viewers' readings of mass media texts, attention should be paid not only to the issue of *agreement* (acceptance/rejection) but also to *comprehension, relevance,* and *enjoyment* (Morley 1981, 10 and 1992, 126–7, 136). There is thus considerable scope for variety in the ways in which individuals engage with such codes.

The most basic task of interpretation involves the identification of what is represented, which requires some degree of familiarity with the medium and the representational codes involved. This is particularly obvious in the case of verbal texts, but it also applies to visual and audio-visual media such as photographs and films. Some cultural theorists would not grant this low-level process the label of 'interpretation' at all, limiting this term to such processes as the extraction of a 'moral' from a narrative text. However, many theorists take the stance that comprehension and interpretation are inseparable (e.g. Mick and Politi 1989, 85).

SOCIAL CODES

All codes are social since their conventions are constructed in social and cultural contexts. Regular repetition of patterns of behaviour establishes or reinforces a social code. The three categories of codes offered here are not clear-cut but it can be analytically useful to consider collectively codes which play key roles in the construction and maintenance of social realities and identities. The human subject does not exist independently of the semiotic systems of meaning provided by language and culture. We live in 'a society of signs' (Harris 1996). David Halperin writes: 'I consider semiotic codes to be constitutive of the meanings out of which individual subjectivity is born. They define the social and symbolic context within which subjectivity takes shape' (2012, 335). They therefore play key roles in the social formation of identities.

Constructionists argue that linguistic codes play a key role in social construction. This includes many sociologists, who would nonetheless justifiably insist that social life is not a free-floating 'social text': it cannot be methodologically reduced to codes ungrounded by referents. We have already noted the impossibility of 'seeing things as they are'; categories are not 'in the world' but are generated by perceptual and semiotic systems. Through discourses, the stories with which we explain our world, we learn not 'the world' but the codes into which it has been structured – without which the world as we know it cannot exist. This is consistent with the Whorfian hypothesis that, as one social constructionist puts it, 'Persons who live in various cultures and historical epochs do not "merely" communicate differently, but experience different ways of being human *because* they communicate differently' (Pearce 1989, xvii). The realities in which we dwell and the meanings we construct are not universal, but they are not purely individual either – they are 'to a large extent unconsciously built upon the language habits of the group' (Sapir 1929, 69), and on other social codes shared within a culture or subculture (see Figure 2.1).

Language use acts as a key marker of social identity. 'It ain't what you say but the way that you say it', as the popular English expression puts it. People's 'choice' of certain words is still a social indicator. For instance, in England, indicating that you didn't hear what someone said by saying 'Sorry?' or 'Pardon?' would suggest that you are middle class (respectively upper middle class or lower middle class). Alternatively, saying 'What?' would be more typical of either the upper class or the working class. Similarly, it tends to be only among the upper and working classes that you are likely to hear references to a toilet as 'the bog' (for which the middle classes have a host of euphemisms). The anthropologist Kate Fox (2014, 214) suggests that in England certain social markers are not shared by adjacent classes because 'each class particularly despises the one immediately below it, and the prospect of being mistaken for a member of this adjacent class is therefore especially abhorrent'. A controversial distinction regarding British linguistic usage was introduced in the 1960s by the sociologist Basil Bernstein between so-called 'restricted code' and 'elaborated code' (Bernstein 1971). His main argument is that working class children are disadvantaged in schools because they tend to rely on a more informal, context-bound ('restricted') style of language than that favoured by schools and the middle classes. Core values and understandings are taken for granted within close-knit communities so there is less need to make meanings explicit. Although the theory has attracted criticism from some linguists (see Crystal 1987, 40), we still routinely use such linguistic cues as a basis for making inferences about people's social backgrounds.

Within a culture, social differentiation is reinforced by a multitude of social codes. Established social categories such as age, sex, and social status are 'ready-made codes' in that visual signs are routinely interpreted as reflecting them (Kjørup 1977, 31, 37). We communicate our social identities through the work we do, the way we talk, the clothes we wear, our hairstyles, our eating habits, our domestic environments and possessions, our use of leisure time, our modes of travelling and so on. Umberto Eco refers to clothes as 'semiotic devices, machines for communicating' (1987, 195), and Roland Barthes declares that with clothes 'it is the meaning that sells' (1967b, xii). Clothing codes are systems of signification; as we have noted, Barthes identifies both syntagmatic and paradigmatic dimensions of 'the garment system'. The conventions are not static but change over time, though some features are remarkably long-lived, such as the arbitrary and symbolic direction of buttoning (left over right for males, right over left for females). Eco (1973, 59) comments that 'obviously, fashion codes are less articulate, more subject to historical fluctuations than linguistic codes are. But a code is no less a code for the fact that it is weaker than other stronger ones'.

Dress codes regulate social distinctions such as of gender, age, class, and status. In 1899, Thorstein Veblen noted that the highly impractical finery of 'the leisure class', which restricted their freedom of action, performed the symbolic function of indicating that they did not do any manual work. Wearing the appropriate 'uniform' represents an endorsement of the code and the power relations it helps to reproduce. Gendered clothing is a clear example. Even those who reject the dominant code find their performance judged with reference to it. Wearing clothes closely identified with 'the opposite sex' constitutes a strong statement of nonconformity. I have encountered shocked reactions to the suggestion that 'we are all in drag, whether we wear conventional clothing or cross-dress, in that we are always imitating some convention of masculinity and femininity' (Weinberg 2005, 167). The historian Jonathan Ned Katz (2007, 15) comments on the markedness involved: 'We name and talk of a problematic "trans-vestism", the desire to dress in the clothes of the other sex. We do not usually name and speak of the strong desire to dress in the clothes of one's own sex. But why would most of us feel intense anxiety at dressing publicly in the clothes of the other sex? Does not our fervid desire to dress in the clothes of our own sex suggest a mystery to be explained?' Structuralists argue that the shock, confusion, embarrassment, or frisson generated by marked transgressions of our customary social rules or conventions reflect the power of cultural symbolism and myths and the degree of importance attached to the tidy organization of the social categories into which we 'carve up the social environment' (Leach 1973, 51). The stability of our conceptual structures is perpetually under threat – as is evident in, for instance, the endless need for the performance of gender identities (Butler 1999). Fred Davis (1992, 17–18) notes that fashion has 'drawn upon certain recurrent instabilities in the social identities of Western men and women', such as masculinity–femininity, youth–age, inclusiveness–exclusiveness, work–play, domesticity–worldliness, revelation–concealment, licence– restraint, and conformity–rebellion. Such oppositions serve as points of reference in the performance of personal and social identity, operating through the expressive use of material features such as colour (hue, saturation, luminance), texture (rough–smooth), weight (heavy–light), and line (straight–curved) (Sahlins 1976, 88).

Codes are sometimes termed 'restricted' in a more everyday sense (unrelated to Bernstein's theories) – notably in relation to the construction of gender differentiation. For instance, since the nineteenth century, Western clothing norms (especially for formal apparel), have offered women far more options than men. A similar pattern applies to the gendering of objects (as in marketing): colour codes for males tend to be more restricted than for females. Even in relation to the connotations of fonts, 'masculine' options (typically big and bold) are much more restricted than 'feminine' ones. All of these patterns are consistent with the alignment of masculinity–femininity with other mutually reinforcing oppositions, such as plain–fancy, heavy–light, colourless–colourful, instrumental–expressive, observer–observed, and also with the markedness of femininity and the exnomination of masculinity (discussed in Chapter 3).

Research in social psychology has consistently shown that the two most important dimensions of interpersonal relations expressed in both nonverbal and verbal behaviour are *liking* and *dominance* (Argyle 1988, 86). As we have seen (Table 4.9), Gombrich maps

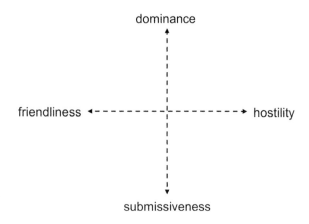

FIGURE 5.1 Key poles in social relationships

Source: Adapted from Argyle 1988, 86

particular sensations, sights, and sounds in relation to connotations of friendliness–hostility. A wide range of situational relationships can be usefully mapped onto the quadrants generated by the interaction of liking and dominance (Figure 5.1). Nonverbal cues for both include facial expression, gaze, touch, posture, and vocal pitch (ibid., 97; Argyle 1994, 46). Such cues both reflect and dynamically shape interpersonal power relations.

Everything we do communicates. Most of the time we communicate without being conscious of doing so, and when we attribute emotions and attitudes to 'body language', we are rarely aware of reading signs. The psychologist Ray Birdwhistell (1971) devised *kinesics* – a 'linguistics' of nonverbal communication, identifying 50 to 60 basic units (or 'kinemes') of bodily movement (analogous to linguistic phonemes), into which most nonverbal messages can be decomposed. According to Paul Ekman (2004), another psychologist, the most language-like forms of nonverbal communication are hand, head, or facial movements which he terms *emblems*. These are typically deliberate gestures with specific meanings recognizable to most members of a culture or subculture. Like verbal languages they are socially learned, culturally variable, and communicate messages, but emblems are not normally used as sequences and they lack a 'syntax'. Research in the United States (Johnson *et al.* 1975) has identified over a dozen emblems for which the message decoded exactly matched that encoded in a sample of fifty-three white, middle-class, college-educated, third-generation Americans living in the San Francisco Bay area in 1973. These gestures represented messages including commands, replies, and insults – such as 'you!', 'sit down beside me!', 'be silent/hush!', 'come here!', 'wait/hold it!', 'I can't hear you', 'yes' (or 'I agree' or 'I like it'), 'no' (or 'I disagree'), 'okay', and 'I don't know'. Many others were recognized by at least 70 per cent of the sample.

In the context of the present text, a few examples must suffice to illustrate the importance of nonverbal codes. Those which regulate a 'sensory regime' are of particular interest. 'Codes of looking' regulate how people may look at other people (including taboos on certain kinds of looking). Such codes tend to retreat to transparency when the cultural context is one's own. 'Children are instructed to "look at me", not to stare at strangers, and not to look at certain parts of the body . . . People have to look in order to be polite, but not to look at the wrong people or in the wrong place' (Argyle 1988, 158). People in 'contact cultures' such as Arabs, Latin Americans, and southern Europeans, look more directly; those in 'non-contact cultures', such as Northern Europeans and Asians, look less directly (ibid.). In contact cultures, too little gaze is seen as insincere, dishonest, or impolite, while in non-contact cultures too much gaze ('staring') is seen as threatening, disrespectful and insulting (Argyle 1983, 95 and 1988, 165). Within the bounds of the cultural conventions, people who avoid one's gaze may be seen as nervous, tense, evasive, and lacking in confidence, while people who look a lot may tend to be seen as friendly and self-confident (Argyle 1983, 93). Such codes may sometimes be deliberately violated. In the USA in the 1960s, bigoted white Americans employed a sustained 'hate stare' directed against blacks, which was designed to depersonalize the victims (Goffman 1969).

Codes of looking are particularly important in relation to gender differentiation. One woman reported to a male friend: 'One of the things I really envy about men is the right to look'. She pointed out that in public places, 'men could look freely at women, but women could only glance back surreptitiously' (Dyer 1992, 103). Nancy Henley, a psychologist in the USA, conducted informal studies in 'smile elicitation' through the observation of about 300 people in public places (evenly divided between males and females). In her book *Body Politics* (1977) she reports her findings that people generally tended to return a smile, that women returned smiles more often than males did (and especially tended to return smiles to males), and that males were more inhibited at smiling back (especially to other males) (see Table 5.2). Henley also explored gaze return by asking her students to look at someone in a public place for about three seconds, noting whether the person returned the gaze (see Table 5.3). In 400 elicitations she found that the dominant tendency was gaze aversion. With an opposite-sex gaze women tended to avert their eyes while men tended to return it, and males showed 'a striking avoidance of eye contact with other males' (ibid., 165).

The performance of unconscious behavioural codes maintains social hierarchies. Complementary dyadic relationships – such as parent/child, employer/employee, teacher/student, doctor/patient – are asymmetrical in terms of dominance–submissiveness or activity–passivity (Henley 1977, 95; Leach 1982, 59). Taking the example of touch, this is of course often used to express friendly support and comfort, as in patting someone's back or putting an arm around their shoulders, but such actions also carry status messages. For instance,

	target persons			
smilers	*male*		*female*	
	% returned	*% not returned*	*% returned*	*% not returned*
male	58	42	93	7
female	67	33	86	14

TABLE 5.2 Patterns of smile return

Source: Derived from data in Henley 1977, 176–7

gazers	target persons			
	male		*female*	
	% returned	*% averted*	*% returned*	*% averted*
male	20	80	41	59
female	60	40	39	61

TABLE 5.3 Patterns of gaze return

Source: Derived from data in Henley 1977, 165

Erving Goffman notes a 'touch system' in hospital wards, where doctors might supportively touch the other ranks, but the other ranks regarded it as presumptuous to reciprocate or initiate such behaviour towards doctors (1967, 73–4).

Our sense of self is a social and relational construction (Berger and Luckmann 1967, Gergen 2009b and 2011). When we first encounter this notion we are likely to find it counter-intuitive: we take our individual identity for granted (we have 'our own' thoughts, emotions, and motivations). However, we learn to read the world in terms of the dominant codes and conventions in the specific socio-cultural contexts and roles within which we are socialized, and in the process of adopting a way of seeing, we also adopt an 'identity'. In perception, internalized codes stabilize experience by maintaining constancies in relationships between shifting relata. The most important constancy in our understanding of reality is our sense of who we are as individuals. This sense of self emerges gradually from the activation of social codes in repeated performances of social relationships. The self is not wholly determined by these internalized codes but, argues Bill Nichols, it 'would be entirely undetermined without them' (1981, 30). We will return later to the notion of our social positioning as 'subjects'.

Nichols notes that society depends upon its members granting a taken-for-granted status to its foundational myths and codes (ibid.). Culturally variable codes are typically inexplicit, and we are not normally conscious of the roles that they play. To users of the dominant, most widespread codes, meanings generated within such codes tend to appear obvious and natural. Stuart Hall comments:

> Certain codes may ... be so widely distributed in a specific language community or culture, and be learned at so early an age, that they appear not to be constructed – the effect of an articulation between sign and referent – but to be 'naturally' given. Simple visual signs appear to have achieved a 'near-universality' in this sense: though evidence remains that even apparently 'natural' visual codes are culture-specific. However, this does not mean that no codes have intervened; rather, that the codes have been profoundly *naturalized*.
>
> (Hall 1973, 132)

Learning these codes involves adopting the values, assumptions, and worldviews which are built into them, without normally being aware of their intervention in the construction of reality. A startling example of this relates to colour codes. When I showed my own students a picture of two teddy bears, one clothed in powder blue and the other in pale pink, this was instantly interpreted as signifying respectively male and female. There followed an almost tangible sense of shock when I confronted them with this passage:

> Pink or blue? Which is intended for boys and which for girls? This question comes from one of our readers this month, and the discussion may be of interest to others. There has been a great diversity of opinion on this subject, but the generally accepted rule is pink for the boy and blue for the girl. The reason is that pink being a more decided and stronger color, is more suitable for the boy; while blue, which is more delicate and dainty is prettier for the girl.

Widely misattributed to the *Ladies' Home Journal*, this is actually from a Chicago-based trade magazine called *The Infants' Department: A Monthly Magazine of Merchandising Helps for the Infants' Wear Buyer* (vol. 1, no. 10, June 1918, 161). Nor is this an isolated source for the same sentiments in the early decades of the twentieth century. Only in more recent times has pink acquired such a powerfully marked status as 'feminine' (Taft 1997, Paoletti 2012). The justification for pink as more suitable for boys than for girls may initially seem an amusing rationalization, but our own rationale for the opposite case is hardly immune from the same judgement. However natural and commonsensical familiar codes may seem to be, they are always social conventions (which clearly need not take their current form). The profound sense of amazement or even disbelief generated by encountering such 'counter-intuitive' gendering of colours highlights the value of semiotics for challenging that which is taken for granted by 'making the familiar strange'.

REPRESENTATIONAL CODES

Some cultural theorists choose to treat all codes as representational or 'textual', reading the world as a 'social text' – a metaphor intended to undermine literalist assumptions about 'the way things are'. 'Every decoding is another encoding', says Morris Zapp, a fictional literary scholar in David Lodge's novel *Small World*. This is more than saying simply that interpretations are texts in themselves. The postmodernist notion that decoding is an endless process of 'translation' from one representation to another is foreshadowed in Peirce's observation that 'the meaning of a representation can be nothing but a representation' (CP 1.339) – although of course Peirce would not have endorsed the notion that there is nothing outside representation. We have already discussed the mediating role of interpretive codes in processes of representation. As with the other broad categories, representational codes are a specific focus of study and, as we saw in Chapter 3, semiotic approaches are often employed in textual analysis.

As should be clear by now, representation is a central concern of semiotics. We have already noted that representational systems mediate our access to reality; if perception is mediated, it is 'always already' representation. Furthermore, social construction and reproduction operate through processes of representation. The mass media endlessly circulate normative images of social identity such as of class, age, gender, and ethnicity. The media do not directly regulate our behaviour, but it is widely accepted that such frequent and pervasive imagery does function as a restrictive frame of reference for social identities. Advertising in particular tends to reproduce conventional expectations for 'appropriate' behaviour because, as the sociologist Erving Goffman puts it, 'advertisers conventionalize our conventions' (1979, 84). Such relentless reality maintenance may seem some basis for the claim, for instance, that 'the representation of gender *is* its construction' (de Lauretis 1987, 3). Deconstructing the ideological processes of representation depends, in the first instance, on dispelling the illusion that representation simply 'reflects reality'.

Representational or textual codes are conventions of form, style, and content for texts in any medium. They are systems of signs and rules which are drawn upon in both the production and interpretation of texts, guiding expectations and reflecting certain values, attitudes, beliefs, assumptions, and practices. Such codes transcend single texts, linking them together in an interpretive framework. In creating our own texts, we select and combine signs in relation to the codes with which we are familiar. These codes help to simplify phenomena in order to make it easier to communicate experiences. The film scholar Richard Dyer (1993, 2) observes that representational forms 'restrict and shape what can be said by and/or about any aspect of reality in a given place in a given society at a given time, but, if that seems like a limitation on saying, it is also what makes saying possible at all' (cf. Barthes 1967b, 161).

Of course, our frame of reference in interpreting representations depends not only on our knowledge of representational codes but also on our knowledge of real world situations and social codes (see Figure 6.5). Texts do not rely solely on textual codes. In reading texts, we interpret signs with reference to what seem to be appropriate codes. This helps to limit their possible meanings. Usually the appropriate codes are obvious, reinforced by all sorts of contextual cues. The medium employed clearly influences the choice of codes. In this sense, we routinely 'judge a book by its cover'. We can typically identify a text as a poem or a menu simply by the way in which it is set out on the page. The use of what is sometimes called 'scholarly apparatus' (such as introductions, acknowledgements, section headings, tables, diagrams, notes, references, bibliographies, appendices, and indexes) is what makes academic texts immediately identifiable as such to readers. Such cueing is part of the *metalingual* function of signs. With familiar codes, we are rarely conscious of our acts of interpretation, but occasionally a text requires us to work a little harder – for instance, by pinning down the most appropriate signified for a key signifier (as in jokes based on word play) – before we can identify the relevant codes for making sense of the text as a whole. Representational codes do not *determine* the meanings of texts but where such codes are dominant they do tend to *constrain* them. Social conventions ensure that signs cannot mean whatever an individual wants them to mean. The use of codes helps to guide us towards what Stuart Hall calls 'a preferred reading' and away from what Umberto Eco calls 'aberrant decoding', though signs and texts do vary in the extent to which they are open to interpretation.

Genre

One of the most fundamental kinds of representational code relates to *genre* (Chandler 1997a), which the literary theorist E. D. Hirsch sees as a primary interpretive frame of reference (1967, 74). Traditional definitions of genres tend to be based on the notion that they constitute particular conventions of content (such as themes or settings) and/or form (including structure and style) which are shared by the texts that are regarded as belonging to them. This mode of defining a genre is deeply problematic. For instance, genres overlap and texts often exhibit the conventions of more than one genre. It is seldom hard to find texts that are exceptions to any given definition of a particular genre. Furthermore, genres are involved in a constant process of change.

An overview of genre taxonomies in various media is beyond the scope of the current text, but it is appropriate here to allude to a few key cross-media genre distinctions. The organization of public libraries suggests that one of the most fundamental contemporary genre distinctions is between *fiction* and *non-fiction* – a categorization that highlights the importance of modality judgements. Even such an apparently basic distinction is revealed to be far from straightforward as soon as one tries to apply it to the books on one's own shelves or to an evening's television viewing. Another binary distinction is based on the kinds of language used: *poetry* and *prose* – the 'norm' being the latter, as Molière's Monsieur Jourdain famously discovered: 'Good Heavens! For more than forty years I have been speaking prose without knowing it!' Even here there are grey areas, with literary prose often being regarded as 'poetic'. This is related to the issue of how librarians, critics, and academics decide what is 'literature' as opposed to mere 'fiction' (or art rather than entertainment). As with the typology of codes in general, no genre taxonomy can be ideologically neutral. Traditional rhetoric distinguishes between four kinds of discourse: *exposition*, *argument*, *description*, and *narration* (Brooks and Warren 1972, 44). These four forms, which relate to primary purposes, are often referred to as different genres (e.g. Fairclough 1995a, 88). However, texts frequently involve any combination of these forms. More widely described as genres are the four 'modes of emplotment', which Hayden White (1973), in his study of historiography, adopted from Northrop Frye: *romance*, *tragedy*, *comedy*, and *satire*. Useful as such interpretive frameworks can be, however, no taxonomy of textual genres adequately represents the diversity of texts.

Despite such theoretical problems, various interpretive communities (at particular periods in time) do operate on the basis of a negotiated (if somewhat loose and fluid) consensus concerning what they regard as the primary genres relevant to their purposes. While there is far more to a genre code than that which may seem to relate to specifically textual features, it can still be useful to consider the distinctive properties attributed to a genre by its users. For instance, if we take the case of film, the textual features typically listed by theorists include:

- *narrative* – similar (sometimes formulaic) plots and structures, predictable situations, sequences, episodes, obstacles, conflicts, and resolutions;
- *characterization* – similar types of characters (sometimes stereotypes), roles, personal qualities, motivations, goals, behaviour;
- basic *themes*, topics, subject-matter (social, cultural, psychological, professional, political, sexual, moral) and values;
- *setting* – geographical and historical;

- *iconography* (echoing the narrative, characterization, themes, and setting) – a familiar stock of images or motifs, the connotations of which have become fixed; primarily but not necessarily visual, including décor, costume, and objects, certain 'typecast' performers (some of whom may have become 'icons'), familiar patterns of dialogue, characteristic music and sounds, and appropriate physical topography; and
- *filmic techniques* – stylistic or formal conventions of camerawork, lighting, sound-recording, use of colour, editing, etc. (viewers are often less conscious of such conventions than of those relating to content).

Some film genres tend to be defined primarily by their *subject-matter* (e.g. detective films), some by their *setting* (e.g. the western) and others by their *narrative* form (e.g. the musical). Less easy to place in one of the traditional categories are *mood* and *tone* (which are key features of *film noir*). In addition to *textual* features, different genres (in any medium) also involve different purposes, pleasures, audiences, modes of involvement, styles of interpretation, and *text–reader relationships* (an issue to which we shall return in Chapter 6).

Some codes employed in cultural texts and performances are more widespread and accessible than others. John Fiske (1982, 78ff.) distinguishes between *broadcast* codes, which are shared by members of a mass audience, and *narrowcast* codes, which are aimed at a more limited audience; pop music is a broadcast code; ballet is a narrowcast code. Broadcast codes are learned through experience; narrowcast codes often involve more deliberate learning (Fiske 1989, 315). Broadcast codes are described as structurally simpler and more repetitive ('overcoded'), having what information theorists call a high degree of *redundancy*. In such codes, several elements serve to emphasize and reinforce preferred meanings. Umberto Eco (1981) describes as 'closed' those texts (such as many mass media texts), which show a strong tendency to encourage a particular interpretation. In contrast, literary writing – in particular poetry – has a minimum of redundancy (Lotman 1976). Some cultural theorists refer to broadcast codes as 'restricted codes' and to narrowcast codes as 'elaborated codes', but this misrepresents Bernstein.

The distinction between broadcast and narrowcast codes tends to reinforce a hierarchy of taste which seeks to elevate a 'highbrow' élite above the 'lowbrow' majority. Cultural élites distinguish 'high' art from 'popular' entertainment, defining the former as more 'original' and unpredictable. Fiske suggests that narrowcast codes have the potential to be more subtle; broadcast codes can lead to cliché. Cultural critics frequently argue that it is a distinctive feature of art that conventional codes are 'more honoured in the breach than the observance' (*Hamlet* I, iv). However, such codes are also regularly subverted in popular culture. Some critics add that aesthetic works are not only 'code-transgressive' but also 'code-productive' (Eagleton 1983, 125), but once again the generation of new codes is also a key feature of popular culture (especially youth culture). Roland Posner suggests that interpreting the 'non-precoded' elements of an artwork requires us both to draw upon existing codes and to infer an aesthetic code which is specific to its own structure and texture: a recursive process that is rewarding for the art lover (Chatman *et al.* 1979, 693). Critics sometimes refer to genre codes as creatively restrictive and deny the status of 'art' to generic forms. The dangers of élitism inherent in such stances make it particularly important that the evidence is closely examined in the context of the particular code under study. Aesthetic texts may tend to veer away from particular codical norms but this is a difference of degree rather than kind (see Table 4.1).

Any text uses not one code, but several. For instance, pictures draw upon codes such as figurative, iconographic, rhetorical, and stylistic codes (often in association with linguistic and typographic codes). Just as signs need to be analysed in their relation to other signs, so codes need to be analysed in relation to other codes. The Russian-born semiotician Yuri Lotman (1922–93) argues that a poem is a 'system of systems' – lexical, syntactical, metrical, morphological, phonological, and so on – and that the relations between such systems generate powerful literary effects (Lotman 1976). A code may set up expectations that other codes reinforce or violate. Becoming aware of the interplay of such codes requires a potentially recursive process of rereading. Such readings are not confined to the internal structure of a text, since the codes utilized within it extend beyond any specific text – an issue of 'intertextuality' to which we shall return.

Aesthetic realisms

From the Renaissance until the nineteenth century, Western art was dominated by a mimetic representational purpose which still prevails in popular culture. Realism involves an instrumental view of the medium as a neutral means of representing a reality independent of the act of representation, as if it were a window on the world. The referent is foregrounded at the expense of the sign vehicle. Realist representational practices tend to mask the processes involved in producing texts, as if they were slices of life 'untouched by human hand'. Such modes of representation generate a deceptive illusion of 'truth', especially in visual media. However, 'realism is not reality', as the film theorist Christian Metz puts it (1968, 21). Its plausibility derives primarily from the familiarity of its conventions rather than from its reflection of the world. Ironically, the 'naturalness' of realist texts comes not from their reflection of reality but from their uses of codes which are derived from other texts. The familiarity of particular semiotic practices renders their mediation invisible. Our recognition of the familiar in realist texts repeatedly confirms the 'objectivity' of our habitual ways of seeing. Yet since we only ever experience reality through systems of representation, we are never in a position to compare any representation with 'naked reality'.

The codes of the various realisms are not always initially familiar. In his influential book, *Languages of Art*, the North American philosopher Nelson Goodman insists that 'realism is relative, determined by the system of representation standard for a given culture or person at a given time' (1968, 37). Semioticians argue that, although exposure over time leads 'visual language' to seem natural, we need to learn how to 'read' even visual and audio-visual texts (though see Messaris 1982 and 1994 for a critique of this stance). In the context of painting, Ernst Gombrich (1977) has illustrated (for instance, in relation to John Constable) how aesthetic codes which now seem 'almost photographic' to many viewers, were regarded at the time of their emergence as strange and radical. Eco adds that early viewers of Impressionist art could not recognize the subjects represented and declared that real life is not like this (1976, 254; Gombrich 1982, 279). Most people had not previously noticed coloured shadows in nature (Gombrich 1982, 27, 30, 34).

Even photography involves transformations (such as flatness, decontextualization, and rescaling): photographs are not replicas and require 'translation'. Anthropologists have often reported the initial difficulties experienced by people in primal tribes in making sense of photographs and films (Deregowski 1980), while historians note that even in recent times the first instant snapshots confounded Western viewers because they were not accustomed to arrested images of transient movements and needed to go through a process of cultural habituation or training in order to interpret them (Gombrich 1982, 100, 273). Photography involved a new 'way of seeing' (to use John Berger's phrase) which had to be learned before it could become transparent. When we look at things around us in everyday life, we gain a sense of depth from our binocular vision, by rotating our head or by moving in relation to what we are looking at. To get a clearer view, we can adjust the focus of our eyes. But for making sense of depth when we look at a photograph, none of this helps. We have to decode the cues, drawing on our knowledge of the world and of the medium.

What human beings see in the world does not resemble a filmic sequence of rectangular frames, and camerawork and editing conventions are not direct replications of the way in which we see the everyday world. When the pioneering American film-maker D. W. Griffith initially proposed the use of close-ups, his producers warned him that the audience would be disconcerted since the rest of the actor is missing (Rosenblum and Karen 1979, 37–8). What count as realistic modes of representation are both culturally and historically variable. To most contemporary Western audiences, the familiarity of the conventions of contemporary American cinema makes them seem more realistic than those of early silent movies or modern Indian cinema. Even within a culture, over historical time particular codes become increasingly less familiar, and as we look back at texts produced centuries ago we are struck by the strangeness of their codes – their maintenance systems having long since been superseded.

Peirce refers to signs in (unedited) photographic media as being *indexical* as well as *iconic* – meaning that the sign vehicles do not simply resemble their referents but are mechanical recordings and reproductions of them (within the limitations of the medium). John Berger also argues that photographs are automatic 'records of things seen' and that 'photography has no language of its own' (1968, 179, 181). Understanding a photograph seems to require only knowledge of the world, which it appears to represent directly, and not knowledge of the medium, which is generally experienced as uncoded. In 'The photographic message' (1961, 17), Roland Barthes famously declared that 'the photographic image . . . is a *message without a code*'. Since this phrase is frequently misunderstood, it may be worth clarifying its context with reference to this essay together with another published three years later – 'The rhetoric of the image' (1964).

Barthes grants that photography involves both mechanical *reduction* (flattening, perspective, proportion, and colour) and human *intervention* (choice of subject, framing, composition, optical point of view, distance, angle, lighting, focus, speed, exposure, printing, and 'trick effects'). In other words, he acknowledges the existence of photographic conventions. When we look at photographs we can often recognize the conventions of particular historical periods, of particular genres (e.g. news photos, snapshots, portraits, passport photos), and of individual styles (composition/framing, lighting, point of view) – sometimes we can even identify the photographer from the ways in which they use and 'break' conventions.

However, the relation of the photographic image to its referent is clearly not arbitrary (ibid., 35). Despite the transformations we noted earlier, Barthes argues that 'in the photograph – at least at the level of the literal message – the representational relation is not one of "transformation" but of "recording"'. Although the photographer is unavoidably selective, the lens is not: unlike a drawing or a painting, a photograph reproduces 'everything' within its scope. Barthes refers to the 'absolutely analogical, which is to say, *continuous*' character of the medium (1961, 20). 'Is it possible', he asks, 'to conceive of an analogical code (as opposed to a digital one)?' (1964, 32). Unlike a language, photography does not involve dividing up reality into units and constituting these units as signs that are 'substantially different from the object they communicate; there is no necessity to set up . . . a code, between the object and its image' (1961, 17). In other words, no one has succeeded in identifying discrete units into which all photographs can be decomposed, or syntactic rules for their combination, and in this sense there is no language-like code (cf. Langer 1957, 93–7). In consequence, Barthes notes, photographs cannot be reduced to words and photography is only metaphorically a 'language'.

Nevertheless, Barthes accepts that 'every sign supposes a code' and at a level higher than the 'literal' level of denotation, he identifies a *connotative* code (recall his identification of orders of signification, as in Figure 4.5). At the 'level of production', 'the press photograph is an object that has been worked on, chosen, composed, constructed, treated according to professional or ideological norms' and, at the 'level of reception', the photograph 'is not only perceived, received, it is *read*, connected by the public that consumes it to a traditional stock of signs' (1961, 19). Reading a photograph involves relating it to 'a rhetoric' (by which he means a sort of mental inventory of cultural connotations). In addition to the photographic techniques already noted, he refers for instance to the signifying functions of: postures, expressions, and gestures; the associations evoked by depicted objects and settings; syntagmatic sequences of photographs, such as in magazines; and relationships with accompanying text (ibid., 21–5). He adds that 'thanks to the code of connotation the reading of the photograph is . . . always historical; it depends on the reader's "knowledge" just as though it were a matter of a real language, intelligible only if one has learned the signs' (ibid., 28).

Clearly, therefore, it would be a misinterpretation of Barthes' declaration that 'the photographic image . . . is a *message without a code*' to suggest that he meant that no codes are involved in producing or 'reading' photographs. His main point is that it did not seem possible to reduce the photographic image itself to elementary 'signifying units'. Far from suggesting that photographs are purely denotative, he suggests that the 'purely "denotative" status' attributed to them is 'mythical'. Barthes is convinced that connotation comes into play even at the level of the analogue image (ibid., 19). Citing Bruner and Piaget, he acknowledges the possibility that 'there is no perception without immediate categorization' (ibid., 28). Reading a photograph also depends closely on the reader's culture, knowledge of the world, and ethical and ideological stances (ibid., 29). Barthes adds that 'the viewer receives *at one and the same time* the perceptual message and the cultural message' (1964, 36).

In *Writing Degree Zero*, Barthes sought to demonstrate that the classical textual codes of French writing (from the mid-seventeenth century until the mid-nineteenth century) had been used to suggest that such codes are natural, neutral, and transparent conduits for an innocent and objective reflection of reality (i.e. the operation of the codes is masked). Barthes (1953) argues that while generating the illusion of a 'zero-degree' of style, these codes serve the purpose of fabricating reality in accord with the bourgeois view of the world and covertly propagating bourgeois values as self-evident. In 'The rhetoric of the image', Barthes develops this line of argument in relation to the medium of photography, arguing that because it appears to record rather than to transform or signify, it serves an ideological function. The fact that the image is 'captured mechanically' reinforces the myth of its 'objectivity' (1964, 44). The photographer Richard Avedon declares that 'All photographs are accurate. None of them is the truth' (Arrigo 2003, 1232). There is nothing 'natural' or necessary about *how* reality is represented in a photograph. 'Photographs do not "show how things look", since there is no one way that anything looks' (Coleman 1998, 57). Yet, argues Barthes (because of its indexicality) photography 'seems to found in nature the signs of culture . . . masking the constructed meaning under the appearance of the given meaning' (1964, 45–6). In her famous book of essays *On Photography*, Susan Sontag notes that 'nobody takes the same picture of the same thing', so 'photographs are evidence not only of what's there but of what an individual sees, not just a record but an evaluation of the world' (1979, 88). Or, as Berger (1972, 8) puts it, 'Every image embodies a way of seeing. Even a photograph'. In this unavoidably selective medium, some features are foregrounded and others excluded. Photographs are taken (or rather made) for a variety of purposes. Provocatively, Sontag proposes that 'photographs are as much an interpretation of the world as paintings and drawings are' (1979, 6–7).

Most semioticians emphasize that photography involves visual codes, and that film and television involve both visual and aural codes. John Tagg argues that 'the camera is never neutral. The representations it produces are highly coded' (1988, 63–4). Cinematic and televisual codes include: genre; camerawork (shot size, focus, lens movement, camera movement, angle, lens choice, composition); editing (cuts and fades, cutting rate and rhythm); manipulation of time (compression, flashbacks, flashforwards, slow motion); lighting; colour; sound (soundtrack, music); graphics; and narrative style. Christian Metz adds authorial style, and distinguishes codes from subcodes, where a subcode is a particular choice from within a code (e.g. western within genre, or naturalistic or expressionist lighting subcodes within the lighting code). The syntagmatic dimension is a relation of combination between different codes and subcodes; the paradigmatic dimension is that of the film-maker's choice of particular subcodes within a code. Since, as Metz (1971, 63) notes, 'a film is not "cinema" from one end to another', film and television involve many codes that are not specific to these media.

While some photographic and filmic codes are relatively arbitrary, many of the codes employed in realistic photographic images or films simulate familiar aspects of our everyday perception of the physical world (Nichols 1981, 35; cf. Messaris 1982 and 1994). This is a key reason for their perceived realism. The depiction of reality even in iconic signs involves variable codes which have to be learned, yet which, with experience, come to be taken for granted as transparent and obvious. Eco (1976, 190ff.) argues that it is misleading to regard such signs as less conventional than other kinds of signs: even photography and film involve conventional codes. Paul Messaris (1994), however, stresses that the formal conventions of representational visual codes (including paintings and drawings) are not arbitrary, and Ernst Gombrich (1982, 278–97) offers a critique of what he sees as the 'extreme conventionalism' of Nelson Goodman's stance (see the discussion of iconicity in Chapter 1), stressing that 'the so-called conventions of the visual image [vary] according to the relative ease or difficulty with which they can be learned' (1994, 283) – a notion familiar from the Peircean ranking of sign relations in terms of relative conventionality.

Invisible editing

Semioticians often refer to 'reading' film or television – a notion that may seem strange since the meaning of filmic images appears not to need decoding at all. When we encounter a shot in which someone is looking off screen, we usually interpret the next shot as what he or she is looking at. Consider the following example offered by Ralph Rosenblum, a major professional film editor. In an initial shot, 'a man awakens suddenly in the middle of the night, bolts up in bed, stares ahead intensely, and twitches his nose'. If we then cut to 'a room where two people are desperately fighting a billowing blaze, the viewers realize that through clairvoyance, a warning dream, or the smell of smoke, the man in bed has become aware of danger'. Alternatively, if we cut from the first shot to 'a distraught wife defending her decision to commit her husband to a mental institution, they will understand that the man in bed is her husband and that the dramatic tension will surround the couple'. If it's a Hitchcock movie 'the juxtaposition of the man and the wife will immediately raise questions in the viewers' minds about foul play on the part of the woman'. This form of editing may alert us not only to a link between the two consecutive shots but in some cases to a genre. If we cut to an image of clouds drifting before the full moon, we know that we can expect a 'wolf-man' adventure (Rosenblum and Karen 1979, 2).

Such interpretations are not 'self-evident': they are a feature of a filmic editing code. Having internalized such codes at a very young age, we then cease to be conscious of their existence. Once we know the code, decoding it is almost automatic and the code retreats to invisibility (a key to its effectiveness). The convention just described is known as an *eyeline match* and it is part of the dominant editing code in film and television narrative which is referred to as 'the continuity system' or as 'invisible editing' (Reisz and Millar 1972; Bordwell *et al.* 1988, Chapter 16). While minor elements within the code have been modified over time, most of the main elements are still much the same now as when they were developed many decades ago. This code was originally developed in Hollywood feature films but most narrative films and television dramas now routinely employ it. Editing supports rather than dominates the narrative: the story and the behaviour of its characters are the centre of attention. While nowadays there may be cuts every few seconds, these are traditionally intended to be unobtrusive. The technique gives the impression that the edits are always required and are motivated by the events in the reality that the camera is recording rather than the result of a desire to tell a story in a particular way. The seamlessness convinces us of its realism, but the code consists of an integrated system of technical conventions. These conventions serve to assist viewers in transforming the two-dimensional screen into a plausible three-dimensional world in which they can become absorbed.

Another traditional cinematic convention is the use of the *establishing shot*: soon after a cut to a new scene we are given a long shot of it, allowing us to survey the overall space – followed by closer 'cut-in' shots focusing on details of the scene. Re-establishing shots are used when needed, as in the case of the entry of a new character. Another key convention involved in helping the viewer to make sense of the spatial organization of a scene is the so-called *180° rule*. Successive shots are not shown from both sides of the 'axis of action' since this would produce apparent changes of direction on screen. For instance, traditionally, a character moving right to left across the screen in one shot is not shown moving left to right in the next shot. This helps to establish where the viewer is in relation to the action. In separate shots of speakers in a dialogue, one speaker always looks left while the other looks right. Even in telephone conversations the characters are oriented as if facing each other.

In *point-of-view (POV) shots*, the camera is placed (usually briefly) in the spatial position of a character to provide a subjective point of view. This is often in the form of alternating shots between two characters – a technique known as *shot/reverse-shot*. Once the 'axis of action' has been established, the alternation of shots with reverse-shots allows the viewer to glance back and forth at the participants in a dialogue (*matched shots* are used in which the shot-size and framing of the subject is similar). In such sequences, some of these shots are *reaction shots*. All of the techniques described so far reflect the goal of ensuring that the same characters are always in the same parts of the screen.

Because this code foregrounds the narrative, it employs what are called *motivated cuts*: changes of view or scene occur only when the action requires it and the viewer expects it. When cuts from one distance and/or angle to another are made, they are normally *matches on action*: cuts are usually made when the subject is *moving*, so that viewers are sufficiently distracted by the action to be unaware of the cut. Within this code there is a studious avoidance of *jump-cuts*: the so-called *30° rule* is that a shot of the same subject as the previous shot must differ in camera angle by at least 30° (otherwise it will feel to the viewer like an apparently pointless shift in position).

This long-established cinematic editing code has become so familiar to us that we no longer consciously notice its conventions until they are broken. Indeed, it seems so natural that some will feel that it closely reflects phenomenal reality and thus find it hard to accept it as a code at all. Do we not mentally 'cut' from one image to another all of the time in everyday visual perception? This case seems strongest when all that is involved is a shift corresponding to a turn of our head or a refocusing of our eyes (Reisz and Millar 1972, 213–16). But of course many cuts would require us to change our viewing position. A common response to this – at least if we limit ourselves to moderate changes of angle or distance and ignore changes of scene – is to say that the editing technique represents a reasonable analogy with the normal mental processes involved in everyday perception. A cut to close-up can thus be seen to reflect as well as direct a purposive shift in attention. Of course, when the shot shifts so radically that it would be a physical impossibility to imitate this in everyday life, then the argument by perceptual analogy breaks down. Cuts reflect such shifts more often than not; only fleetingly does film editing closely reflect the perceptual experience of 'being there' in person. But of course a gripping narrative may already have led to our 'suspension of disbelief'. We thus routinely and unconsciously grant the film-maker the same 'dramatic licence' with which we are familiar not only from the majority of films that we watch but also from analogous codes employed in other media – such as theatre, the novel, or the comic-strip.

For an argument questioning the interpretive importance of a cinematic editing code and emphasizing real-life analogies, see the lively and interesting book by Paul Messaris entitled *Visual Literacy* (1994, 71ff.). However, his main focus of attack is on the stance that the cinematic editing code is *totally arbitrary* – a position which few would defend. Clearly these techniques were designed where possible to be analogous to familiar codes so that they would quickly become invisible to viewers once they were habituated to them. Messaris argues that context is more important than code; it is likely that where the viewer is in doubt about the meaning of a specific cut, interpretation may be aided by applying knowledge either from other representational codes (such as the logic of the narrative) or from relevant social codes (such as behavioural expectations in analogous situations in everyday life). The interpretation of film draws on knowledge of multiple codes. Adopting a semiotic approach to cinematic editing is not simply to acknowledge the importance of conventions and conventionality but to highlight the process of naturalization involved in the 'editing out' of what 'goes without saying'.

The emphasis given to *visual* codes by most theorists may derive from a Western tendency to privilege the visual over other channels. We need to remind ourselves that it is not only the visual image which is mediated, constructed, and codified in the various media – in film, television, and radio, this also applies to *sound*. Film and television are not simply visual media but *audio-visual* media. Even where the mediated character of the visual is acknowledged, there is a tendency for sound to be regarded as largely unmediated. But codes are involved in the choice and positioning of microphones, the use of particular equipment for recording, editing, and reproduction, the use of diegetic sound (ostensibly emanating from the action in the story) versus non-diegetic sound (such as a musical soundtrack), direct versus post-synchronous (dubbed) recording, simulated sounds, and so on (Altman 1992; Stam 2000, 212–23). In the dominant Hollywood tradition, conventional sound codes included features such as:

- diegesis: sounds should be relevant to the story;
- hierarchy: dialogue should override background sound;
- seamlessness: no gaps or abrupt changes in sound;
- integration: no sounds without images or vice versa;
- readability: all sounds should be identifiable;
- motivation: unusual sounds should be what characters are supposed to be hearing (Stam 2000, 216–17).

Sound can also assist in making visual editing 'invisible': within the same scene a 'sound-bridge' (carrying the same unbroken sound sequence) is used across a cut from one shot to another, as if there had been no cut at all.

CODIFICATION

To paraphrase Sir Francis Bacon in the epigraph prefacing this book, the subtlety of nature is greater many times over than the subtlety of our attempts to codify it. Reality always eludes our representational codes, or as Richard Dyer (1993, 3) puts it, 'Representation never "gets" reality, which is why human history has produced so many different and changing ways of trying to get it'. The synchronic perspective often associated with structuralism tends to give the impression that codes are static. But codes have origins and they do evolve, and studying their evolution is a legitimate semiotic endeavour. Guiraud argues that there is a gradual process of 'codification' whereby systems of implicit interpretation acquire the status of codes (1975, 41). Codes are dynamic systems which change over time and are thus historically as well as socioculturally situated. Codification is a *process* whereby conventions are established. For instance, Metz (1968) notes how, in Hollywood cinema, the white hat became codified as signifying a 'good' cowboy; eventually this convention became over-used and was abandoned.

In the commercial application of semiotics to market research (where consumer trends are of course a key concern), a distinction has been made between three kinds of consumer codes, based loosely on categories outlined by the British cultural theorist Raymond Williams (1977): dominant codes (the prevailing codes of the present day); residual codes (codes in decline), and emergent codes (Alexander 2000). In structuralist accounts, codes tend to be presented as if they evolve autonomously, but socially oriented semioticians emphasize human agency: as Eco puts it, 'in exchanging messages and texts . . . *people* contribute to the changing of codes' (1976, 152; my emphasis). It is not only in aesthetic contexts that we witness code transgression and code production. Eco adds that there is 'a dialectic between codes and messages, whereby the codes control the emission of messages, but new messages can restructure the codes' (ibid., 161). For those in marketing, this comes as no surprise.

In historical perspective, many of the codes of a new medium evolve from those of related existing media (for instance, many televisual techniques owe their origins to their use in film and photography). New conventions are also developed to match the technical potential of the medium and the uses to which it is put. Some codes are unique to (or at least characteristic of) a specific medium or to closely related media (e.g. 'fade to black' in film and television); others are shared by (or similar in) several media (e.g. scene breaks); and some are drawn from cultural practices that are not tied to a medium (e.g. body language). Some are more specific to particular genres within a medium. Some are more broadly linked either to the domain of science ('logical codes', suppressing connotation and diversity of interpretation) or to that of the arts ('aesthetic codes', celebrating connotation and diversity of interpretation), though such differences are differences of degree rather than of kind.

Whatever the nature of any 'embedded' ideology, it is often claimed that as a consequence of their internalization of the codes of the medium, those born in the age of a new medium such as the Web or mobile communication perceive the world differently from those who grew up without such media. Critics have objected to the degree of technological determinism which is involved in such stances, but such tools and techniques may indeed influence our habits of mind. The subtle phenomenology of new media is worthy of closer attention than is typically accorded to it. Whatever the medium, learning to notice the operation of codes when representations and meanings seem natural, obvious, and transparent is clearly not an easy task. Understanding what semioticians have observed about the operation of codes can help us to denaturalize such codes by making their implicit conventions explicit and amenable to analysis. Semiotics offers us some conceptual crowbars with which to deconstruct the codes at work in particular texts and practices, providing that we can find some gaps or fissures, which offer us the chance to exert some leverage.

LIMITATIONS

Codes cannot account for everything in human culture and communication: social behaviour and textual practices cannot simply be reduced to the operation of semiotic codes. They are not autonomous determinants of human action – historical changes in social and textual patterns attest to the importance of human agency and textual 'transgression'. Even in terms of structure and style, few texts (especially those of enduring importance) can be wholly mapped onto existing generic codes. Unless semioticians wish to restrict themselves to trivial codes of limited scope, they must take into account the possibility that at least some of the most significant codes in human meaning-making may be quite loosely and transitorily defined. Certainly many social codes have no clearly definable boundaries, and the study of human culture requires explorers who are prepared to venture into the shifting sands of border zones as well as beyond them into codically unmapped (and sometimes, perhaps, codically unmappable) territory. However, recognizing the limitations of the concept of *code* does not mean that it has no utility, that there are no recognizable codes, that there is no value in seeking to identify patterns in textual and social practices, or even that codes never appear to exhibit some degree of 'relative autonomy'. Nor, as we will see in the next chapter, does endorsement of the concept necessarily require meaning to be related purely to codes – even in structuralist models of human communication. Nevertheless, a poststructuralist shift within the theoretical discourse of cultural theory from the metaphor of society as a text towards that of society as an image may reflect a change in interpretive emphasis from decoding to inference.

REFLECTIONS

1 A television commercial called *Fish on a Bicycle* is used here to illustrate Stuart Hall's three interpretive codes: dominant, negotiated, and oppositional. Find an example of your own for which you can outline similar interpretive stances.

2 Which 'emblems' (gestures) are interpreted in exactly the same way by all of your friends?

3 Which features of 'body language' are most commonly associated with the stereotypical construction of gender? Can these be regarded as constituting a code?

4 Sol Worth (1981) asserts that 'pictures can't say ain't'. In what ways are pictorial codes used to signify negation (e.g. in social media)?

5 In film, the traditional code of 'invisible editing' (or continuity editing) has increasingly become eroded as an acknowledgement of audience sophistication. What examples of this have struck you?

6 What examples have you spotted of currently dominant, residual, and emergent cultural codes?

7 Before reading further, turn to Figure 6.1, which depicts the etched marks on a plaque, which was attached to a spacecraft launched in 1972. Consider what codes would need to be shared in order for alien beings to understand this message from Earth. What problems might they have in making sense of it? You can compare your own reflections with the commentary.

FURTHER READING

Barthes 1974 and 1977a; Birdwhistell 1971; Bouissac 1998, entries for 'articulation', 'code', 'photography'; Corner 1980; Fiske 1989; Guiraud 1975; Hall 1966; Hall 1973; Henley 1977; Messaris 1982; Mitchell 1987; Morley 1980; Nichols 1981 and 1991; Sebeok 1994b, entries for 'articulation', 'Barthes', 'code', 'photography'; Sontag 1979; Williamson 1978; Worth 1981.

INTERACTIONS

In this chapter, we will consider forms and processes of interaction in semiosis. First, we will explore the issue of what structuralists refer to as the 'encoding' and 'decoding' of texts and the ways in which readers are 'positioned' in this process. Then we will consider *intertextuality* – or the interactions between texts.

MODELS OF COMMUNICATION

In 1972, Pioneer 10, a 'deep-space probe', was launched into inter-stellar space by NASA; attached to the craft (and to the later Pioneer 11) was a plaque bearing the image shown in Figure 6.1. A press release noted the possibility that, during its long journey, the spacecraft might be intercepted by 'intelligent scientifically educated beings'. One of the designers wrote that the plaque was intended to 'convey, in what is hoped is easily understood scientific language, some information on the locale, epoch, and nature of the builders of the spacecraft' (Sagan 1977, 235). Ernst Gombrich (1972, 55–6) wrote an insightful

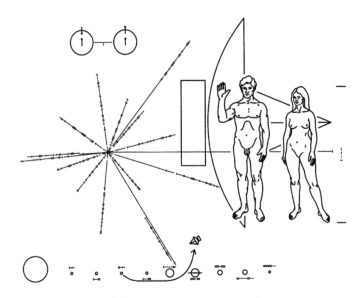

FIGURE 6.1 Pictorial plaque on Pioneer 10 spacecraft (1972)

Source: Produced by the Pioneer Project at NASA Ames Research Center and obtained from NASA's National Space Science Data Center

commentary on this endeavour. He notes that alien beings 'could not possibly get the message'. The most obvious reason is that, on the sensory level, they would have to be tuned to the same narrow range of the electromagnetic spectrum as we are, whereas even on Earth other creatures do not share the same sensory apparatus.

Gombrich's main point is that 'reading an image, like the reception of any other message, is dependent on prior knowledge of possibilities; we can only recognize what we know' (ibid., 56). Communication depends on a shared frame of reference, which includes at least a basic ontology (a conceptualization of entities and their relations); we need to be able to recognize the referents. These alien beings would have no knowledge of what sort of things exist in our world. In the unlikely event that the alien beings shared our visual capabilities, without direct experience of human life they would have no understanding of our 'ways of seeing'. As Wittgenstein declares,

'If a lion could talk, we wouldn't be able to understand it' (1953, 235). Communication also requires a common set of signs in the minds of those seeking to communicate with each other. Since the plaque cannot enable viewers to experience our earthly realities other than through its social and representational codes, their frame of reference would also need to include these codes (which on first contact would be impossible). For alien beings encountering the plaque before encountering human beings and life on Earth, the entire system of representation would be impenetrable.

They could not even begin to understand the plaque without first inferring an intention to communicate (or at least social meaningfulness). They might be able to infer that the scratches are purposeful rather than random and that the plaque is intended to have some function, but simply examining it would not enable them to establish whether this function is communicative, decorative, technical, or even magical. How can we expect alien beings to be able to identify the function of the Pioneer plaque when our archaeological experts can't even agree on the function of prehistoric 'cave art', which features recognizable animals and human figures? Even if a hypothesis of communicative intent were to be explored, no such examination would indicate *how* the markings were intended to be understood. The plaque can't explain itself. It would not even be possible to ascertain whether such a communicative intent is to inform, to persuade, or to please (as art or entertainment). Linear B, a Mycenaean script predating the Greek alphabet by several centuries, could not have been deciphered if linguists had not been able to recognize both its formal similarities to known syllabic systems and its pictorial representations of familiar objects (providing an interpretive starting point for decades of analysis). To alien beings, the Pioneer plaque would simply be a series of meaningless marks without some prior knowledge of the relevant signs, referents, and codes. 'It is this information alone that enables us to separate the code from the message' (Gombrich 1972, 56). The utilization of this prior knowledge is what Gombrich calls 'the beholder's share': the viewer's essential contribution to the process of representation (ibid., 53).

Our knowledge of the affordances of the medium allows us, for instance, to discount issues of scale and the lack of colour in the depiction of recognizable objects. We don't need to think twice about which way up the plaque needs to be: the orientation of the human figures makes this seem obvious. For us, the human figures are immediately identifiable as such within the overall configuration of lines. We are so familiar with a range of visual conventions used to depict human beings that we are rarely conscious of the intervention of representational codes – after all, we routinely decode far more schematic images indicating 'male' or 'female' on toilet doors. The basis of this mode of representation in 'similarity' seems to us to be self-evident. But as Gombrich puts it, 'the innocent eye is a myth' (1977, 252). We have learned how to read such images (and if alien beings actually made contact with us they might learn to do so too).

Our knowledge of representational codes helps us to break the whole ensemble into separate parts: we know which bits seem to 'belong together' even if we don't know exactly what they all represent. This is not purely due to the apparently global invariance of the gestalt theorists' perceptual code (e.g. *good continuity* and *closure* – which enable us, for instance, to fill in the gaps in the large but backgrounded outline of Pioneer itself), but because we can distinguish several cohesive sets of representational conventions with different degrees of modality (even when they are superimposed). Gombrich notes that, in relation to the human figures, we recognize which lines are contours and which are conventional modelling. He adds: 'Our "scientifically educated" fellow creatures in space might be forgiven if they saw the figures as wire constructs with loose bits and pieces hovering weightlessly in between. Even if they deciphered this aspect of the code, what would they make of the woman's right arm that tapers off like a flamingo's neck and beak?' (1972, 56). This latter point will give most readers pause for thought because it draws our attention to the familiar – and therefore normally invisible – convention that this represents the occlusion of one shape by another.

As for social codes, although the man's raised right hand is presumably intended to signify a greeting, this is a nonverbal code which would be alien to those living on large parts of our own planet. This gesture can only be interpreted according to the preferred reading because we have social knowledge of the source of the craft and can infer the likely intentions of its makers: without this knowledge we might assume (from other contexts) that it signified 'stop' (e.g. traffic police); 'go' (as a signal for a train to depart), 'goodbye', or even 'I curse you!'. Furthermore, we might wonder why these figures are naked. It seems a little forward for a first attempt at communicating with strangers. Who are they supposed to be anyway? How can we be sure whether these figures are intended to represent 'humankind', Adam and Eve, 'a man and a woman', 'masculinity and femininity', or 'this man and this woman' (perhaps the designers or senders of the plaque)? They would be most likely to be seen as generic representatives of humanity by those whose culture gave birth to them. Even naked their bodies carry the baggage of white middle-class American culture of the early 1970s (discernible in their hairstyles). If they were intended to be seen as representing the male and female of the species (as in a naturalist's field guide), one might expect them both to be posed fully frontal with their hands by their sides (and to be displayed in greater anatomical detail: why do they lack body hair, for instance?). Embedded in the nonverbal codes of posture and gesture are assumptions about gender which no doubt escaped designers who dwelt in a cultural bubble beyond which all others are aliens. Most notably masculinity is aligned with activity (the male figure initiates contact with his gesture) and femininity with passivity (the female figure poses like a model). Furthermore, male dominance is reinforced by the symbolic priority given to the left-hand side in left-to-right reading and writing systems (an issue explored in Chapter 3).

Relatively few of us have access to the scientific codes that would enable us to interpret the large starburst-like pattern as 'the 14 pulsars of the Milky Way' – it could easily represent an explosion. In case the alien beings would like to track us down to discuss this further, there is a helpful route-map at the bottom of the picture, but since it adopts spatial conventions analogous to those of the London Underground map we probably won't be hearing from them soon, unless that is, they realize that the key to decoding it is the image at the top, which to most of us looks like dumb-bells or eye-glasses, whereas it is apparently intended to represent two hydrogen atoms engaged in 'hyperfine transition'. This symbolic representation is clearly part of a narrowcast code that could only be recognized by the scientific community on Earth. The Rosetta Stone famously provided linguists with a key to deciphering the writings of ancient Egypt, allowing the hieroglyphic and hieratic scripts to be related to the known language of ancient Greek, but on this plaque an alien creature would be unable to recognize a link with anything known. Even the 'universal' scientific symbols and diagrammatic conventions employed are (of course) Earth-bound. As Gombrich points out, even if alien beings cracked the coded 'route-map', 'the trajectory . . . is endowed with a directional arrowhead; it seems to have escaped the designers that this is a conventional symbol unknown to a race that never had the equivalent of bows and arrows' (1972, 56). The message, one fears, seems likely to be 'lost in translation'.

Gombrich's observations on making sense of the Pioneer plaque capture very well the processes of 'decoding' outlined by semioticians in the structuralist tradition. Paired with the term 'encoding', this sometimes has the unfortunate consequence of making the processes of constructing and interpreting texts (visual, verbal, or otherwise) sound too programmatic (implying also that 'the real meaning' is embedded within the text, awaiting decipherment). The Pioneer plaque example shows that reading (or viewing, or listening) requires reference to relevant codes (*relevance* itself requiring inference and hypothesis-testing). We have seen that we need prior knowledge of such codes in order to disembed the message. Although with practice the interpretive process can become transparent (so that it can seem strange to say that pictures require 'reading'), it is clearly a cognitively active process. What is 'meant' is invariably more than what is 'said', so *inference* is required to go 'beyond the information given'. While psychologists refer to the generation of inferences by invoking familiar social and textual 'scripts', semioticians refer to accessing social and representational codes (and sometimes to the modality judgements needed to compare these codes).

In contrast to the notion of interpretation as a cognitively active process, everyday references to communication are based on a 'transmission' model in which a sender transmits a message to a passive receiver – a formula that reduces meaning to explicit or literal 'content' which resides within the text and is delivered like a parcel (Reddy 1979). This model is implicit, for instance, in the Pioneer-plaque designer's reference to the intention to 'convey . . . information'.

Transmission is also the basis of Claude Shannon and Warren Weaver's well-known model of communication (1949), which makes no allowance for the importance of social codes or contexts – though ironically, to criticize that particular model for this reason would be to ignore the context of telephone engineering for which it was developed.

Figure 6.2 shows Saussure's 'speech circuit'. At first glance, it seems to represent a transmission model. However, the social semiotician Paul Thibault (1997) offers a persuasive alternative interpretation. On the evidence from the *Cours*, he argues that the speech circuit does not reflect the common sense 'conduit metaphor' identified by Reddy; nor can it be accurately described as a 'code model' or 'decoding model' (as it is in Sperber and Wilson 1995). In the *Cours*, there is no suggestion of thoughts, ideas, or information being encoded and transmitted to a passive 'decoder'. The circuit needs to be seen in terms of the co-production of meaning rather than the

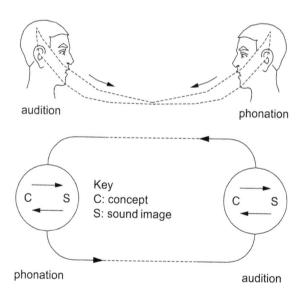

FIGURE 6.2 Saussure's speech circuit

Source: Based on Saussure 1916/1995, 27, 28

communication of pre-established ideas. The interactants already share a socially-learned mental system for associating acoustic images with concepts, and they collaboratively deploy the resources of the language system in a genuinely reciprocal relationship. The Saussurean speech circuit can be seen as representing 'signifying acts' of *parole* which unite 'psychic' (psychological) activity with social meaning.

In 1960, Roman Jakobson proposed his own model of inter-personal verbal communication (see Figure 6.3; cf. Eco 1976, 141). His model was influenced by cybernetics and information theory (including the work of Shannon and Weaver). However, he moved beyond a basic transmission model of communication (which excludes meaning), drawing on work in the 1930s by the German psychologist Karl Bühler. Jakobson outlines what he regards as the six 'constitutive factors . . . in any act of verbal communication' thus:

> The *addresser* sends a *message* to the *addressee*. To be operative the message requires a *context* referred to ('referent' in another, somewhat ambivalent, nomenclature), seizable by the addressee, and either verbal or capable of being verbalized, a *code* fully, or at least partially, common to the addresser and addressee (or in other words, to the encoder and decoder of the message); and finally, a *contact*, a physical channel and psychological connection between the addresser and the addressee, enabling both of them to stay in communication.
>
> (Jakobson 1960, 353)

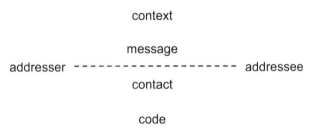

FIGURE 6.3 Jakobson's model of communication

Source: Jakobson 1960, 353

In any speech act, the speaker composes utterances 'out of the word stock supplied by the code' and 'the listener correlates the incoming message with the code common to himself and the speaker' (1956, 71, 33). For Jakobson, a 'code' correlates pre-existing signifieds with predetermined signifiers (a structuralist conception, rejected by the deconstructionists, which is not at all Saussurean). The mediational factors between the *encoder* and the *decoder* in Jakobson's model are: the *message* (the signs), the *contact* (the medium), the *context* (the relevant situational frame), and the *code* (the correlational system). Jakobson's basic visualization of his model does not indicate the relationships between its parts; Figure 6.4 is an attempt to do so (note the overlapping codes *and* contexts of the addresser and the addressee, representing their shared frames of reference). Jakobson established the principle already noted that we cannot make sense of messages (signs which are also chains of signs) without relating them to relevant codes.

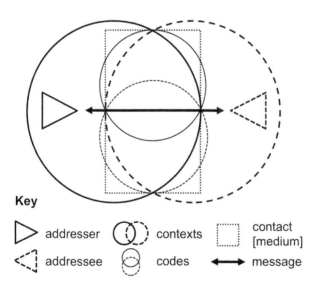

FIGURE 6.4 A revisualization of Jakobson's model

Source: © 2016 Daniel Chandler

In response to Bertrand Russell's point that 'no one can understand the word "cheese" unless he has a nonlinguistic acquaintance with cheese', Jakobson (1958, 261) replied that (likewise) 'the meaning of the word "cheese" cannot be inferred from a nonlinguistic acquaintance with cheddar or with camembert without the assistance of the verbal code'. From a Saussurean perspective, of course, the difference between cheddar and camembert is a difference of values within the language system.

Although Jakobson was greatly influenced by Peirce, he did not, of course, owe his emphasis on encoding and decoding to him. Peirce does refer to the determinative role of 'the community' in interpretation, but one Peircean scholar comments that 'there is no reflection at all, to speak of, on the system to which any individual sign belongs or on the process that produces it . . . His interest is neither in the construction of the message nor in the larger code from which its components are drawn' (Bruss 1978, 93). Jakobson did not derive the concept from Saussure either; there is only one explicit reference in the *Cours* to the speaker's use of 'the language code' (*CLG* 31; 14), and there is no reference there to encoding and decoding. Indeed, insofar as such terms imply pre-existing meanings, they are incompatible with Saussure's model.

CONTEXT

We have already noted that communication requires a shared frame of reference (previously unaccounted for in transmission models of communication), and shared codes clearly function as an interpretive framework. However, Jakobson's model does not account for acts of communication purely in terms of encoding and decoding. It highlights the importance not only of systemic codes but also of the contexts involved. Jakobson argues that the extralinguistic context is as interpretively important as relations within the language system (1956, 75; 1960, 353). All signs appear in a context of use. Although Saussure sees *langue* and *parole* as complementary, the focus of the *Cours* on the language system at the expense of the *use* of language raises interpretive issues. Critics argue that the intended meaning of polysemic utterances cannot be established without reference to the context of use. How do we know what 'duck' signifies on any given occasion: is it a reference to a waterbird or an urgent warning? In nonverbal behaviour the situational context is even more important (Birdwhistell 1971). However, the backgrounding of the contextual use of language within the *Cours* does not mean that it cannot be adequately accounted for (see, for instance, Thibault 1997). In Saussurean terms, *valeur* depends upon the system of *langue* and *signification* upon processes of *parole* (which are tied to particular contexts). Hjelmslev asserts that 'any sign meaning arises in a context, by which we mean a situational context' (1961, 45). Jakobson notes that 'there are two references which serve to interpret the sign – one to the code, and the other to the context' (1956, 75), and insists that 'it is not enough to know the code in order to grasp the message . . . you need to know the context' (1953, 233). Without such knowledge, we would have no idea that something is a sign or what it is a sign of. Without relation to code and/or context, a sign is not a sign, an expression lacks content, a 'message' is an empty form.

We noted in Chapter 4 that the identification of irony requires reference to contextual factors in the form of perceived intent and truth status. As a linguist, Jakobson was initially wary of trespassing too far beyond the notion of linguistic contexts into the more philosophical territory of referentiality. For instance, he notes that 'truth values . . . as far as they are . . . "extralinguistic entities," obviously exceed the bounds of . . . linguistics in general'. Nevertheless, it was clear that he would not seek to exclude from his concerns 'the question of relations between the word and the world' (1960, 351). 'Speech events' take place in the social world, and Jakobson was a linguist who emphasized the social functions of language. He quickly recognized the importance of both 'the place occupied by the given messages within the context of surrounding messages . . . and . . . the relation of the given message to the universe of discourse' (1968a, 697).

The philosophical concept of a *universe of discourse* refers to a semantic frame of reference shared by participants in an act of communication. Jakobson declared that 'Linguistics is likely to explore all possible problems of relation between discourse and the "universe of discourse": what of this universe is verbalized by a given discourse and how it is verbalized' (1960, 351). Later he ventured further, noting that 'the sometimes equivalent term "context" means not only the verbalized context but also the partly or nonverbalized context' (1973, 319). By 1972 he felt able to issue a unequivocal declaration on this issue:

> Fourteen years ago [1958], Quine [the American philosopher] and I agreed diplomatically that the signified (*signatum*) belonged to linguistics and the referent (*designatum*) to logic. Now I think that the referent also belongs to linguistics . . . This does not mean to linguistics only, but it has a linguistic aspect, namely, what we call contextual meaning. The general meaning belongs to semantics; the contextual meaning, given by the whole context, by the universe of discourse, is also a linguistic fact.
>
> (Jakobson 1973, 320)

Elsewhere, he is even more explicit – adding that contextual meaning included *situational* meanings (1972, 44). Communication depends on an adequate overlap in the participants' implicit definitions of the situation in which it takes place. Effective communication also requires shared knowledge of normative roles and purposes in 'stock situations'.

In definitively including context as well as code, Jakobson's model moves beyond the focus of the *Cours*. It is important for general semiotics because it is not restricted to internal relations within the semiotic system. Jakobson's model supports not only the symbolic mode featured in both the Saussurean and the Peircean models but also the referential character of Peirce's iconic and indexical relations. However problematic Jakobson's model of the sign may be, his model of communication constitutes a conceptual bridge between the two major semiotic traditions (see Figure 7.1). While the determination of meaning in the Saussurean model depends upon the system of relations within a code and in the Peircean model upon a referential context, the Jakobsonian model seeks to account for both.

A model of communication that incorporates both code and context underlines the interpretive importance of the processes of decoding and inference (even though neither of these processes are

FIGURE 6.5 Decoding and inference in sign relations

Source: © 2016 Daniel Chandler

actually made explicit within it). It may be helpful to envisage the interpretation of sign relations as a spectrum in relation to the relative importance of these processes (see Figure 6.5; cf. Table 1.11). Understanding signs and messages requires prior knowledge, but the extent to which this is knowledge of representational conventions and/or real world situations is variable. In general, the more symbolic the mode, the more decoding is required; the more indexical it is, the greater the dependence on inference.

All communication and representation depends on the interaction between code and context and involves both decoding and inference. Structuralists give interpretive priority to decoding while 'relevance theorists' give priority to inference (Sperber and Wilson 1995). Relevance theorists dismiss a 'decoding model' of communication in favour of a cognitivist 'inference model' (sometimes even dismissing semiotics in favour of pragmatics). Interpretation is not simply a matter of 'decoding': understanding also requires inference. However, in my own view, seeking to explain communication (or representation) in terms of inference at the expense of decoding is linked to the fallacy of regarding comprehension (or perception) as taking place prior to interpretation. I am convinced by the arguments that these processes are inseparable.

There is no doubt that inferring communicative intentions involves the pragmatic assessment of *relevance*. For the British philosopher of language, Paul Grice (1975), the assumption that utterances are relevant is one of the basic maxims of cooperative conversation, and the cognitive scientists Dan Sperber and Deirdre Wilson (1995) argue that this assumption is fundamental in communication. Establishing what can be taken for granted involves a dynamic cognitive process of ruling out irrelevant 'noise' and identifying which representational codes and ways of framing the situational context lead to the most plausible and coherent interpretation. This process is largely automatic when the situation and the code are fairly standardized (for the parties involved), as in much of everyday interaction. It should be added that relevance is relative to a point-of-view, so in social interaction establishing communicative relevance involves not only cognitive processes but also situational negotiation (which of course is tied to power relations).

In information theory, codes are often described as 'context-free' sets of rules, but semiotic codes are no more context-free than contexts are code-free. The relative openness of signs to interpretation depends on both representational code and situational context. Within the *Highway Code* (with which all British drivers are required to be familiar), a road sign consisting of a black S-bend shape within a red triangle functions as an iconic symbol which warns of a double bend in the road ahead. In its proper (indexical) context, its meaning is clear to the intended audience, but if the same sign were to be encountered in an art gallery it could reasonably be construed as a work of art, the meaning of which is entirely open to interpretation (though viewers often try to infer the artist's intentions). Torn away from its intended location and hung by a teenager on their bedroom wall, it loses its normative locational indexicality and is likely to be interpreted as a marked 'statement' symbolizing rebellious youth. In such cases, it may seem reasonable to claim that context may function as the ultimate anchor. The meaning of a sign depends on the code with which it is interpreted, but we cannot identify what might be relevant codes without knowing the situational context. When we are seeking to establish plausible interpretations of utterances and representations, decontextualization is a legitimate criticism. Arbitrary contexts play havoc with meaning. Even in surrealistic art, viewers search for the possible significance of particular recontextualizations. It is a fundamental principle in pragmatics that meaning is 'context-bound', but even the context of the 'here and now' is clearly not a shared frame of reference for interpreters and message-makers who are not co-present.

Context cannot be divorced from code. Linguistic categorization creates contexts. 'Situations' do not exist in the world, but only within systems of classification. We cannot encounter 'the same context' on different occasions, but we do broadly codify culturally shared understandings of common situations in terms of functional equivalence (shopping, dining out, and so on). Such standardized situations are closely associated with particular codes, and vice versa: our recognition of one generates expectations of the other. The relative dominance of these factors is dynamically variable. Context is not a fixed point of reference 'within' which meaning may be determined; contextual frames shift from moment to moment. Context is not a determinative 'given': it requires interpretation just like any other set of signs (Culler 1988, ix). It is a very slippery term, the scope of which is frequently taken for granted – as historical, sociocultural, individual, situational, representational, and so on (Chandler and Munday 2011, 72–3). For instance, 'context' is prominent in Marxist theory, where it refers primarily to socioeconomic conditions. 'All contexts have levels' (Wilden 1972, xxiii). We have already encountered (in Chapter 2) the 'Thomas Theorem' in which what is real in social interaction depends on how a situation is defined (Thomas and Thomas 1928, 573). In communication and representation, context depends on a frame of reference and a point of view. Any situation can be reconstrued: there are multiple ways of contextualizing any situation. 'Context' is 'a context' rather than 'the context'. As the anthropologist Edmund Leach observes, 'social behaviour is "coded" so that it makes statements about what the social situation is and where the actor is positioned in that social situation' (1982, 177). We need to ask *whose* contexts we are referring to in any given instance, and the extent to which these are shared. Successful communication depends on a (sufficiently) shared definition of the situation (only in highly technical contexts could such definitions come close to being identical). Clearly those from different cultural and subcultural backgrounds may have very different understandings of particular situations, but even at the level of our physical surroundings, what most of us see as objects would not be what a scientist would see at a molecular level. Furthermore, in 'constitutive models' of communication neither context nor code is predetermined – both are dynamically constructed in the course of communicative interaction. Neither constitutes a fixed point of reference, and code-switching is dynamically matched by context-switching (or recontextualization).

This is not a counsel of despair in the determination of meaning: most of the time we manage remarkably well to infer appropriate frames of reference in relation to texts and utterances. The point here is simply that context is not as determinative as is often supposed: it can be as loosely defined as the loosest of codes (it is unbounded and never completely specifiable), and (as with codes) an over emphasis on context veers towards relativism. Such is the interaction between code and context that no clearcut distinction can be made between them (see Figure 6.6). It can indeed be instructive to reframe 'situational contexts' and 'representational codes' as 'situational codes' and 'representational contexts'. Situational contexts are not 'fragments of reality' but are themselves coded (as in stock situations). There is nothing to stop pedestrians from choosing to regard road signs as artworks (a form of code-switching) in the interests of 'making the familiar strange', though a driver charged with dangerous driving

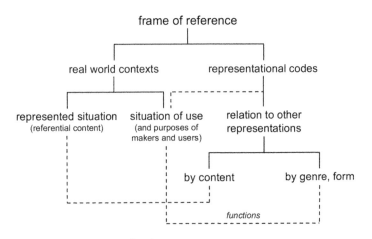

FIGURE 6.6 Context and code in representation

Source: © 2016 Daniel Chandler

through such 'aberrant decoding' would get short shrift in court. There are circumstances in which we cannot establish a situational context until we have identified the code to which signs belong. For instance, in archaeology traces of an identifiable code are often essential in reconstructing the original context.

Karl Bühler published his 'organon model' of linguistic communication in the early 1930s, identifying three basic communicational functions: representational, expressive, and conative (Bühler 1934; Innis 1982). Jakobson adopted Bühler's functions (the representational function becoming the referential function) and added the poetic, phatic, and metalingual functions (see Table 6.7). Jakobson proposed that each of the six factors in his own model (context, addresser, addressee,

type	oriented towards	function	example
referential	context	imparting information	It's raining.
expressive	addresser	expressing feelings or attitudes	It's bloody pissing down again!
conative	addressee	influencing behaviour	Wait here till it stops raining!
phatic	contact	establishing or maintaining social relationships	Nasty weather again, isn't it?
metalingual	code	referring to the nature of the interaction (e.g. genre)	This is the weather forecast.
poetic	message	foregrounding textual features	It droppeth as the gentle rain from heaven.

TABLE 6.7 Jakobson's six functions of language

Source: © 2016 Daniel Chandler

contact, code, and message) determines a different function of language (1960, 353). Unlike the basic transmission model, Jakobson's model thus avoids the reduction of language to purely informational communication (although reducing language to communication neglects the logically prior function of categorization; see Whorf 1956, 55 and Ellis 1993). Though one of the potential communicative functions is referential (or informational), this function is not always foregrounded in texts and discourse. Jakobson argues that in any given situation several functions may operate in a 'hierarchical order', but that a dominant function influences the general character of the 'message'. For instance, the *poetic* function (which is intended to refer to any creative use of language rather than simply to poetry) focuses on the message for its own sake. It highlights 'the palpability of signs', undermining any sense of natural or transparent representation (1960, 356). In this aesthetic function, we must expect the unexpected: 'messages' are far less predictable and meaning less determinable than in the referential function (see also Figure 4.1). This code-transgressive and code-productive feature leads many to deny that it is appropriate to apply the concepts of 'communication' or 'information' to art. The distinctive features of aesthetic codes are lost in translation. The *metalingual* (or metacommunicational) function (communication about communication, messages about messages) reminds us that communication operates on several levels, the code operating at a higher logical level than the message. Wilden (1972, 166) suggests that the referential (cognitive) and metalingual functions are digital modes, the others being analogical.

In Jakobson's model, messages and meanings cannot be isolated from functional factors. He adds that 'the question of presence and hierarchy of those basic functions which we observe in language ... must be applied also to the other semiotic systems ... A parallel investigation of verbal, musical, pictorial, choreographic, theatrical, and cinematographic arts belongs to the most imperative and fruitful duties of semiotic science' (1970, 458; see Lévi-Strauss 1969, 29–30 on music and Ashwin 1989 on graphic design).

As we have seen, Jakobson allocates a role for a situational context and stresses the importance of *parole* – the contingency of 'speech events'. However, his embedded *functions* are systemic representations of 'frozen' human purposes and he did not address the dynamic, shifting purposes of those involved in particular acts of communication or the social frameworks within which communication occurs. Each communicative function implies normative expectations about the complementary roles of the parties involved. For instance, in a referential function their expected roles are respectively to inform and to understand, while in the case of the conative function they are to persuade and to decide. 'In a sense, the participants enter into a communication relationship with a kind of contract governing their performance . . . When we ask road directions we expect a simple and helpful answer . . . The person who is directing us expects us to listen carefully and to be grateful for what he has told us' (Schramm 1973, 44). Relationships may precede the interaction as social roles or established power relations and/or be established or modified (at least temporarily) by it. Jakobson's theoretical frameworks opened up new pathways but he left to sociolinguists and socio-semiotic researchers the task of investigating specific, socially situated acts of communication: this, in practice, was beyond the scope of even the most radical of the original structuralist linguists.

While these earlier models had focused on interpersonal communication, the British sociologist Stuart Hall, in an essay entitled 'Encoding/decoding' (1973), proposes a model of mass communication which highlights the importance of signifying practices within relevant codes. A televisual text emerges as 'meaningful' discourse from processes of encoding and decoding. Each of these processes involves 'meaning structures', which consist of 'frameworks of knowledge', 'relations of production', and 'technical infrastructure'. Despite the apparent symmetry, Hall rejects textual determinism, noting that 'decodings do not follow inevitably from encodings' (1973, 136). Hall gives a significant role to the 'decoder' as well as to the 'encoder' and presents communication as a socially contingent practice. Mass media codes offer their readers social identities that some may adopt as their own. However, readers do not necessarily accept such codes. Where those involved in communicating do not share common codes and social positions, decodings are likely to be different from the encoder's intended meaning. Umberto Eco (1965) uses the term 'aberrant decoding' to refer to a text that has been decoded by means of a different code from that used to encode it. As we noted in Chapter 5, Hall incorporated into his model a series of alternative, socially-inflected 'reading positions' for decoders.

This necessarily brief review of key structuralist models of communication has shown that while systemic codes (and the *processes* of encoding and decoding) are a central feature, post-Saussurean semiotics also came to recognize the importance of contexts (including social contexts) in the determination of meanings. Implicit in such models (for instance in the reference of Jakobson's functions to the roles and modes of relation of the 'addresser' and the 'addressee') there are also implications for the construction of social identities. In the structuralist tradition, through the processes of human communication and representation, the structures of language and texts came to be seen by some cultural theorists as involved in 'positioning the subject'.

THE POSITIONING OF THE SUBJECT

While the relation between system and usage is a key issue in linguistics, the binary of structure–agency is central in sociological theory (Jenks 1998). This enduring debate can be framed as a spectrum of views ranging from structural determinism (human agency being subordinated to social structures) to social determinism (vice versa). Such relations can be seen as dynamically variable, and softer stances refer to *constraints* rather than *determination*. Social institutions (such as the family, the state, and the law) are the most obvious structures, and it is such social structures that individuals are most likely to experience as constraining their actions. Other structures, such as languages, media, and genres may seem more like tools, which we can subordinate to our purposes, but in subtle ways we can be shaped (and our purposes modified) by all sorts of structures, often beyond our conscious awareness. This was a key insight of the Canadian media theorist, Marshall McLuhan (1911–80) in relation to media and technologies, and we do not need to subscribe to 'hard determinism' to acknowledge such influences (Chandler 1995b). Like metaphors, structures facilitate some possibilities while restricting others (which is not necessarily disempowering).

As an antidote to dominant myths of individualism, it is instructive to be reminded that individuals are not unconstrained in their construction of meanings. Common sense suggests that 'I' am a unique individual with a stable, unified identity and ideas of my own. Semiotics can help us to realize that such notions are created and maintained by our engagement with sign systems: our sense of identity is established through signs. We derive a sense of self from drawing upon conventional, pre-existing repertoires of signs and codes, which we did not ourselves create. As the sociologist Stuart Hall puts it, our 'systems of signs . . . *speak us* as much as we speak in and through them' (1977, 328). We are thus the subjects of our sign systems rather than being simply instrumental 'users' who are fully in control of them. While we are not puppets who are determined by semiotic systems we are shaped by them far more than we realize.

Structuralism attributes agency to the language system rather than to the individual – wholly contrary to the *Cours* (Holdcroft 1991, 154; Thibault 1997, 48). Readers who feel immune to the influence of linguistic structures may care to reflect on how 'menu-driven' much of our everyday interaction can be. Raymond Tallis suggests that 'most of our talk consists of standard phrases and responses (so much that an original phrase stands out)' (1995, 209). Jonathan Culler remarks that even in our most intimate interactions, 'I love you' is really a quotation (1983, 120). Even novelists report that the structures that they create for themselves limit their options, and that as they proceed, their options narrow (Chandler 1995a, Chapter 5). Although all structures limit options, the structures of natural language are less restrictive than those of media and genres with more specific functions. In the design of technological structures for a broad user base, options are frequently restricted in the interests of ease of use. However, in limiting our options, structures can be seen as embodying ideologies (Chandler 1990). For instance, in communication networks such as the internet, different network topologies have implications for information flow, gatekeeping, influence, and power relations (Chandler and Munday 2016).

Building our own structures is enabling and empowering but it can also be technically demanding. Until the early 1990s, the BASIC programming language was routinely built into the firmware of personal computers; the discontinuance of this practice discouraged users from being makers. Later, the structural restrictions of 'user-friendly' Web 2.0 also excluded amateurs from webpage construction. In the 1990s online personal profiles were 'personal home pages', the design of which was controlled by their makers rather than limited to standardized templates (Chandler and Roberts-Young 1999, Chandler 2006). Although such designs were not always elegant and the user-base was limited, this unregulated regime encouraged diversity and reflexive self-presentation. Social media (including blogs) have massified the user-base and fostered its interconnectedness through obliging users to operate within prefabricated templates. As with all shared codes, this foregrounds content over form but deprives users of the expressive potential of formal diversity. Such platforms offer us convenient communication hubs but they involve a form of social engineering which reductively positions users within their structures and sorts content beyond their own control using algorithms, which serve commercial agendas. The database structure of Facebook (like many template-driven profile sites) limits users to 'multiple-choice identities' and a 'one size fits all' format, semi-automating self-presentation (Lanier 2011, 48ff.). Users of social media are encouraged to become 'curators' and distributors of fragments of commoditized content, and to inhabit ideological 'echo chambers' of like-minded people. Such structures are not irresistible, though having built up a personal presence within a site such as Facebook is a strong disincentive to seeking alternatives. Declining to be boxed, critical users can still use them to communicate in their own distinctive ways. Used reflectively by such users, social media have the pro-social potential to become tools of democratic engagement (Chandler 2016). Structures cannot be divorced from the pragmatics of use.

In cultural theory, a mediating concept in the structure–agency debate is that of 'subject position'. 'The positioning of the subject' is a structuralist notion that is absent from the *Cours* and from early structuralist discourse. The terms 'subject' and 'position' need some initial explanation. In 'theories of subjectivity' a distinction is made between 'the subject' and 'the individual'. While the *individual* is an actual person, the *subject* is a set of what would traditionally have been called 'roles', defined by primary sociocultural categories (e.g. in terms of class, age, gender, and ethnicity). In contrast to the liberal humanist emphasis on 'free' individuals with pre-given essences (such as talent or laziness), in structuralist cultural theory human subjectivity is 'constituted' (constructed) by pre-given structures. Subjects can be seen as relational perspectives which are adopted and constructed through the use of signs in texts and discourse (teacher/student, father/daughter, and so on). Jacques Lacan undermined the traditional notion of a unified and consistent subject. The individual can occupy multiple subject positions, some of them contradictory, and 'identity' can be seen as the contextual interaction of subject positions. This fluid, processual, and dynamic conception of 'selves' and 'identities' is what leads constructionists to favour the term 'subject position' over the modernist notion of 'role' (Davies and Harré 1990).

'Positioning theory' has been widely adopted by cultural theorists. According to theorists of textual positioning, understanding the meaning of a text obliges the reader to adopt a subject position in relation to it. For instance, to understand an advertisement, we would have to adopt the identity of a consumer who desired the advertised product. Some theorists argue that this position already exists within the structure and codes of the text. 'Narratives or images always imply or construct a position or positions from which they are to be read or viewed' (Johnson 1996, 101). What Colin MacCabe (1974) famously called the 'classic realist text' is structured to effect interpretive closure: contradictions are suppressed and the reader is encouraged to adopt a position from which everything seems 'obvious'. This stance assumes both that a text is homogeneous and that it has only one meaning – that intended by its makers – whereas contemporary theorists contend that there may be several alternative (even contra-dictory) subject-positions from which a text may make sense. While these may sometimes be anticipated by the author, they are not necessarily built into the text itself. Not every reader is the 'ideal reader' envisaged by the producer(s) of the text. In structuralist discourse, 'the positioning of the subject' implies a 'necessary "subjection" to the text' (Johnson 1996), and is thus problematic since there is always some freedom of interpretation. We may for instance choose to regard a poorly translated set of instructions for assembling flat-pack furniture as a text constructed purely for our amusement.

The French neo-Marxist philosopher Louis Althusser (1918–90) was the first ideological theorist to give prominence to the notion of the subject. For him, ideology is a system of representations of reality offering individuals certain subject positions. Ideology turns individuals into subjects. Althusser famously declared that 'what is represented in ideology is . . . not the system of real relations which govern the existence of individuals, but the imaginary relation of these individuals to the real relations in which they live' (Althusser 1971, 155). Individuals are called into being as subjects through the ideological mechanism, which he calls *interpellation* – literally, being addressed or 'hailed' (ibid., 174). For instance, if a police officer tells you to 'Stop where you are!', you become a suspect; if a salesperson asks, 'Can I help you?', you become a customer (Gergen 2009b, 38).

The Althusserian concept of interpellation is used by Marxist media theorists to explain the political function of mass media texts. According to this view, the subject (viewer, listener, reader) is constituted by the text, and the power of the mass media resides in their ability to position the subject in such a way that their representations are taken to be reflections of everyday reality. Such structuralist framings of positioning reflect a stance of *textual determinism*, which has been challenged by contemporary social semioticians who tend to emphasize the 'polysemic' nature of texts (their plurality of meanings) together with the diversity of their use and interpretation by different audiences ('multiaccentuality'). While resistance at the level of the message is always possible, resistance at the level of the code is generally much more difficult when the code is a dominant one. The familiarity of the codes in realist texts (especially photographic and filmic texts) leads us to routinely 'suspend our disbelief' in the form (even if not necessarily in the manifest content). Recognition of the familiar (in the guise of the natural) repeatedly confirms our conventional ways of seeing and thus reinforces our sense of self, while at the same time invisibly contributing to its *construction*. 'When we say "I see (what the image means)" this act simultaneously installs us in a place of knowledge and slips us into place as subject to this meaning

. . . All the viewer need do is fall into place as subject' (Nichols 1981, 38). Falling into place in a realist text can be a pleasurable experience that few would wish to disrupt with reflective analysis (which would throw the security of our sense of self into question). According to this perspective, where this occurs we are seduced into submitting freely to the ideological processes which construct our sense of ourselves as free-thinking individuals.

A primary representational code involved in the construction of the subject is that of *genre* (discussed at length in Chapter 5). Genres are ostensibly neutral, functioning to make *form* (the conventions of the genre) more transparent to those familiar with the genre, foregrounding the distinctive *content* of individual texts. Certainly genre provides an important frame of reference that helps readers to identify, select, and interpret texts (as well as helping writers to compose economically within the medium). However, a genre can also be seen as embodying certain values and ideological assumptions and as seeking to establish a particular worldview. Changes in genre conventions may both reflect and help to shape the dominant ideological climate of the time. Some Marxist commentators see genre as an instrument of social control which reproduces the dominant ideology. Within this perspective, the genre is seen as positioning the audience in order to naturalize the reassuringly conservative ideologies which are typically embedded in the text. Certainly, genres and narrative structures are far from being ideologically neutral and analysts cannot ignore the politics of representation. Different genres produce different positionings of the subject which are reflected in the modes of address employed within generic texts. Thus, over and above the specific content of the individual text, genres can be seen as involved in the construction of their readers.

Film and television add a narrative dimension to the positioning of the subject, incorporating dominant narrative devices specific to filmic media. Film theorists refer to the use of 'suture' (surgical stitching) – the 'invisible editing' of shot relationships which seeks to foreground the narrative and mask the ideological processes which shape the subjectivity of viewers. Some Lacanian theorists argue that, in the context of conventional narrative (with its possibilities of identification and opposition), the unique character of the cinema (e.g. watching a large bright screen in the dark) offers us the seductive sense of a 'return' to the pre-linguistic 'mirror-phase' of the 'imaginary' in which the self is constructed (Nichols 1981, 300).

In order to communicate, a producer of any text must make some assumptions about an intended audience; reflections of such assumptions may be discerned in the text (advertisements offer particularly clear examples of this). 'A sign . . . addresses somebody,' Charles Peirce declares (CP 2.228). Signs 'address' us within particular codes. For instance, a genre is a semiotic code within which we are 'positioned' as 'ideal readers' through the use of particular 'modes of address'. Modes of address can be defined as the formal ways in which relations between addresser and addressee are constructed in a text.

MODES OF ADDRESS

Linguists generally regard modes of address as a matter of 'register' (a variety of language defined situationally) rather than of genre (a text type typically defined structurally), but these perspectives are closely inter-related in the construction of text–reader relations in any medium (diverse definitions are reviewed in Lee 2001).

The *modes of address* employed by texts are influenced primarily by three interrelated factors:

- *textual context*: the conventions of the genre and of a specific syntagmatic structure;
- *social context* (e.g. the presence or absence of the producer of the text, the scale and social composition of the audience, institutional and economic factors); and
- *technological constraints* (features of the medium employed).

Modes of address differ in their directness, their formality and their narrative point of view. The various narrative points of view in literature are as follows:

- *third-person* narration
  - omniscient narrator
    - intrusive (e.g. Dickens)
    - self-effacing (e.g. Flaubert)

- selective point of view of character(s) presented by self-effacing narrator (e.g. Henry James)
- *first-person* narration: narrated directly by a character (e.g. Salinger's *Catcher in the Rye*).

In television and film drama, the camera typically offers the viewer a relatively detached perspective on a scene which is independent of any single character in the narrative. This can be seen as resembling the 'third-person' narrative style of an omniscient and self-effacing narrator – which of course does not necessarily entail such a narrator 'revealing all' to the viewer (indeed, in genres such as the 'whodunit' and the thriller the positioning of the subject is most obvious in relation to what information is withheld and when it is disclosed). Camera treatment is called 'subjective' when the camera shows us events as if from a particular participant's visual point of view (encouraging viewers to identify with that person's way of seeing events or even to feel like an eye-witness to the events themselves). This first-person style in filmic media is rarely sustained, however (or we would never see that character). The point of view is *selective* when we are mainly concerned with a single character but the camerawork is not subjective. Voice-overs are sometimes used for first-person narration by a character in a drama; they are also common as a third-person narrative mode in genres such as documentary. Where first-person commentary shifts from person to person within a text, this produces 'polyvocality' (multiple voices) – contrasting strongly with the interpretive omniscience of 'univocal' narrative, which offers a single reading of an event. Where the agency of a narrator is backgrounded, events or facts deceptively seem to 'speak for themselves'.

Modes of address also differ in their *directness*. In linguistic codes, this is related to whether 'you' are explicitly addressed, which, in literary modes, is quite rare. In Laurence Sterne's highly 'unconventional' novel *Tristram Shandy* (1760), one chapter begins thus: 'How could you, Madam, be so inattentive in reading the last chapter?' (vol. 1, ch. 20). Realist fiction avoids such alienatory strategies. In representational visual codes, directness is related to whether or not a depicted person appears to look directly at the viewer (in the case of television, film and photography, via the camera lens). A direct gaze simulates interaction with each individual viewer (an impossibility, of course, outside one-to-one communicative media, but a feature of 'cam-to-cam' communication on the internet or in video-conferences). In film and television, directness of address is reflected in linguistic codes as well as camerawork. Films and (especially) television programmes within the documentary genre frequently employ a disembodied voice-over which directly addresses the audience, as do television com-mercials. On television, directness of address is also a matter of the extent to which participants look directly into the camera lens. In this way too, commercials frequently include direct address. As for programmes, in a book entitled *The Grammar of Television*, an industry professional warned: 'Never let a performer look straight into the lens of a camera unless it is necessary to give the impression that he is speaking directly to the viewer personally' (Davis 1960, 54). In television programmes, a direct mode of address is largely confined to newsreaders, weather forecasters, presenters, and interviewers – which is why it seems so strange on the rare occasions when we notice an interviewee glancing at the camera lens. In short, people from outside the television industry are seldom allowed to talk to us directly on television. The head of state or the leader of a political party are among the few outsiders allowed to look directly at the viewer, and then typically only within special genres such as a party political broadcast or an 'address to the nation'. Direct address reflects the power of the addresser and typically signifies 'authority'. It is rare in the cinema, and when it is used it tends to be for comic effect. *Indirect address* is the principal mode employed in conventional narrative, masking authorial agency in the interests of foregrounding the story. Conventional film and television drama, of course, depends on the illusion that the participants do not know they are being watched.

Additionally, the mode of address varies in its *formality* or *social distance*. Following Edward T. Hall's distinctions, we may distinguish between 'intimate', 'personal', 'social', and 'public' (or 'impersonal') modes of address (Hall 1966). In relation to language, formality is quite closely tied to explicitness, so that intimate language tends to be minimally explicit and maximally dependent on nonverbal cues, while public language tends to reverse these features (especially in print). As we saw in Chapter 4, social distance can also established through the use of loaded quasi-synonyms to reflect ideological distinctions of 'us' from 'them', as in '*I* am a patriot; *you* are a nationalist; *they* are xenophobes' (see Figure 4.5).

In visual representation, social distance is related in part to *apparent proximity*. In camerawork, degrees of formality are reflected in *shot sizes* – close-ups signifying intimate or personal modes, medium shots a social mode, and long shots an impersonal mode (Kress and van Leeuwen 1996, 130–5; cf. Tuchman 1978, 116–20). In visual media, the represented physical distance between the observed and the observer often reflects attempts to encourage feelings of emotional involvement or critical detachment in the viewer. The cultural variability of the degree of formality signified by different zones of proximity is highlighted in relation to face-to-face interaction in Edward T. Hall's influential book – *The Hidden Dimension* (Hall 1966). Proximity is not the only marker of social distance in the visual media: *angles of view* are also significant. High angles (looking down on a depicted person from above) are widely interpreted as making that person look small and insignificant, and low angles (looking up at them from below) are usually seen as making them look powerful and superior (Messaris 1997, 34–5 and 1994, 158; Kress and van Leeuwen 1996, 146).

Representational codes construct possible subject positions for the addresser and addressee. Building upon Jakobson's model, Thwaites *et al.* define 'the functions of address' in terms of the construction of such subjects and of relationships between them. The *expressive function* involves the construction of an addresser (authorial persona); the *conative function* involves the construction of an addressee (ideal reader); the *phatic function* involves the construction of a relationship between the addresser and the addressee (Thwaites *et al.* 1994, 14–15). Not everyone has access to the relevant codes for reading (or writing) a text. The phatic function excludes as well as includes certain readers. Those who share the code are members of the same 'interpretive community' (Fish 1980, 167ff., 335–6, 338). Familiarity with particular codes is related to social position, in terms of such factors as class, ethnicity, nationality, education, occupation, political affiliation, age, gender, and sexuality.

INTERTEXTUALITY

As we have seen, Saussure stresses that signs only function in relation to other signs. Jonathan Culler notes that to read is 'always to read in relation to other texts' (1981, 12). However, one of the weaknesses of some forms of textual analysis is a tendency to treat individual texts as discrete, closed-off entities and to focus exclusively on internal structures. Even where texts are studied as a 'corpus' (a unified collection), the overall generic structures tend themselves to be treated as strictly bounded. The structuralist's first analytical task is often to delimit the boundaries of the system (what is to be included and what excluded), which is logistically understandable but ontologically problematic. Codes transcend texts. The semiotic notion of 'intertextuality' introduced by the literary theorist Julia Kristeva is associated primarily with poststructuralist theorists. Kristeva (1980, 69) refers to texts in terms of two axes: a *horizontal axis* connecting the author and reader of a text, and a *vertical axis*, which connects the text to other texts. Uniting these two axes are shared codes: every text and every reading depends on prior codes. Kristeva declares that 'every text is from the outset under the jurisdiction of other discourses which impose a universe on it' (1974, 388–9; translation by Culler 1981, 105). She argues that rather than confining our attention to the structure of a text, we should study its 'structuration' (how the structure came into being). This involves siting it 'within the totality of previous or synchronic texts' of which it is a 'transformation' (Kristeva 1970, 67–9; translation by Coward and Ellis 1977, 52).

Intertextuality refers to far more than the 'influences' of writers on each other. For structuralists, language has powers which not only exceed individual control but also determine subjectivity. Structuralists sought to counter what they saw as a deep-rooted bias in literary and aesthetic thought which emphasized the uniqueness of both texts and authors. The ideological myth of individualism (with its associated concepts of authorial 'originality', 'creativity', and 'expressiveness') is a post-Renaissance legacy which reached its peak in Romanticism but which still dominates popular discourse. 'Authorship' was a historical invention. Concepts such as authorship and 'plagiarism' did not exist in the Middle Ages.

Language is a system which pre-exists the individual speaker. For structuralists and poststructuralists alike, we are always already positioned by semiotic systems – and most clearly by language. Contemporary theorists have referred to the subject as being *spoken by* language. Barthes declares that 'it is language which speaks, not the author; to write is . . . to reach the point where only language acts, "performs", and not "me"' (1977a, 143). This is strikingly similar to Peirce's comment that 'thought thinks in us, rather than we in it' (CP 5.289n1). When writers write they are also *written*. To communicate, we must utilize existing concepts and conventions. Consequently, while our intention to communicate and *what* we intend to communicate are both important to us as individuals, meaning cannot be reduced to authorial 'intention'. To define meaning in terms of authorial intention is the so-called 'intentional fallacy' identified by the literary critics W. K. Wimsatt and M. C. Beardsley (1954). We may, for instance, communicate without being aware of doing so. As Michel de Montaigne wrote in 1580, 'the work, by its own force and fortune, may second the workman, and sometimes out-strip him, beyond his invention and knowledge' (*Essays*, trans. Charles Cotton, 1685: 'Of the art of conferring' III, 8). Furthermore, in conforming to any of the conventions of our medium, we act as a medium for perpetuating such conventions.

PROBLEMATIZING AUTHORSHIP

Theorists of intertextuality problematize the status of 'authorship', treating the writer of a text as the orchestrator of what Roland Barthes refers to as the 'already-written' rather than as its originator (1974, 21). 'A text is . . . a multidimensional space in which a variety of writings, none of them original, blend and clash. The text is a tissue of quotations' (1977a, 146). In his book *S/Z*, Barthes deconstructs Balzac's short story *Sarrasine*, seeking to 'deoriginate' the text – to demonstrate that it reflects many voices, not just that of Balzac (Barthes 1974). It would be pure idealism to regard Balzac as 'expressing himself' in language since we do not precede language but are *produced* by it. For Barthes, writing did not involve an instrumental process of recording pre-formed thoughts and feelings (Chandler 1995a, 60ff.).

One of the founding texts of semiotics, the *Course in General Linguistics*, itself problematizes the status of authorship. While the text published in French by Payot in Paris bears the name of Ferdinand de Saussure as its author, it is in fact not the work of Saussure at all. Saussure died in 1913 and the *Cours* was first published posthumously in 1916. It was assembled by Charles Bally and Albert Sechehaye ('with the collaboration of Albert Riedlinger') on the basis of the notes that had been taken by at least seven students, together with a few personal notes that had been written by Saussure himself. The students' notes referred to three separate courses on general linguistics, which Saussure had taught at the University of Geneva over the period of 1906–11. Saussure thus neither wrote nor read the book that bears his name, although we continually imply that he did by attaching his name to it. It is hardly surprising that various contradictions and inconsistencies and a lack of cohesion in the text have often been noted. Clearly, the *Cours* cannot be seen as 'a faithful reflection' of Saussure's ideas. On top of all this, English readers have two competing translations of the *Cours* (Saussure 1916/2011; Saussure 1916/1983). Each translation is, of course, a re-authoring. No neutral translation is possible, since languages involve different value systems – as is noted in the *Cours* itself. Nor can specialist translators be expected to be entirely disinterested. Furthermore, anyone who treats the *Cours* as a founding text in semiotics does so by effectively 'rewriting' it, since its treatment of semiology is fragmentary. Finally, we are hardly short of persuasive interpretations (e.g. Harris 1987; Holdcroft 1991; Tallis 1995; Thibault 1997). Indeed, Saussure's supposed principles are best known through their refraction via interpreters and critics of the *Cours* such as Jakobson, Lévi-Strauss, Barthes, and Derrida (Harris 2003).

This rather extreme but important example thus serves to highlight that every reading is always a rewriting. It is by no means an isolated example. The first critique of the ideas outlined in the *Cours* was in a book entitled *Marxism and the Philosophy of Language*, which was published (in Russian) in 1929 under the name Valentin Voloshinov (1895–1936), but it has subsequently been claimed that this book had in fact been written by the literary critic Mikhail Bakhtin (1895–1975), and the authorship of this text is still contested (Morris

1994, 1). Readers, in any case, construct authors. They perform a kind of amateur archaeology, reconstructing them from textual shards while at the same time feeling able to say about anyone whose writings they have read, 'I *know* her (or him).' The reader's 'Roland Barthes' (for example) never existed. If one had total access to everything he had ever written throughout his life it would be marked by contradiction. The best we can do to reduce such contradictions is to construct yet more authors, such as 'the early Barthes' and 'the later Barthes'. Barthes died in 1981, but every invocation of his name creates another Barthes.

In 1968, Barthes announced 'the death of the author' and 'the birth of the reader', declaring that 'a text's unity lies not in its origin but in its destination' (1977a, 148). The framing of texts by other texts has implications not only for their *writers* but also for their *readers*. Fredric Jameson argues that 'texts come before us as the always-already-read; we apprehend them through the sedimented layers of previous interpretations, or – if the text is brand-new – through the sedimented reading habits and categories developed by those inherited interpretive traditions' (Jameson 1981, 9). A famous text has a history of readings. 'All literary works ... are "rewritten", if only unconsciously, by the societies which read them' (Eagleton 1983, 12). No one today – even for the first time – can read a famous novel or poem, look at a famous painting, drawing, or sculpture, listen to a famous piece of music, or watch a famous play or film without being conscious of the contexts in which the text had been reproduced, drawn upon, alluded to, parodied, and so on. Such contexts constitute a primary frame which the reader cannot avoid drawing upon in interpreting the text.

Claude Lévi-Strauss's notion of the *bricoleur* who creates improvised structures by appropriating pre-existing materials which are ready to hand is now fairly well known within cultural studies (1962, 16–33, 35–6, 150n.; cf. 1964). Lévi-Strauss sees 'mythical thought' as 'a kind of bricolage' (1962, 17): 'it builds ideological castles out of the debris of what was once a social discourse' (ibid., 21n.). The *bricoleur* works with signs, constructing new arrangements by 'speaking' 'through the medium of things' – by the choices made from 'limited possibilities' (ibid., 20, 21). 'The first aspect of bricolage is ... to construct a system of paradigms with the fragments of syntagmatic chains', leading in turn to new syntagms (ibid., 150n.). 'Authorship' could be seen in similar terms. Lévi-Strauss certainly sees artistic creation as in part a dialogue with the materials (ibid., 18, 27, 29). Logically (following Quintilian), the practice of *bricolage* can be seen as operating through several key transformations: addition, deletion, substitution, and transposition. Elsewhere, I have explored *bricolage* in relation to the construction of personal profiles on the web (Chandler 2006).

NO TEXT IS AN ISLAND

The concept of intertextuality reminds us that each text exists in relation to others – a fundamental semiotic principle for both Saussure and Peirce. In fact, texts owe more to other texts than to their own makers. Michel Foucault declares that 'the frontiers of a book are never clear-cut ... It is caught up in a system of references to other books, other texts, other sentences: it is a node within a network' (1974, 23).

Texts are framed by others in many ways. Most obvious are formal frames: a television programme, for instance, may be part of a series and part of a genre (such as *soap* or *sitcom)*. Our understanding of any individual text relates to such framings. Texts provide contexts within which other texts may be created and interpreted. The art historian Ernst Gombrich goes further, arguing that all art, however naturalistic, is 'a manipulation of vocabulary' rather than a reflection of the world (1982, 70, 78, 100). Texts draw upon multiple codes from wider contexts – both textual and social. The assignment of a text to a genre provides the interpreter of the text with a key intertextual framework. Genre theory is an important field in its own right, and genre theorists do not necessarily embrace semiotics. Within semiotics genres can be seen as sign systems or codes – conventionalized but dynamic structures. Each example of a genre utilizes conventions that link it to other members of that genre. Such conventions are at their most obvious in 'spoof' versions of the genre. But intertextuality is also reflected in the fluidity of genre boundaries and in the blurring of genres and their functions, which is reflected in such recent coinages as 'advertorials', 'infomercials', 'edutainment', 'docudrama', and 'faction'.

The debts of a text to other texts are seldom acknowledged (other than in the scholarly apparatus of academic writing). This serves to further the mythology of authorial 'originality'. However, some texts allude directly to each other – as in 'remakes' of films, extra-diegetic references to the media in the animated cartoon *The Simpsons*, and many amusing contemporary TV ads. This is a particularly self-conscious form of intertextuality: it credits its audience with the necessary experience to make sense of such allusions and offers them the pleasure of recognition. By alluding to other texts and other media, this practice reminds us that we are in a mediated reality, so it can also be seen as an alienatory mode, which runs counter to the dominant realist tradition, which focuses on persuading the audience to believe in the ongoing reality of the narrative. It appeals to the pleasures of critical detachment rather than of emotional involvement.

In order to make sense of many contemporary advertisements, one needs to be familiar with others in the same series. Expectations are established by reference to one's previous experience in looking at related advertisements. Modern visual advertisements make extensive use of intertextuality in this way. Sometimes there is no direct reference to the product at all. Instant identification of the appropriate interpretive code serves to identify the interpreter of the advertisement as a member of an exclusive club, with each act of interpretation serving to renew one's membership.

The notion of intertextuality problematizes the idea of a text having boundaries and questions the dichotomy of inside–outside: where does a text 'begin' and 'end'? What is 'text' and what is 'context'? The medium of television highlights this issue: it is productive to think of television in terms of a concept which Raymond Williams calls 'flow' rather than as a series of discrete texts (1974, 86, 93). Much the same applies to the Web, where hypertext links on a page can link it directly to many others. However, texts in any medium can be thought of in similar terms. The boundaries of texts are permeable. Each text exists within a vast 'society of texts' in various genres and media: no text is an island entire of itself. A useful semiotic technique is comparison and contrast between differing treatments of similar themes (or similar treatments of different themes), *within* or *between* different genres or media.

INTRATEXTUALITY

While the term intertextuality would normally be used to refer to allusions to other texts, a related kind of allusion is intratextuality – involving internal relations within the text. Within a single code (e.g. a photographic code) these would be simply syntagmatic relationships (e.g. the relationship of the image of one person to another within the same photograph). However, a text may involve several codes: a newspaper photograph, for instance, may have a caption (such an example serves to remind us that what we may choose to regard as a discrete 'text' for analysis lacks clear-cut boundaries: the notion of intertextuality emphasizes that texts have contexts).

Roland Barthes introduces the concept of *anchorage* (1964, 38ff.). Linguistic elements can serve to 'anchor' (or constrain) the preferred readings of an image: 'to *fix* the floating chain of signifieds' (ibid., 39). Barthes employs this concept primarily in relation to advertisements, but it applies of course to other genres such as captioned photographs, maps, narrated television and film documentaries, and cartoons and comics ('comic books' to North Americans) with their speech and thought 'balloons'. Barthes argues that the principal function of anchorage is ideological (ibid., 40). This is perhaps most obvious when photographs are used in contexts such as newspapers. Photograph captions typically present themselves as neutral labels for what self-evidently exists in the depicted world while actually serving to define the terms of reference and point of view from which it is to be seen. For instance, 'It is a very common practice for the captions to news photographs to tell us, in words, exactly how the subject's expression *ought to be read*' (Hall 1981, 229). You may check your daily newspaper to verify this claim.

Barthes uses the term *relay* to describe text–image relationships which are 'complementary', instancing cartoons, comic strips, and narrative film (1964, 41). He did not coin a term for 'the paradoxical case where the image is constructed according to the text' (ibid., 40). Even if it were true in the 1950s and early 1960s that the verbal text was primary in the relation between texts and images, in contemporary society visual images have acquired far more importance in contexts such as advertising, so that what he called 'relay' is far more common. There are also many instances where the 'illustrative use' of an image provides anchorage for ambiguous text – as in assembly instructions for flat-pack furniture (note that when we talk about 'illustrating' and 'captioning' we logocentrically imply the primacy of verbal text over images). Awareness of the importance of intertextuality should lead us to examine the functions of those images and written or spoken text used in close association within a text, not only in terms of their respective codes, but also in terms of their overall rhetorical orchestration.

In media such as film, television, and the Web, multiple codes are involved. As the film theorist Christian Metz puts it, codes 'are not . . . added to one another, or juxtaposed in just any manner; they are organized, articulated in terms of one another in accordance with a certain order, they contract unilateral hierarchies . . . Thus a veritable *system of intercodical relations* is generated which is itself, in some sort, another code' (1971, 242). The interaction of film and soundtrack in chart music videos offers a good example of the dynamic nature of their modes of relationship and patterns of relative dominance. The codes involved in such textual systems clearly cannot be considered in isolation: the dynamic patterns of dominance between them contribute to the generation of meaning. Nor need they be assumed to be always in complete accord with each other – indeed, the interplay of codes may be particularly revealing of incoherences, ambiguities, contradictions, and omissions, which may offer the interpreter scope for deconstructing the text.

TYPES OF INTERTEXTUALITY

Gérard Genette proposes the term 'transtextuality' as a more inclusive term than 'intertextuality' (Genette 1997). He lists five subtypes:

- *intertextuality*: quotation, plagiarism, allusion;
- *paratextuality*: the relation between a text and its 'paratext': that which surrounds the main body of the text – such as titles,

headings, prefaces, epigraphs, dedications, acknowledgements, footnotes, illustrations, dust jackets, etc.;

- *architextuality*: designation of a text as part of a genre or genres (Genette refers to designation by the text itself, but this could also be applied to its framing by readers);
- *metatextuality*: explicit or implicit critical commentary of one text on another text (metatextuality can be hard to distinguish from the following category);
- *hypotextuality* (Genette's term is *hypertextuality*): the relation between a text and a preceding 'hypotext' – a text or genre on which it is based but which it transforms, modifies, elaborates or extends (including parody, spoof, sequel, translation).

To such a list, computer-based *hypertextuality* should be added: text that can take the reader directly to other texts (regardless of authorship or location) – as in online hyperlinks. This kind of intertextuality disrupts the conventional 'linearity' of texts. Reading such texts is seldom a question of following standard sequences predetermined by their authors.

Useful as the concept can be, it is important to remember that intertextuality is not purely a relation between texts. Nor does Kristeva's horizontal axis – that connecting the author and reader of a text – adequately represent the frequently neglected dimension of intertextuality. As the Peircean model suggests, the meaning of a sign is in its interpretation. Long before Barthes announced the death of the author, Plato (in the *Phaedrus*) had foreseen (with regret) that once the text leaves the author, the *reader* is in control. Socrates observes:

> The fact is, Phaedrus, that writing involves a similar disadvantage to painting. The productions of painting look like living beings, but if you ask them a question they maintain a solemn silence. The same holds true of written words; you might suppose that they understand what they are saying, but if you ask them what they mean by anything they simply return the same answer over and over again. Besides, once a thing is committed to writing it

circulates equally among those who understand the subject and those who have no business with it; a writing cannot distinguish between suitable and unsuitable readers.

(Plato 1973, 97)

Ultimately readers, not authors, are the determinants of the meaning of texts and the relations between them – textual interactions do not even exist without readers ('suitable' or otherwise). This is not to suggest that texts may mean whatever their readers want them to mean or relate to whatever readers decide they relate to. Nor is it only textual support that the reader must seek for a sustainable reading. Meanings and meaningful textual relations are socially negotiated; readings don't last without interpretive communities. Similarly, the intergeneric blending and blurring that characterizes the evolution of genres depends not on texts but on shifting expectations within interpretive communities. Genre codes are a key intertextual framework, but we noted in Chapter 5 the frequent absence of text–reader relations in the classification of generic features. Intertextuality is not about purely textual features. Although assumptions about 'model' readers may be discerned in textual cues, text–reader relations cannot be determined by them. Readers do not necessarily adopt the anticipated 'reading positions', even if they have access to the relevant codes. Nor should we neglect the *pleasures* of recognition that have made intelligent television programmes such as *The Simpsons* so popular and amusing.

Confounding the realist agenda that 'art imitates life', intertextuality suggests that art imitates art. Oscar Wilde (typically) took this notion further, declaring provocatively that 'life imitates art' (1891, 32). Texts are instrumental not only in the construction of other texts but in the construction of experiences. Our behaviour is not determined by texts, but much of what we know about the world is derived from what we have read, seen, or heard in the mass media or online. 'Photographs that changed the world' (the title of several popular books) are a primary frame of reference for interpreting pivotal cultural moments. Life is lived through texts and framed by texts to a greater extent than we are normally aware of. Intertextuality blurs the boundaries not only between texts but between texts and the world of lived experience, reminding us that we live within representations of reality.

We have seen that both textual and social relations are central in, and produced through, semiosis, and that the meanings of texts are dependent on the frames of reference within which they are produced and interpreted (both codes and contexts). One key implication of such semiotic perspectives for students of cultural studies and allied disciplines is that 'textual analysis' makes no sense without reference to such interactions.

REFLECTIONS

1   In order to make sense of a verbal or pictorial text we need to go beyond the information given. What knowledge do you draw upon in making sense of the following text (let's assume here that it is in a child's reading book): 'Janet: That isn't a very good ball you have. Give it to me and I'll give you my lollipop' (an example cited in Dreyfus 1992, 10). Schank (1991) offers a very useful discussion of this issue.

2   Search YouTube for the photographic montage in the film *The Parallax View* (1974, Dir. Alan J. Pakula). It consists of single words (in bold white block capitals on black), each followed by a sequence of photographs. Without regard to its context within the film, what sense do you make of this sequence and how do you do so? In what ways do you draw on social knowledge and representational knowledge? How do you make sense of juxtapositions?

3   Find some full-page or double-page magazine advertisements which illustrate how target readers are positioned. How do you know who you are supposed to be?

4   In what ways are you positioned by algorithms when you use social media?

5   What examples can you find in newspapers of photographs with captions, which seek to influence the reader's interpretation?

6   In what ways do you practise bricolage in everyday life?

FURTHER READING

Allen 2000; Bouissac 1998, entry for 'communication'; Gombrich 1972; Hall 1966; Jakobson 1960; Lidov 1998; Sebeok 1994b, entries for 'communication', 'genre', 'intertextuality'.

PROSPECT AND RETROSPECT

The definition, scope, and methodologies of semiotics vary from theorist to theorist, so it is important for newcomers to be clear about whose version of semiotics they are dealing with. This book has referred to the two great traditions of structuralist and Peircean semiotics, with a particular emphasis on Jakobson as a bridge between them. There are many semioticians whose work has not been discussed in this brief introduction to the subject (see Figure 7.1), and some theorists – notably Derrida and Foucault – have been included because they address semiotic issues even though they are not semioticians. This introductory text cannot perform the functions of the encyclopedias of semiotics (Sebeok 1994b, Bouissac 1998) or of Nöth's magisterial handbook (Nöth 1990). Even in these three great reference works, the only dedicated entries appearing in all of them are for Barthes, Hjelmslev, Jakobson, Peirce, and Saussure. My own account of semiotics is partial in both senses; the biases of which I am conscious were outlined in the Preface – the critical reader will no doubt discern others. Regarding semiotics as unavoidably ideological alienates those semioticians who see it as a purely objective science,

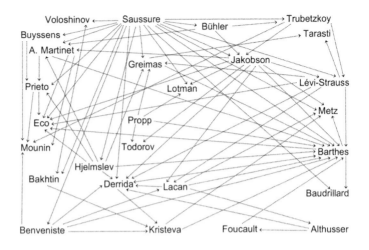

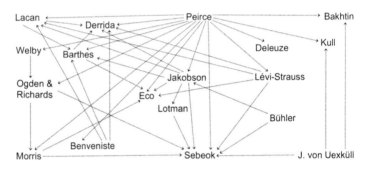

Key to names

Althusser, Louis (1918–1990)
Bakhtin, Mikhail (1895–1975)
Barthes, Roland (1915–1980)
Baudrillard, Jean (1929–2007)
Benveniste, Émile (1902–1976)
Bühler, Karl (1879–1963)
Buyssens, Eric (1900–2000)
Deleuze, Gilles (1925–1995)
Derrida, Jacques (1930–2004)
Eco, Umberto (1932–2016)
Foucault, Michel (1926–1984)
Greimas, Algirdas J. (1917–1992)
Hjelmslev, Louis (1899–1965)
Jakobson, Roman (1896–1982)
Kristeva, Julia (b.1941)
Kull, Kalevi (b.1952)
Lacan, Jacques (1901–1981)
Lévi-Strauss, Claude (1908–2009)

Lotman, Yuri (1922–1993)
Martinet, André (1908–1999)
Metz, Christian (1931–1993)
Morris, Charles W. (1901–1979)
Mounin, Georges (1910–1993)
Ogden, Charles K. (1889–1957)
Peirce, Charles S. (1839–1914)
Prieto, Luis J. (1926–1996)
Propp, Vladimir (1895–1970)
Richards, Ivor A. (1893–1979)
Saussure, Ferdinand de (1857–1913)
Sebeok, Thomas (1920–2001)
Tarasti, Eero (b.1948)
Todorov, Tzvetan (1939–2017)
Trubetzkoy, Nicholai (1890–1938)
Voloshinov, Valentin (1895–1936)
von Uexküll, Jakob (1864–1944)
Welby, Victoria (1837–1912)

FIGURE 7.1 Lines of influence in the structuralist and Peircean traditions

Source: © 2016 Daniel Chandler

but the history of its exposition reveals that semiotics is clearly a 'site of struggle'.

STRUCTURALIST SEMIOTICS

In cultural studies, semiotics has often been identified with structuralist approaches. However, it is not tied to any particular theory or methodology and it has continued to evolve. The current review has focused primarily on the European tradition deriving from Saussure and the structuralists but has also explored the increasing impact of the Peircean approach. Even the 'semiological' tradition has been far from monolithic: there have been various inflections of both structuralist and poststructuralist semiotics. Whatever the limitations of some of its manifestations, the legacy of structuralism is a toolkit of analytical methods and concepts, which have not all outlived their usefulness. Particular tools have subsequently been applied, adapted, replaced, or discarded. Some have even been used 'to dismantle the master's house'. Saussure's framework was dismantled not only by deconstructionists such as Jacques Derrida, but also by the structuralist linguist Roman Jakobson. It is thus notable primarily as a point of departure for ongoing debates about the nature of signs and sign systems – the most obvious structuralist departures from the *Cours* being a shift of focus from *systems* to *structures* and from differential relations to binary oppositions.

Jakobson argues that the radical arbitrariness of the linguistic sign is an 'illusory' 'dogma' (1963a, 19). Even language incorporates iconic and indexical modes (ibid., 59; 1966, 419–20). As we have seen, Saussure alludes to 'relative arbitrariness', although this potentiality is little more than a footnote in his exposition of the 'first principle' of the sign. Nevertheless, the enduring value of Saussure's emphasis on unmotivated signs lies in alerting us to the conventional character of many signs which we experience as natural. All signs, texts, and codes need to be read. When we interpret television or photography as 'a window on the world' (simply reflecting a pre-existing external reality) we treat the referent as unmediated and the sign vehicle as transparent. Saussurean-inspired semiotics demonstrates that the transparency of the medium is illusory.

Post-Saussurean structuralists sought to apply verbal language as a model to media which are nonverbal or not solely or primarily verbal. Roland Barthes declared in 1964 that he had been 'engaged in a series of structural analyses, all of which aim at defining a certain number of extralinguistic "languages"' (1972, 151–2). Many cultural practices can be productively viewed, if not as 'languages' as such, but as systems of signification which are *structured like languages*. Attempts at a unifying approach were seen by critics as failing to allow for the diversity of media, though Jakobson rejects this criticism: 'I have looked forward to the development of semiotics, which helps to delineate the specificity of language among all the various systems of signs, as well as the invariants binding language to related sign systems' (1981, 65). Despite the Jakobsonian stance, a key example of the problem identified by critics is that analogical images (such as in figurative art and in photography) cannot be unproblematically reduced to discrete and meaningfully recombinable units in the way that verbal language can. Yet some semioticians have insisted that a 'grammar' can nevertheless be discerned at some level of analysis in visual and audio-visual media. While we may acknowledge the role of conventions in painting, in the case of an indexical medium such as photography, common sense suggests that we are dealing with 'a message without a code'. Thus, semiotic references to 'reading' photographs, films, and television lead some to dispute that we need to learn the formal codes of such media, and to argue that the resemblance of their images to observable reality is not merely a matter of cultural convention: 'to a substantial degree the formal conventions encountered in still or motion pictures should make a good deal of sense even to a first-time viewer' (Messaris 1994, 7). Semioticians in the structuralist tradition insist that such stances underestimate the intervention of codes in the interpretation of these media (even if their familiarity renders them transparent): relative arbitrariness should not be equated with an absence of conventions. The indexical character of the medium of film does not mean that a documentary film lacks formal codes or guarantee its 'reflection of reality' (Nichols 1991).

While the concept of codes that need to be read can shed light on familiar phenomena, critics have objected to the way in which some semioticians have treated almost anything as a code, while leaving the details of some of these codes inexplicit. It has been argued that we draw on both social and representational codes in making sense even of figurative art, as indeed we do, but we also draw more broadly on both social and representational *knowledge*. Not all of such knowledge is reducible to codes. We cannot identify which codes to invoke in making sense of any act of communication without knowing the situational context (or alternatively, being there). The single word 'coffee', spoken with the rising inflection we associate with a question, can be interpreted in a host of ways depending largely on the context in which it is spoken (just try stopping yourself thinking of some!). It is only in social contexts that codes can be learned and applied. However, as we have seen, excluding context is not necessarily a defining feature of structuralist approaches. Roman Jakobson showed that the context counts at least as much as the code in interpreting signs. Such a stance challenges the reductive transmission model of communication.

Semiotics is invaluable if we wish to look beyond the manifest content of texts. Structuralist semioticians seek to infer organizational relations from the explicit features of texts. The more obvious the structural organization of a text or code may seem to be, the more difficult it may be to see beyond such features, but this approach can lead to fruitful insights. The identification of meaningful oppositions, markedness, and conceptual alignments, undoubtedly has the potential to reveal the workings of ideological biases. However, in structuralist discourse the pervasive metaphor of textual 'surfaces' and 'underlying' meanings implies a foundational level where 'the real meaning' can be found – a concept rightly challenged by the deconstructionists. No such notion is found in the *Cours* (where *langue* and *parole* are interdependent). Critics argue that the focus that characterizes the structural formalism of theorists such as Propp, Greimas, and Lévi-Strauss tends to over-emphasize the similarities between texts and to deny their distinctive features. This is particularly vexatious for aesthetic critics, for whom issues of stylistic difference are a central concern. Some structuralist analysis has been criticized as nothing more than an abstract and 'arid formalism'. Frederic Jameson notes that structuralist criticism is characterized by 'a kind of transformation of form into content' (1972, 198–9). Lévi-Strauss is explicit about his lack of interest in specific *content* – for him, form *is* the content (e.g. 1962, 75–6).

Structuralist studies (such as Jakobson and Lévi-Strauss 1970) have tended to be purely textual analyses and socially-oriented critics complain that the social dimension tends to be dismissed as (or reduced to) 'just another text'. Purely structuralist approaches have not addressed processes of textual production or audience interpretation. They have downplayed or even ignored the contingencies of particular practices, institutional frameworks, and cultural, social, economic, and political contexts. Even Roland Barthes, who argues that texts are codified to encourage a reading that favours the interests of the dominant class, did not investigate the social context of interpretation (though his ideological analysis will be discussed in relation to poststructuralist semiotics). It cannot be assumed that preferred readings will go unchallenged (Hall 1973; Morley 1980). Structuralist semiotics failed to relate texts to social relations (Slater 1983, 259). Sociologists insist that we must consider not only *how* signs signify (structurally) but also *why* (socially): structures are not causes. The creation and interpretation of texts must be related to social factors outside the structures of texts.

POSTSTRUCTURALIST SEMIOTICS

The structuralist movement was short-lived, its intellectual ascendancy in France lasting only from the end of the Second World War to the late 1960s, when it began to be undermined by increasingly trenchant academic criticism (Dosse 1997). The structuralist label was frequently disavowed by those seeking to distance themselves from its excesses. Most contemporary theorists have rejected a purely structuralist semiotics, though as we have seen, structuralism has taken a variety of forms, and not all of them are subject to the same catalogue of criticisms. However, even those who choose to reject structuralist priorities need not abandon every tool employed by structuralists, and whether they do or not, they need not reject semiotics wholesale. Influential as it has been in cultural studies, structuralist analysis is but one approach to semiotics. Many of the criticisms of semiotics are directed at a form of semiotics to which few contemporary semioticians adhere. It is only fair to note that much of the criticism of semiotics has taken the form of self-criticism by those within the field. The theoretical literature of semiotics reflects a constant attempt by many semioticians to grapple with the implications of new theories for their framing of the semiotic enterprise. Poststructuralism evolved from the structuralist tradition in the late 1960s, problematizing many of its assumptions. By then, most of the leading theorists who had previously been associated with structuralism – Barthes, Lacan, and Foucault – had distanced themselves from its goals. For many, Derrida's reading of Saussure in his book *On Grammatology*, first published in French in 1967, signals the end of the structuralist project. As Daylight (2011) shows, Derrida's criticisms are more applicable to French structuralism than to Saussure, whose ideas can indeed be seen as more post-structuralist than structuralist. Seeking to account for the role of social change and the role of the subject, poststructuralist semiotics has sometimes adopted Marxist and/or psychoanalytical inflections. Another inflection derives from Foucault – emphasizing power relations in discursive practices. Such shifts of direction are not an abandonment of semiotics but of the limitations of purely structuralist semiotics.

Theorists such as Roland Barthes used semiotics for the 'revelatory' political purpose of 'demystifying' society. However, the semiotic 'decoding' and denaturalization of textual and social codes tends to suggest that there is a literal truth or pre-given objective reality underlying the coded version, which can be revealed by the skilled analyst's banishing of 'distortions'. This strategy is itself ideological. Poststructuralist theorists have argued that the structuralist enterprise is impossible – we cannot stand outside our sign systems. While we may be able to bypass one set of conventions we can never escape the framing of experience by convention. The notion of 'codes within codes' spells doom for a structuralist quest for a fundamental and universal underlying structure but it does not represent the demise of the semiotic enterprise conceived more broadly.

Poststructuralist theory derived some of its inspiration from Peircean concepts. Derrida wrote that 'Peirce goes very far in the direction that I have called the deconstruction of the transcendental signified, which . . . would place a reassuring end to the reference from sign to sign' (1967a, 49). For Peirce, of course, 'an endless series of representations . . . may be considered to have an absolute object as its limit' (CP 1.339). He would have rejected the relativistic notion that there is nothing outside representation. The Peircean model has become increasingly influential since the late 1960s in cultural studies, particularly in relation to film and photography – though (much as with Saussure) often on a 'pick and mix' basis. Roman Jakobson's advocacy of Peirce helped to counter negative associations with Peirce's behaviourist disciple, Charles Morris. Peirce's model of the sign is attractive to many visual theorists, for instance, because it embraces motivated as well as unmotivated signs. Peter Wollen's influential *Signs and Meaning in the Cinema* (1969) accepts some structuralist notions (such as shared codes, and systems of differences and oppositions) but since cinema involves all forms of sign relations he sees the Peircean triadic model as 'necessary'. In his own cinematic studies, the French philosopher Gilles Deleuze (1925–95) also rejects the linguistic model and selectively adopts the Peircean model (1989), but, like so many other cultural theorists, he reductively interprets symbolic, iconic, and indexical sign relations in terms of the Saussurean terms *signifier* and *signified*, neglecting genuine triadicity and the function of the interpretant. Subsequently within the same field more wholeheartedly Peircean approaches have been increasingly adopted (e.g. Ehrat 2005).

Whereas both common sense and positivist realism involve an insistence that reality is independent of the signs that refer to it, socially oriented semioticians tend to adopt constructionist stances, emphasizing the role of sign systems in the construction of reality. They refer to 'social reality' (rather than physical reality) as constructed. Some argue that there is nothing natural about our values: they are social constructions, which are peculiar to our location in space and time. Assertions which seem to us to be obvious, natural, universal, given, permanent, and incontrovertible may be generated by the ways in which sign systems operate in our discourse communities. The social constructionist stance is that while things may exist independently of signs, we know them only through the mediation of signs; our socially generated sign systems are our experiential frameworks.

As noted in Chapter 2, the emphasis on the mediation of reality (and on representational conventions in the form of codes) is criticized by many realists as relativism (or conventionalism). Such philosophical critics often fear an extreme relativism in which every representation of reality is regarded as being as good as any other. There are understandable objections to any apparent sidelining of referential concerns such as truth, facts, accuracy, objectivity, bias, and distortion. Socially oriented semioticians are very much aware that representations are far from equal. If signs do not merely reflect (social) reality but are involved in its construction, then those who control the sign systems control the construction of reality. Dominant social groups seek to limit the meanings of signs to those that suit their interests, and to naturalize such meanings. For Roland Barthes, various codes contributed to reproducing dominant bourgeois ideology, making it seem natural, proper, and inevitable. One need not be a Marxist to appreciate that it can be liberating to become aware of whose view of reality is being privileged in the process. What we are led to accept as 'common sense' involves incoherences, ambiguities, inconsistencies, contradictions, omissions, gaps, and silences, which offer leverage points for potential social change. The role of ideology is to suppress these in the interests of dominant groups. Consequently, reality construction occurs on 'sites of struggle'. Socially oriented semioticians accept that there can be no 'exhaustive' semiotic analyses because every analysis is located in its own particular social and historical circumstances. In his widely cited essays on the history of photographic practices, John Tagg comments that he is 'not concerned with exposing the manipulation of a pristine "truth", or with unmasking some conspiracy, but rather with the analysis of the specific "political economy" within which the "mode of production" of "truth" is operative' (1988, 174–5).

Since the second half of the 1980s, 'Social Semiotics' has been adopted as a label by members and associates of the Sydney semiotics circle, much-influenced by Michael Halliday's *Language as Social Semiotic* (1978). Halliday (b. 1925) is a British linguist who retired from a chair in Sydney in 1987 and whose functionalist approach to language stresses the contextual importance of social roles. The original Sydney group included Gunther Kress, Theo van Leeuwen,

Paul J. Thibault, Terry Threadgold, and Anne Cranny-Francis; other associates include Bob Hodge, Jay Lemke, Ron Scollon, and Suzanne Wong-Scollon. Members of the group established the journal *Social Semiotics* in 1991. The Sydney school version of social semiotics is not a branch of semiotics in the same sense as visual semiotics: it is a brand of semiotics positioned in opposition to Saussurean semiology, which it tends to hold responsible for the later excesses of structuralism. It describes itself as an alternative to 'mainstream semiotics' (Hodge and Kress 1988, 18). While the terminology of this school is often distinctive, many of its concepts derive from structuralism (and others from Peirce). Seeking to establish a wholeheartedly social semiotics, Bob Hodge and Gunther Kress (ibid., 1) declare that 'the social dimensions of semiotic systems are so intrinsic to their nature and function that the systems cannot be studied in isolation'. There is, of course, nothing new about semiotics having a social dimension (albeit widely neglected): the roots of social semiotics can be traced to the early theorists. Neither Saussure nor Peirce studied the social use of signs, but Saussure envisioned semiotics as a science that studies the life of signs in society, while Peirce accorded a determinative role in interpretation to the 'community'. The road to social semiotics had already been paved.

As we have seen, the structuralist Jakobson (stressing the interpretive importance of both code and context) had already upturned the Saussurean priorities along some of the lines outlined by Hodge and Kress, while Derrida's *On Grammatology* (1967a) had focused on deconstructing and overturning principles of structuralism which he misattributed to Saussure (see Daylight 2011). The Sydney school has adopted and adapted some of its analytical concepts partly from (primarily Jakobsonian) structuralism (with a Hallidayan twist) while (like Jakobson) defining itself largely in opposition to Saussure's analytical priorities, which they characterize in terms of the privileging of verbal over nonverbal systems, speech over writing, internal relations over external reference, arbitrariness over motivation, *langue* over *parole*, code over context, form over substance, and synchrony over diachrony (for a critique see McDonald 2012a). For Hodge and Kress (1988, 17), social semiotics represents 'the return of the repressed'. They declare that 'social semiotics is primarily concerned with human semiosis as an inherently social phenomenon in its sources, functions, contexts, and effects' (ibid., 261). The key difference in this respect is that the Australian school has set itself the task of investigating actual meaning-making practices (theoretically prioritized but not pursued by Jakobson). A major concern of socially oriented semioticians is with 'specific signifying practices' or 'situated social semiosis' (Jensen 1995, 57). This is, of course, in strong contrast to the focus in the *Cours* on *langue* rather than *parole*. The Sydney school has nailed its colours to the mast in reprioritizing the social (Hodge and Kress 1988, van Leeuwen 2005; for a critique see McDonald 2012b).

Distancing itself from system-based semiotics, but employing some of 'the master's tools', this critical form of social semiotics also emphasizes the ideological dimension of semiosis, acknowledging the influence of Voloshinov (1929). The Sydney school semioticians explore the role of signs and sign systems in power relations and in maintaining the hegemony of dominant groups. This is of course reminiscent of Roland Barthes' semiotic mission, as part of which we have already encountered his notion of exnomination (ideological unmarkedness). However, like the sociologist Stuart Hall (whose interpretive codes were discussed in Chapter 5), critical social semioticians resist structural determinism by accounting for resistant readings. This ideological focus is not limited to the Sydney school: a similar approach is found in the work of the American sociologists Robert Goldman and Stephen Papson, who have applied semiotic analysis to advertising sign systems (1996, 1998).

The Australian strategy is not the only game in town – socially-oriented semiotics is not limited to those adopting it. Mark Gottdiener, an American sociologist, has chronicled and played a part in the development of a materialist socio-semiotics which seeks to relate symbolic processes to social life. He sees cultural artefacts as the material expression of ideology (in the sense of values). Hjelmslev's model of the sign, which acknowledged its materiality, was adopted by Eco and Metz, who in turn have influenced others. Gottdiener (1995, 56) argues that a materialist approach, in contrast to the idealism of both Marxism and deconstructionism, helps to explain how ideology is codified in the material environment through the articulation of the 'substance of the expression' with the 'form of the content'

(Figure 1.13; Table 1.14). He notes that Peirce and Bakhtin have inspired socio-semiotic work through concepts such as polysemy, the interpretant, and semiosis, which were notable by their absence from the Saussurean model. Gottdiener cites the early work of both Barthes and Baudrillard as socio-semiotic examples of the materialist analysis of everyday life and popular culture. Not the least of the values of socio-semiotic stances is the potential to attract back to semiotics some of those who were alienated by structuralist excesses and who had reductively defined semiotics according to these. The extent to which socially-oriented semiotics has so far met the concerns of sociologists is debatable. However, social semiotics is still under construction. Semiotics transcends its various schools, but as Umberto Eco declares (1973, 71), 'semiotics is a discipline which must be concerned with the whole of social life'.

Another growing brand of semiotic inquiry is 'cognitive semiotics', which its advocates insist is neither a branch of semiotics nor a school of thought within it (Zlatev 2012, 2). Broadly, it adopts a transdisciplinary, integrationist approach to semiosis with an emphasis on empirical research. It emerged from cognitive science – already linked to the social sciences through psychology (primarily cognitive and developmental) and linguistics, and to the humanities through philosophy (particularly phenomenology). However, it is something of a splinter group which seeks stronger links with the humanities than in mainstream 'physicalist' cognitive science (which is more closely associated with computer science, neuroscience, and a reductionist philosophy of mind). Some cognitivist approaches have emerged in opposition to structuralist semiotics, as in the case of David Bordwell's cognitive film theory (in contrast to the cognitive semiotics of many European film theorists). The arrival of cognitive semiotics was heralded in 1995 in Thomas Daddesio's *On Minds and Symbols: The Relevance of Cognitive Science for Semiotics*, building upon existing studies such as that of Lakoff and Johnson (1980). The journal *Cognitive Semiotics* was launched in 2007 and a Centre for Cognitive Semiotics was set up at Lund University in 2009, with the eminent semiotician Göran Sonesson as its research director. It was here that the International Association for Cognitive Semiotics (IACS) was founded in 2013.

THE RETURN OF SAUSSURE

We know already that Saussure did not write the *Cours*, which was published posthumously in 1916. It is hardly surprising that it features tensions and contradictions, and its treatment of semiology is fragmentary, leaving considerable scope for interpretation (Harris 2003, Tallis 1995, Thibault 1997, Daylight 2011). Indeed, simply inverting the perceived priorities of the *Cours* has served to generate alternative semiotic manifestos (Voloshinov 1973, Derrida 1967a and 1967b, Jakobson 1984, Hodge and Kress 1988). Many Saussurean concepts have been reinterpreted by structuralists and poststructuralists in unSaussurean ways. The 'faux Saussure' was real in its consequences and cannot be unwritten; it shaped the development both of structuralism and of reactions against it.

However, in 1996 came the important discovery of long-lost manuscripts in the orangery of Saussure's family home. This included his own handwritten notes for his *Cours* (1907–11), together with earlier material – notes for lectures given in 1891 and for a book on general linguistics (1893–4), and a draft of a book on the philosophy of language (*De l'essence double du langage*). Finally, we can encounter Saussure in his own words (2002). An English translation was first published in 2006 (when the previous edition of this book was going to press). The resurrected Saussure does not overturn the theories attributed to him, but he does disarm his critics with a richer, more nuanced stance than that of his stand-in.

In these various texts, Saussure notes that whatever is perceived by the mind becomes a sign (ibid., 26). Semiology, which he also refers to occasionally as 'signology', is 'the study of what occurs when a person tries to represent thought through a necessary convention' (188). The study of a semiotic system such as language can be seen as 'the study of the representation of ideas' through the 'use of forms' (15). It includes 'morphology, grammar, syntax, synonymy, rhetoric, stylistics, lexicology etc., *all of which are inseparable*' (26). Saussure emphasizes that language is 'a historical product' (145) and that the diachronic point of view is as necessary as the synchronic one (7). His conception of language is not at all 'static', as critics such as Jakobson suggest. He acknowledges a succession of *états de langue* (language states) and asserts that 'it is clearly impossible to understand what *langue* is, without establishing its many modifications from one period to another' (34). Nevertheless, he argues that we can only study how the language system works 'at a given time' (250). Contrary to a position attributed to him by his critics, Saussure denies that language is a 'single, unified entity' (161). Nor does he show any sign of phonocentrism when he declares that 'the relationship between graphical mark and spoken sound is the same as that between spoken sound and idea' (30).

He readily acknowledges the importance of *parole*. 'A word only exists ... in actual use' (56). He repeatedly refers to 'speaking subjects'. Language is 'a sign system as it exists in the mind of speaking subjects' (25). 'Innovation comes about through improvisation' in discourse (65). He emphasizes that we should not focus on individual usage; the language system is a social phenomenon (120). *Langue* cannot be 'divorced from its social reality' because it depends on its use by a community of speakers (238). A sign system exists only as part of a community, from which its values arise (202–3).

It is the 'principle of oppositions or reciprocal values' which creates the language system (10, 13). 'Signs and meanings only exist by virtue of the *difference between signs*' (20). The negative, oppositional basis of the sign system is indeed the 'fundamental principle of semiology' (46). 'Any linguistic fact consists of a relationship, and nothing but a relationship' (188).

He reveals himself as less dualistic than in the *Cours*, insisting on 'three irreducible relationships': between a sign and its meaning, a sign and another sign, and a meaning and another meaning (22). Within what he calls 'the last quaternion' (Figure 7.2), any particular sign 'presupposes four irreducible terms and three relationships between these four terms, all three of which must be borne in the mind of the speaking subject' (26). As if in response to those who misinterpret his system as based on 'one-to-one correspondence', he declares that 'there is no such thing as *a* form and a corresponding idea; nor any such thing as *a* meaning and a corresponding sign' (24). There are only differences between forms and between meanings. Saussure rejects the 'traditional' assumption that words correspond 'even very partially' to specific material objects. Since a distinction

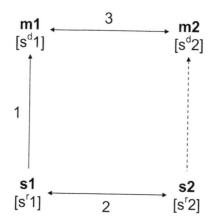

FIGURE 7.2 Saussure's three irreducible relationships

Source: © 2016 Daniel Chandler

between figurative and literal meaning (or 'direct use') depends on such an assumption, he rejects this too (50, 53, 54). He adds that 'it hardly needs pointing out that the difference between terms making up a language system in no way corresponds . . . to the real relationships between things' (50).

Distancing himself from the traditional stance that language is the vehicle of thought, he adopts a position that is close to the Sapir-Whorf hypothesis: 'it is not thought that creates the sign, but the sign that fundamentally guides thought (and thus in fact creates it), causing it in turn to create signs of its own' (27–8). 'What distinguishes something . . . constitutes it' (188). 'The whole object of the science of language finds itself in the realm of relativity' (43) because the objects it deals with 'never have any innate reality', being defined only in terms of relational differences (42). Language 'depends on an object' but its relation to the object is arbitrary and unnatural (140, 147); linguistic symbols are independent of their objects, unlike representations such as portraits, which are visibly linked to them (145).

Saussure tells us that in linguistics the object is not given in itself (8). Linguistic objects have no intrinsic and independent existence

(139). Viewpoints create such objects and define linguistic facts (9, 44, 137, 139). 'The link we establish between things, in this domain, comes *before the things themselves*, and serves to determine them' (138). It is 'a very fraught question' whether meanings, ideas, and categories may exist 'outside the linguistic domain' (48). He acknowledges that 'something external' could be 'sufficiently defined in itself to *elude* the general law of the sign' (71). However, it is not a matter for the linguist to determine 'whether certain categories pre-exist and others post-exist the vocal sign; whether some are thus absolute and necessary for the mind and others relative and contingent; whether some can continue to exist outside the sign' (26). Saussure does not dispute the real existence of moral phenomena such as crime, lies, deception, hypocrisy, honesty, and respect, and he notes that it is a 'fundamental shortcoming' of language that such categories can never be 'exactly and exclusively captured by a certain term' (20). Although he is wary of venturing beyond what he sees as the scope of linguistics he declares that 'objects can only ever be known through the idea we create of them' (50). He takes for granted the existence of material objects which are 'directly apprehensible' and external to the mind (3), but he stresses that these have no bearing on the language system (51). Reality is unavoidably mediated: 'material phenomena . . . always come to our knowledge very indirectly and incompletely' (21). In the light of such observations, it is thus misleading to refer to Saussure's philosophical stance as 'anti-referential'.

METHODOLOGIES

Semiotics has not become widely institutionalized as a formal academic discipline and there is little sense of a unified enterprise building on cumulative research findings. As we have seen, the field is characterized by competing theories and models, and indeed some would champion the diversity of approaches over a quest for unification. Semiotics as such is not a methodology. Although it is often assumed to be synonymous with structuralist analytical practices, it is not committed to any particular methodology. A major strength of the techniques in the semiotic toolkit is that they are not bound to a particular domain, but a semiotic approach suits some purposes better than others and makes certain kinds of questions easier to ask than others. Signs in various media are not alike – different types need to be studied in different ways. The empirical testing of semiotic claims requires a variety of methods. Structuralist analysis is just one of many techniques that may be used to explore sign practices. In relation to textual analysis, other approaches include critical discourse analysis (e.g. Fairclough 1995b) and content analysis. Whereas semiotics is now closely associated with cultural studies, content analysis is well established within the mainstream tradition of social science research. Content analysis involves a quantitative approach to the analysis of the manifest content of texts, while semiotics seeks to analyse texts as structured wholes and investigates latent, connotative meanings. Semioticians have often rejected quantitative approaches: just because an item occurs frequently in a text or cultural practice does not make it significant. The structuralist semiotician is more concerned with the relation of elements to each other while a social semiotician would also emphasize the importance of the significance which readers attach to the signs within a text. Whereas content analysis focuses on explicit content and tends to suggest that this represents a single, fixed meaning, semiotic studies focus on the system of rules governing the discourse involved in texts and practices, stressing the role of semiotic context in shaping meaning. However, some researchers have combined semiotic analysis and content analysis (e.g. Glasgow University Media Group 1980; McQuarrie and Mick 1992; Chandler and Griffiths 2000). Semiotics is not incompatible with quantitative methods – for instance, a highly enlightening study of the signification of domestic objects for their owners made effective use of both qualitative and quantitative data (Csikszentmihalyi and Rochberg-Halton 1981).

Rejecting content analysis, Bob Hodge and David Tripp's classic empirical study of *Children and Television* (1986) links semiotics with both psychology and social and political theory, employing structural analysis, interviews, and a developmental perspective. Semiotic investigations need to range beyond textual analysis, which does not shed light on how people in particular social contexts actually interpret signs – an issue that may require ethno-graphic and phenomenological approaches (McQuarrie and Mick 1992).

AN ECOLOGICAL AND MULTIMODAL APPROACH

The primary value of semiotics is its central concern for the investigation of meaning-making and representation, which conventional academic disciplines have tended to treat as peripheral. Within cultural studies and related disciplines, specific semiotic modalities are addressed by such specialists as linguists, art historians, musicologists, and anthropologists, but we must turn to semioticians if our investigations are to span a range of modalities. Semiotic analysis has been applied to a vast range of modes and media – including gesture, posture, dress, writing, speech, photography, the mass media, and the internet. Since this involves 'invading' the territory of different academic disciplines, it is understandable that semiotics has often been criticized as imperialistic. Aldous Huxley once wryly noted, 'our universities possess no chair of synthesis' (1941, 276). Semiotics has an important synthesizing function, seeking to study meaning-making and representation in cultural artefacts and practices of whatever kind on the basis of unified principles, at its best counteracting cultural chauvinism and bringing some coherence to communication theory and cultural studies. While semiotic analysis has been widely applied to the literary, artistic, and musical canon, it has also been applied to a wide variety of popular cultural phenomena. It has thus helped to stimulate the serious study of popular culture.

While all verbal language is communication, most communication is non-verbal. In an increasingly multimodal culture, an important contribution of semiotics from Roland Barthes onwards has been a concern with advertising, photography, and audio-visual media. Semiotics may encourage us not to dismiss a particular medium as of less worth than another: literary and film critics often regard television as of less worth than 'literary' fiction or 'artistic' film. To élitist critics, of course, this would be a weakness of semiotics. Potentially, semiotics could help us to avoid the routine privileging of one semiotic mode over another, such as the spoken over the written or the verbal over the non-verbal. For many, the 'linguistic turn' has gone too far. Horst Ruthrof (1997) proposes a 'corporeal turn', arguing that interpreting events normally involves correlating several different semiotic systems: not only the language system, but also the various perceptual systems that ground experience (however mediatedly) in physical reality – vision, hearing, the cutaneous senses, the chemical senses, proprioception and kinaesthesia, and the vestibular sense. We need to realize the affordances and constraints of different semiotic modes, as well as the culturally and historically variability of sensory ecologies (Classen 1993). We live within an ecology of signs that both reflects and gives shape to our experience (Csikszentmihalyi and Rochberg-Halton 1981, 16–17). We must identify and recognize the importance of new 'literacies' in this ever-changing semiotic ecology. Thinking in 'ecological' terms about the interaction of different semiotic structures and languages led the Tartu school cultural semiotician Yuri Lotman to coin the term 'semiosphere' to refer to 'the whole semiotic space of the culture in question' (1990, 124–5). This conception of a semiosphere may once again connote semiotic imperialism, but it also offers a more unified and dynamic vision of semiosis than the study of a specific medium as if each existed in a vacuum.

Human experience is inherently multisensory, and every representation of experience is subject to the affordances of the medium involved. Every medium is constrained by the channels that it utilizes. For instance, even in the very flexible medium of language 'words fail us' in attempting to represent some experiences, and we have no way at all of representing smell or touch with conventional media. Different media and genres provide different frameworks for representing experience, facilitating some forms of expression and inhibiting others. The psychologist Lev Vygotsky (1962, 1978) famously argued that both material and semiotic 'tools' are essential for developing more complex modes of thinking (a concept insightfully explored by Salomon 1979). The differences between media led Émile Benveniste to argue that the 'first principle' of semiotic systems is that they are not 'synonymous': 'we are not able to say "the same thing"' in systems based on different units (1969, 235). There is a growing theoretical interest in 'multimodality' (e.g. Kress and van Leeuwen 2001 and Finnegan 2002). This is 'the combination of different semiotic modes – for example, language and music – in a communicative artefact or event' (van Leeuwen 2005, 281). It was foreshadowed in structuralist studies of what Metz called 'intercodical relations' (1971, 242), including Barthes' exploration of relations such as anchorage between images and words.

In the educational framing of such relations, images are still the marked category, as also are makers as opposed to users. At present, 'with regard to images, most people in most societies are mostly confined to the role of spectator of other people's productions' (Messaris 1994, 121). Most people feel unable to draw, paint, or use graphics software, and even among those who own cameras and camcorders not everyone knows how to make effective use of them (the disparity is very evident in social media). This is a legacy of an educational system, which still focuses on the acquisition of one kind of symbolic literacy (that of verbal language) at the expense of other semiotic modes. This institutional bias disempowers people not only by excluding many from engaging in those representational practices, which are not purely linguistic but by handicapping them as critical readers of the majority of texts to which they are routinely exposed throughout their lives.

The ubiquity of social media and mobile communication since the first decade of the twenty-first century has made the development of critical media literacy skills an even more pressing concern for educators. Marshall McLuhan once observed that 'we are all robots when uncritically involved with our technologies' (McLuhan and Fiore 1968, 18). We can be critical users without being luddites. Of course it is true that 'savvy users' exist, but such competence and reflexivity is far from evenly distributed (even among the young, where such competence is often naively assumed). These media have rapidly spawned a range of new tools and techniques, many of which are likely to be unknown to most readers of this book, but which shape our everyday experience (Chandler and Munday 2016). Search engines maintain a 'regime of truth' based on 'popularity', social media algorithmically filter our identities, mobile media make us accessible '24/7', we act as agents of our own surveillance by voluntarily 'sharing' our personal data, and we are commodified by our patterns of online behaviour. Most of us have become dependent on these tools, not least as sources of social and cultural capital, without having subjected them to deep scrutiny. Deepening our understanding of their potent, pervasive, but hidden structures is certainly not purely a matter of what many would regard as 'semiotic analysis', but a semiotic toolkit can offer considerable leverage for reflective users in taking apart that which we take for granted. A working understanding of key concepts in semiotics – including their practical application – remains valuable in understanding the complex and dynamic communication ecologies within which we live, and the 'sign wars' of competition for 'mindshare' (Goldman and Papson 1996).

Semiotics has often been declared dead, but each time it bounces back stronger than ever, with new research centres, new courses, new books, and new journals. If anything, it has experienced a resurgence since the millennium. News of its supposed death is thus greatly exaggerated. Semiotics continues to reassert what Saussure saw as its 'right to exist' (*CLG* 33; 16). Rights bring with them duties, among which is the duty of its practitioners to make it ever more accessible. The late great Umberto Eco, who in 1971 became the first professor of semiotics at Bologna, Europe's oldest university, shattered an oxymoron by becoming a globally famous semiotician. Like Roland Barthes in France, beyond the academy Eco wrote popular articles that raised interest in semiotic topics among the general public (e.g. 1987). Furthermore, not only did he also write popular novels reflecting his academic concerns, but in 1986 his bestselling novel, *The Name of the Rose* (1980), became an award-winning film starring Sean Connery.

Even among 'professional semioticians' there is more than one kind. Semiotics has spread and flourished beyond academia, having been widely adopted since the 1990s as a practical tool in marketing and brand management, for which special tribute should be paid to the British pioneers Virginia Valentine (1939–2010) and Monty Alexander (1928–2008). It is largely because of their influence that the concept of a 'commercial semiotician' is not another oxymoron. 'Semiotician' (or 'semiotics consultant') has become an occupation from which it is possible to earn a living. Beyond those who are full-time practitioners of 'applied semiotics', there are also hosts of amateur semioticians. Some, such as designers and advertising 'creatives', regularly use semiotic concepts and strategies as part of their professional work. Others do so in course of their everyday lives without necessarily being aware that they are 'doing semiotics'. Living within what Umberto Eco refers to as a 'metasemiotic culture', savvy 'prosumers' have already shown themselves to be 'instinctive semioticians' (1987, 210). Semiotic gatekeepers may dismiss popular practitioners as dilettantes, but for Barthes (1970, 8) there is no semiology without 'semioclasm', and this includes contesting the myth of 'scientific' semiotics. In popular journalism semiotics is often dismissed as an 'arcane' subject but many cultural bricoleurs already gain valuable insights from adopting a semiotic point of view.

As Peirce famously put it, 'the universe . . . is perfused with signs' (CP 5.449n.). This introduction has focused on the cultural semiotics of human communication and representation, but beyond these pages the whole world of signification beckons the inquiring mind of the semiotic detective.

REFLECTIONS

1 Gather a range of reputable definitions of semiotics. What are their notable similarities and differences?
2 Referring to Figure 7.1, investigate the ways in which any one semiotician discussed in this book influenced another.
3 What key events should feature on a timeline of the evolution of modern semiotics?
4 How might a semiotic approach be productive for the analysis of social media or selfies?
5 How would you respond to those who declare that semiotics is dead?

FURTHER READING

Daddesio 1995; Eco 1999; Gottdiener 1995; Hodge and Kress 1988; Jackson 1991; Lakoff and Johnson 1980; Pettit 1977; Protevi 2005, entry for 'structuralism'; Sebeok 1994b, entry for 'structuralism and post-structuralism'; Simpkins 1998; Thibault 1991 and 1997; van Leeuwen 2005; Zlatev 2012.

GOING FURTHER

There are several useful works of general reference on semiotics in English, including: Greimas and Courtés 1982, Krampen *et al.* (eds) 1987, Nöth 1990, Colapietro 1993, Sebeok 1994b, Bouissac 1998, Danesi 2000, Martin and Ringham 2000, Cobley 2001, and Trifonas 2015. There are two English translations of the *Cours* – that by Wade Baskin dating from 1959 (Saussure 1916/2011) and a later British translation by Roy Harris (Saussure 1916/1983). Saussure's own notes are available in English translation (2006). There are also bilingual French/English editions of the notebooks of some of Saussure's students (Saussure 1993, 1996, 1997). Peirce's writings are available in the *Collected Papers* (1931–58), an ongoing chronological edition (1982–), and useful selections (e.g. 1966, 1992).

The main works of the leading semioticians are listed here in the references. An accessible introduction to Barthes' version of cultural semiotics is found in *Mythologies* (1957) and *Image–Music–Text* (1977a). His *Elements of Semiology* (1967a) is a short introductory handbook. The work of Jakobson (e.g. 1990) and Lévi-Strauss (e.g. 1972) is an essential foundation for structuralist theory. Greimas's *On Meaning* (1987) is not for beginners. Eco's *Theory of Semiotics* (Eco 1976) is widely cited but difficult – it should be read in conjunction with *Kant and the Platypus* (Eco 1999). The writings of the key poststructuralists, Derrida (1967a, 1967b), Foucault (1970, 1974), and Lacan (1977), are initially daunting, and a beginner's guide may be helpful (e.g. Sarup 1993). Hodge and Kress 1988 and van Leeuwen 2005 offer introductions to social semiotics.

Semiotics is served by a range of journals. These include (in order of date established): *Sign Systems Studies* (1964), *Transactions of the Charles S. Peirce Society* (1965), *Semiotica* (1969), *Kodikas/Code: An International Journal of Semiotics* (1977), *Zeitschrift für Semiotik* (1979), *American Journal of Semiotics* (1982), *International Journal for the Semiotics of Law* (1988), *European Journal for Semiotic Studies* (1989), *Semiotic Review* (1990, formerly *Semiotic Review of Books*), *Social Semiotics* (1991), *Elementa: Journal of Slavic Studies and Comparative Cultural Semiotics* (1993), *Interdisciplinary Journal for Germanic Linguistics and Semiotic Analysis* (1996), *Visio: Revue internationale de sémiotique visuelle/International Journal for Visual Semiotics* (1996), *Applied Semiotics/Sémiotique appliquée* (1996), *International Journal of Applied Semiotics* (1999), *Cognitive Semiotics* (2007), *Chinese Semiotic Studies* (2009), *International Journal of Signs and Semiotic Systems* (2011; from 2017 *International Journal of Semiotics and Visual Rhetoric*), *Signs and Society* (2013), *International Journal of Marketing Semiotics* (2015), *Punctum: International Journal of Semiotics* (2015).

The scholarly societies and associations for semiotics at an international level include the International Association for Semiotic Studies (1969), the International Association for the Semiotics of Law (1987), the International Association for Visual Semiotics (1988), the International Association for Biosemiotic Studies (2005), and the International Association for Cognitive Semiotics (2013). There are also regional and national bodies. Current contact details are best obtained via a search engine. Some useful online resources at the time of writing included the following.

WEBSITES

- Arisbe: The Peirce Gateway
  www.iupui.edu/~arisbe/
- Charles S. Peirce Society
  www.peircesociety.org/
- Charles S. Peirce Studies
  www.peirce.org/
- Commens: Digital Companion to C. S. Peirce
  www.commens.org/
- Guide to the Papers of Roman Jakobson at MIT
  https://libraries.mit.edu/archives/research/collections/
  collections-mc/mc72.html
- Institut Ferdinand de Saussure
  www.revue-texto.net/Saussure/Saussure.html
- International Association for Cognitive Semiotics (IACS)
  www.iacs.dk/
- International Association for Semiotic Studies (IASS)
  http://iass-ais.org/
- International Association for Visual Semiotics (IAVS)
  https://aisviavs.wordpress.com/
- International Semiotics Institute (ISI)
  www.isisemiotics.fi/
- International Society for Biosemiotic Studies (ISBS)
  www.biosemiotics.org/
- Roland Barthes archives
  www.roland-barthes.org/archives.html
- Semioticon: Open Semiotics Resource Center
  http://semioticon.com/
- Semiotic Society of America
  https://semioticsocietyofamerica.org/
- Signo
  www.signosemio.com/
- Umberto Eco
  www.umbertoeco.com/

FACEBOOK GROUPS

- Charles S. Peirce Society
  www.facebook.com/811615495641111/
- Cybersemiotics
  www.facebook.com/412474728811238/
- International Association for Semiotic Studies
  www.facebook.com/1444164299186265/
- International Semiotics Institute
  www.facebook.com/228656963970694/
- Linguistics/Semiology
  www.facebook.com/773241702693814/
- Peirce Matters
  www.facebook.com/159237477450823/
- Semiofest
  www.facebook.com/117451241747426/
- Semiothink
  www.facebook.com/901983096522145/
- Semiotic Research Group
  www.facebook.com/1461217324192312/
- Semiotics, Book, Links, News
  www.facebook.com/373930009449106/
- Semiotic Society of America
  www.facebook.com/1404260749842760/
- Semiotics of Video Games
  www.facebook.com/109655655733219/
- Semiotiek Semiotica . . .
  www.facebook.com/308659098812/
- Signo
  www.facebook.com/206646132726475/

REFERENCES

Abrams, Meyer H. (1971) *The Mirror and the Lamp*. London: Oxford University Press.

Alcoff, Linda and Elizabeth Potter (eds) (1993) *Feminist Epistemologies*. London: Routledge.

Alexander, Monty (1995) 'Big Talk, Small Talk' [WWW document] www.semioticsolutions.com/ref.aspx?id=72 [no longer available online].

—— (2000) 'Codes and Contexts' [WWW document] www.semiotic solutions.com/ref.aspx?id=78 [no longer available online].

Allen, Graham (2000) *Intertextuality*. London: Routledge.

Allport, Gordon W. and Leo J. Postman (1945) 'The basic psychology of rumour', *Transactions of the New York Academy of Sciences*, Series II, 8: 61–81. Reprinted in Eleanor E. Maccoby, Theodore M. Newcomb and Eugene L. Hartley (eds) (1959) *Readings in Social Psychology* (3rd edn). London: Methuen, pp. 54–65.

Althusser, Louis (1971) *Lenin and Philosophy* (trans. Ben Brewster). London: New Left Books.

Altman, Rick (1992) 'The material heterogeneity of recorded sound', in Rick Altman (ed.) (1992) *Sound Theory, Sound Practice*. New York: Routledge, pp. 15–31.

Ang, Ien (1985) *Watching 'Dallas'*. London: Methuen.

Argyle, Michael (1983) *The Psychology of Interpersonal Behaviour* (4th edn). Harmondsworth: Penguin.

—— (1988) *Bodily Communication* (2nd edn). London: Methuen.

—— (1994) *The Psychology of Interpersonal Behaviour* (5th edn). Harmondsworth: Penguin.

Aristotle (2004) *On Interpretation* (trans. E. M. Edghill). Whitefish, MT: Kessinger.

Arnheim, Rudolf (1974) *Art and Visual Perception*. Berkeley, CA: University of California Press.

Arrigo, Jan (2003) 'Photography and photographers', in John McDonough (ed.) *Advertising Age Encyclopedia of Advertising*, vol. 3. New York: Fitzroy Dearborn, pp. 1231–4.

Ashwin, Clive (1989) 'Drawing, design and semiotics', in Victor Margolis (ed.) (1989) *Design Discourse: History, Theory, Criticism*. Chicago: University of Chicago Press, pp. 199–212.

Augustine (397 CE/2009) *On Christian Doctrine*. New York: Dover.

Bakhtin, Mikhail (1981) *The Dialogic Imagination* (trans. C. Emerson and M. Holquist). Austin, TX: University of Texas Press.

Bal, Mieke and Norman Bryson (1991) 'Semiotics and art history: a discussion of context and senders', in Donald Preziosi (ed.) (1998) *The Art of Art History*. Oxford: Oxford University Press, pp. 242–56.

Balzac, Honoré de (1831/1921) 'Le chef-d'œuvre inconnu' (The unknown masterpiece), in Arthur Tilley (ed.) *Balzac: Five Short Stories*. Cambridge: Cambridge University Press.

Barthes, Roland (1953/1967) *Writing Degree Zero* (trans. Annette Lavers and Colin Smith). London: Jonathan Cape.

—— (1957/1987) *Mythologies*. New York: Hill & Wang.

—— (1961) 'The photographic message', in Barthes (1977a), pp. 15–31.

—— (1964) 'The rhetoric of the image', in Barthes (1977a), pp. 32–51.

—— (1967a) *Elements of Semiology* (trans. Annette Lavers and Colin Smith). London: Jonathan Cape.

—— (1967b/1985) *The Fashion System* (trans. Matthew Ward and Richard Howard). London: Jonathan Cape.

—— (1970) 'Preface', in Roland Barthes (1957/1987) *Mythologies*. Paris: Éditions du Seuil.

—— (1972) *Critical Essays*. Evanston, IL: Northwestern University Press.

—— (1974) *S/Z*. London: Jonathan Cape.

—— (1977a) *Image–Music–Text*. London: Fontana.

—— (1977b) *Roland Barthes* (trans. Richard Howard). Berkeley, CA: University of California Press.

—— (1994) *The Semiotic Challenge* (trans. Richard Howard). Berkeley, CA: University of California Press.

Bateson, Gregory (1979) *Mind and Nature*. New York, Dutton.

Baudrillard, Jean (1984) 'The precession of simulacra', in Brian Wallis (ed.) (1984) *Art After Modernism*, vol. 1. New York: Museum of Contemporary Art (reprinted from *Art and Text* 11 (September 1983): 3–47.

—— (1988) *Selected Writings* (ed. Mark Poster). Cambridge: Polity Press.

—— (1995) *The Gulf War Did Not Take Place* (trans. Paul Patton). Bloomington, IN: Indiana University Press.

Bazin, André (1974) *Jean Renoir*. London: W. H. Allen.

Benjamin, Walter (1992) *Illuminations* (ed. Hannah Arendt, trans. Harry Zohn). London: Fontana.

Bensen, Clark (2004) 'Red state blues: did I miss that memo?' [WWW document] www.polidata.org/elections/red_states_blues_de27a.pdf

Benveniste, Émile (1939) 'The nature of the linguistic sign', in Émile Benveniste (1971), *Problems in General Linguistics*. Coral Gables, FL: University of Miami Press, pp. 43–9.

—— (1969/1986) 'The semiology of language', in Robert E. Innis (ed.) (1986), *Semiotics: An Introductory Reader*. London: Hutchinson, pp. 228–46.

Berger, Arthur (2012) *Understanding American Icons*. Walnut Creek, CA: Left Coast Press.

Berger, John (1968) 'Understanding a photograph', in John Berger (1972) *Selected Essays and Articles*. Harmondsworth: Penguin, pp. 178–82.

—— (1972) *Ways of Seeing*. London: BBC/Penguin.

—— (1980) *About Looking*. New York: Pantheon.

Berger, Peter and Thomas Luckmann (1967) *The Social Construction of Reality*. New York: Anchor/Doubleday.

Berkeley, George (1713/1979) *Three Dialogues Between Hylas and Philonous*. Indianapolis, IN: Hackett.

Bernstein, Basil (1971) *Class, Codes and Control*, vol. 1. London: Routledge & Kegan Paul.

Bertalanffy, Ludwig von (1968) *General System Theory*. New York: Braziller.

Birdwhistell, Ray L. (1971) *Kinesics and Context*. London: Allen Lane.

Birren, Faber (1956) *Selling Color to People*. New York: University Books.

Blakemore, Colin (2001) 'Sensation', in Colin Blakemore and Sheila Jennett (eds) *The Oxford Companion to the Body*. Oxford: Oxford University Press, pp. 602–3.

Bloomfield, Leonard (1939) *Linguistic Aspects of Science*. Chicago, IL: University of Chicago Press.

Booker, Christopher (2004) *The Seven Basic Plots*. London: Continuum.

Boorstin, Daniel J. (1961) *The Image*. London: Weidenfeld & Nicolson.

Bordwell, David, Janet Staiger, and Kristin Thompson (1988) *The Classical Hollywood Cinema*. London: Routledge.

Bouissac, Paul (ed.) (1998) *Encyclopedia of Semiotics*. Oxford: Oxford University Press.

Bourdieu, Pierre (1990) 'The social definition of photography', in Jessica Evans and Stuart Hall (eds) (1999) *Visual Culture*. London: Sage, pp. 162–80.

—— (1997) 'The Goffman Prize lecture: masculine domination revisited', *Berkeley Journal of Sociology* 41:189–203.

Brooks, Cleanth and Robert Penn Warren (1972) *Modern Rhetoric* (shorter 3rd edn). New York: Harcourt Brace Jovanovich.

Browne, Ray B., Marshal W. Fishwick, and Kevin O. Browne (1990) *Dominant Symbols in Popular Culture*. Bowling Green, OH: Bowling Green State University Press.

Bruner, Jerome S. (1966) 'Culture and cognitive growth', in J. S. Bruner, R. R. Olver, and P. M. Greenfield (eds) (1966) *Studies in Cognitive Growth*. New York: Wiley.

—— (1973) *Beyond the Information Given*. New York: Norton.

—— (1990) *Acts of Meaning*. Cambridge, MA: Harvard University Press.

Bruner, Jerome S., Jacqueline S. Goodnow, and George A. Austin (1956/1962) *A Study of Thinking*. New York: Wiley.

Bruss, Elizabeth W. (1978) 'Peirce and Jakobson on the nature of the sign', in Richard W. Bailey, Ladislav Matejka, and Peter Steiner (eds) (1978) *The Sign: Semiotics Around the World*. Ann Arbor, MI: University of Michigan Press, pp. 81–98.

Bühler, Karl (1933) 'The axiomatization of the language sciences', in Innis (1982), pp. 75–164.

—— (1934/2011) *Theory of Language* (trans. Donald F. Goodwin). Amsterdam: John Benjamins.

Burke, Kenneth (1969) *A Grammar of Motives*. Berkeley, CA: University of California Press.

Butler, Judith (1999) *Gender Trouble*. London: Routledge.

Callero, Peter L. (2013) *The Myth of Individualism*. Lanham, MD: Rowman & Littlefield.

Chalfen, Richard (1987) *Snapshot Versions of Life*. Bowling Green, OH: Bowling Green State University Popular Press.

Chan, Ting Ting and Benjamin Bergen (2005) 'Writing direction influences spatial cognition'. *Proceedings of the 27th Annual Cognitive Society* Mahwah, NJ: Lawrence Erlbaum, pp. 412–17.

Chandler, Daniel (1990) 'The educational ideology of the computer', *British Journal of Educational Technology* 21(3): 165–74.

—— (1992) 'The phenomenology of writing by hand', *Intelligent Tutoring Media* 3(2/3): 65–74.

—— (1995a) *The Act of Writing*. Aberystwyth: University of Wales, Aberystwyth.

—— (1995b) 'Technological or media determinism' [WWW document] URL http://visual-memory.co.uk/daniel/Documents/tecdet/.

—— (1997a) 'An introduction to genre theory' [WWW document] http://visual-memory.co.uk/daniel/Documents/intgenre/intgenre.html.

—— (1997b) 'Children's understanding of what's "real" on TV: a review of the literature', *Journal of Educational Media* 23(1): 67–82.

—— (2002) *Semiotics: The Basics* (1st edn). London: Routledge.

—— (2006) 'Identities under construction', in Janet Maybin and Joan Swann (eds) (2006) *The Art of English*. Basingstoke: Palgrave Macmillan, pp. 303–11.

—— (2014) 'Icons and indices assert nothing', in Thellefsen and Sørensen (eds) (2014), pp. 131–6.

—— (2016) 'Social media: birds of a feather, or just safety in numbers?' [WWW document] www.oxfordreference.com/newsitem/100/social-media-birds-of-a-feather-or-just-safety-in-numbers.

Chandler, Daniel and Merris Griffiths (2000) 'Gender-differentiated production features in toy commercials', *Journal of Broadcasting and Electronic Media* 44(3): 503–20.

Chandler, Daniel and Rod Munday (2011) *A Dictionary of Media and Communication*. Oxford: Oxford University Press.

Chandler, Daniel and Rod Munday (2016) *A Dictionary of Social Media*. Oxford: Oxford University Press.

Chandler, Daniel and Dilwyn Roberts-Young (1999) 'The construction of identity in adolescent personal home pages', in Pascal Marquet, Alain Jaillet, Stéphanie Mathey, and Elke Nissen (eds) *Internet-Based Teaching and Learning (IN-TELE) 98* (*Internet Communication*, vol. 2). Frankfurt: Peter Lang, pp. 461–6.

Chatman, Seymour, Umberto Eco, and Jean-Marie Klinkenberg (1979) *A Semiotic Landscape/Panorama sémiotique*. The Hague: Mouton.

Clark, Herbert H. (1970) 'Word Associations and Linguistic Theory', in J. Lyons (ed.) *New Horizons in Linguistics*. London: Penguin, pp. 271–86.

Clark, Herbert H. and Eve V. Clark (1977) *Psychology and Language*. New York: Harcourt Brace Jovanovich.

Classen, Constance (1993) *Worlds of Sense*. London: Routledge.

Clifton, N. Roy (1983) *The Figure in Film*. Newark, DE: University of Delaware Press.

Cobley, Paul (ed.) (2001) *The Routledge Companion to Semiotics and Linguistics*. London: Routledge.

Cockburn, Cynthia and Susan Ormrod (1993) *Gender and Technology in the Making*. London: Sage.

Cohen, Stanley and Jock Young (eds) (1981) *The Manufacture of News*. London: Constable.

Colapietro, Vincent Michael (1993) *Glossary of Semiotics*. New York: Paragon House.

Coleman, Allan Douglass (1998) *Depth of Field*. Albuqerque: University of New Mexico Press.

Corner, John (1980) 'Codes and cultural analysis', *Media, Culture and Society* 2: 73–86.

Counihan, Carole and Penny van Esterik (eds) (1997) *Food and Culture*. London: Routledge.

Coward, Rosalind and John Ellis (1977) *Language and Materialism*. London: Routledge & Kegan Paul.

Cross, Mary (ed.) (2002) *A Century of American Icons*. Westport, CT: Greenwood Press.

Crystal, David (1987) *The Cambridge Encyclopedia of Language*. Cambridge: Cambridge University Press.

Csikszentmihalyi, Mihaly and Eugene Rochberg-Halton (1981) *The Meaning of Things*. Cambridge: Cambridge University Press.

Culler, Jonathan (1973) 'The linguistic basis of structuralism', in Robey (ed.) (1973), pp. 20–36.

—— (1975) *Structuralist Poetics*. London: Routledge & Kegan Paul.

—— (1981) *The Pursuit of Signs*. London: Routledge & Kegan Paul.

—— (1983) *On Deconstruction*. London: Routledge & Kegan Paul.

—— (1985) *Saussure*. London: Fontana.

—— (1988) *Framing the Sign*. Oxford: Blackwell.

Daddesio, Thomas (1995) *On Minds and Symbols*. Berlin: Mouton de Gruyter.

Danesi, Marcel (1999) *Of Cigarettes, High Heels, and Other Interesting Things*. London: Macmillan.

—— (2000) *Encyclopedic Dictionary of Semiotics, Media, and Communication*. Toronto: University of Toronto Press.

Daniel, E. Valentine (2008) 'Semiotics', in William A. Darity (ed.) *International Encyclopedia of the Social Sciences* (2nd edn), vol. 7, pp. 436–8.

Davies, Bronwyn and Rom Harré (1990) 'Positioning: the discursive production of selves', *Journal for the Theory of Social Behaviour* 20(1): 43–63.

Davis, Desmond (1960) *The Grammar of Television Production* (rev. John Elliot). London: Barrie & Rockliff.

Davis, Fred (1992) *Fashion, Culture and Identity*. Chicago: University of Chicago Press.

Davis, Howard and Paul Walton (eds) (1983a) *Language, Image, Media*. Oxford: Basil Blackwell.

—— (1983b) 'Death of a premier: consensus and closure in international news', in Davis and Walton (eds) (1983a), pp. 8–49.

Daylight, Russell (2011) *What if Derrida was wrong about Saussure?* Edinburgh: Edinburgh University Press.

—— (2014) 'The difference between semiotics and semiology', *Gramma/Γράμμα: Journal of Theory and Criticism*, 20: 37–50.

Deacon, Terrence W. (1997) *The Symbolic Species*. New York: Norton.

de Lauretis, Teresa (1987) *Technologies of Gender: Essays on Theory, Film and Fiction*. Bloomington, IN: Indiana University Press.

Deledalle, Gérard (2000) *Charles S. Peirce's Philosophy of Signs*. Bloomington, IN: Indiana University Press.

Deleuze, Gilles (1989) *Cinema 2: The Time-Image* (trans. Hugh Tomlinson and Robert Galeta). Minneapolis, MN: University of Minnesota Press.

Deregowski, Jan B. (1980) *Illusions, Patterns and Pictures*. New York: Academic Press.

Derrida, Jacques (1967a/1976) *Of Grammatology* (trans. Gayatri Spivak). Baltimore, MD: Johns Hopkins University Press.

—— (1967b/1978) *Writing and Difference* (trans. Alan Bass). London: Routledge & Kegan Paul.

—— (1974) 'White mythology: metaphor in the text of philosophy', *New Literary History* 6(1): 5–74.

—— (1981) *Positions* (trans. Alan Bass). London: Athlone Press.

Dosse, François (1997) *History of Structuralism*, 2 vols. Minneapolis, MN: University of Minnesota Press.

Douglas, Mary (1966) *Purity and Danger*. London: Routledge & Kegan Paul.

—— (1973a) *Natural Symbols*. Harmondsworth: Penguin.

—— (ed.) (1973b) *Rules and Meanings*. Harmondsworth: Penguin.

—— (1975) 'Deciphering a meal', in Carole Counihan and Penny van Esterik (eds) (1997) *Food and Culture*. London: Routledge, pp. 36–54.

Dreyfus, Hubert (1992) *What Computers Still Can't Do*. Cambridge, MA: MIT Press.

Dyer, Richard (1992) *Only Entertainment*. London: Routledge.

—— (1993) *The Matter of Images*. London: Routledge.

Eagleton, Terry (1983) *Literary Theory*. Oxford: Basil Blackwell.

Easthope, Antony (1990) *What a Man's Gotta Do*. Boston, MA: Unwin Hyman.

Eaton, Marcia (1980) 'Truth in pictures', *Journal of Aesthetics and Art Criticism* 39(1): 15–26.

Eco, Umberto (1965) 'Towards a semiotic enquiry into the television message', in Corner and Hawthorn (eds) (1980), pp. 131–50.

—— (1973) 'Social life as a sign system', in Robey (ed.) (1973), pp. 57–72.

—— (1976) *A Theory of Semiotics*. Bloomington, IN: Indiana University Press/London: Macmillan.

—— (1981) *The Role of the Reader*. London: Hutchinson.

—— (1984) *Semiotics and the Philosophy of Language*. Bloomington, IN: Indiana University Press.

—— (1987) *Travels in Hyperreality* (trans. William Weaver). London: Picador.

—— (1999) *Kant and the Platypus*. London: Secker and Warburg.

Ehrat, Johannes (2005) *Cinema & Semiotic*. Toronto: University of Toronto Press.

Ekman, Paul (2004) 'Emotional and conversational nonverbal signals', in Jesus M. Larrazabal and Luis A. Pérez Miranda (eds) *Language, Knowledge, and Representation*. Dordrecht: Kluwer, pp. 39–50.

Elkins, James (1996) *The Object Stares Back*. New York: Simon & Schuster.

—— (1998) *On Pictures and the Words That Fail Them*. Cambridge: Cambridge University Press.

Ellis, John M. (1993) *Language, Thought, and Logic*. Evanston, IL: Northwestern University Press.

Esland, Geoffrey (1973) *Language and Social Reality*. Bletchley: Open University Press.

Fairclough, Norman (1995a) *Media Discourse*. London: Edward Arnold.

—— (1995b) *Critical Discourse Analysis*. Harlow: Longman.

Feldges, Benedikt (2008) *American Icons*. New York: Routledge.

Finnegan, Ruth (2002) *Communicating*. London: Routledge.

Fish, Stanley (1980) *Is There A Text In This Class?* Cambridge, MA: Harvard University Press.

Fiske, John (1982) *Introduction to Communication Studies*. London: Routledge.

—— (1987) *Television Culture*. London: Routledge.

—— (1989) 'Codes', in Tobia L. Worth (ed.) *International Encyclopedia of Communications*, vol. 1. New York: Oxford University Press, pp. 312–16.

Fleming, Dan (1996) *Powerplay*. Manchester: Manchester University Press.

Floch, Jean-Marie (2000) *Visual Identities* (trans. Pierre Van Osselaer and Alec McHoul). London: Continuum.

Forceville, Charles (1996) *Pictorial Metaphor in Advertising*. London: Routledge.

Foucault, Michel (1970) *The Order of Things*. London: Tavistock.

—— (1974) *The Archaeology of Knowledge*. London: Tavistock.

Fox, Kate (2014) *Watching the English* (2nd edn). London: Hodder & Stoughton.

Freud, Sigmund (1938) *The Basic Writings of Sigmund Freud*. New York: Modern Library.

Fuss, Diane (ed.) (1991) *Inside/Out.* London: Routledge.

Gaffron, Mercedes (1950) 'Right and left in pictures', *Art Quarterly* 13: 312–31.

Gallie, W. B. (1952) *Peirce and Pragmatism*. Harmondsworth: Penguin.

Galtung, Johan and Eric Ruge (1981) 'Structuring and selecting news', in Cohen and Young (eds) (1981), pp. 52–63.

Genette, Gérard (1997) *Palimpsests* (trans. Channa Newman and Claude Doubinsky). Lincoln, NB: University of Nebraska Press.

Gergen, Kenneth J. (2009a) *An Invitation to Social Construction* (2nd edn). London: Sage.

—— (2009b) *Relational Being*. New York: Oxford University Press.

—— (2011) 'The social construction of self', in Shaun Gallagher (ed.) *The Oxford Handbook of the Self*. Oxford: Oxford University Press, pp. 633–53.

Glasgow University Media Group (1980) *More Bad News*. London: Routledge & Kegan Paul.

Goethe, Johann Wolfgang von (1982) *Goethes Werke* (10th edn, ed. E. Trunz), 14 vols. Munich: C. H. Beck.

Goffman, Erving (1959/1971) *The Presentation of Self in Everyday Life*. Harmondsworth: Penguin.

—— (1967) *Interaction Ritual*. Garden City, NY: Doubleday.

—— (1969) *Behaviour in Public Places*. Harmondsworth: Penguin.

—— (1979) *Gender Advertisements*. New York: Harper & Row/London: Macmillan.

Goldman, Robert (1992) *Reading Ads Socially*. London: Routledge.

Goldman, Robert and Stephen Papson (1996) *Sign Wars*. New York: Guilford Press.

Gombrich, Ernst H. (1949) 'Signs, language and behaviour', *Art Bulletin* 31: 68–75; reprinted in E. H. Gombrich (1987) *Reflections on the History of Art* (ed. Richard Woodfield). London: Phaidon, pp. 240–9.

—— (1963) *Meditations on a Hobby Horse*. London: Phaidon.

—— (1972) 'The visual image', in *Scientific American* (eds) *Communication*. San Francisco, CA: Freeman, pp. 46–60; originally in a special issue of *Scientific American*, September 1972; republished in Gombrich (1982), pp. 137–61.

—— (1977) *Art and Illusion*. London: Phaidon.

—— (1982) *The Image and the Eye*. London: Phaidon.

—— (1996) 'Four theories of artistic expression', in Richard Woodfield (ed.) (1996) *Gombrich on Art and Psychology*, Manchester: Manchester University Press.

Goodman, Nelson (1968) *Languages of Art*. London: Oxford University Press.

Gottdiener, Mark (1995) *Postmodern Semiotics*. Oxford: Blackwell.

Goudge, Thomas A. (1950/1969) *The Thought of C. S. Peirce*. New York: Dover.

Gregory, Richard L. (1970) *The Intelligent Eye*. London: Weidenfeld & Nicolson.

—— (1979) 'Feeling the world by perception', in Mick Csáky (ed) *How Does It Feel?* London: Thames and Hudson, pp. 55–64.

—— (1998) *Eye and Brain*. Oxford: Oxford University Press.

Greimas, Algirdas J. (1966/1983) *Structural Semantics*. Lincoln, NB: University of Nebraska Press.

—— (1970) *Du Sens*. Paris: Seuil.

—— (1987) *On Meaning* (trans. Paul J. Perron and Frank H. Collins). London: Frances Pinter.

Greimas, Algirdas J. and J. Courtés (1982) *Semiotics and Language*. Bloomington, IN: Indiana University Press.

Grice, H. Paul (1975) 'Logic and conversation', in Peter Cole and Jerry L. Morgan (eds) *Syntax and Semantics*, vol. 3: *Speech Acts*. New York: Academic Press, pp. 41–58.

Grosz, Elizabeth (1993) 'Bodies and knowledges: feminism and the crisis of reason', in Alcoff and Potter (eds) (1993), pp. 187–215.

Groves, Peter (1998) 'Markedness', in Bouissac (ed.) (1998), pp. 385–7.

Guiraud, Pierre (1975) *Semiology* (trans. George Gross). London: Routledge & Kegan Paul.

Haas, William (1962) 'The theory of translation', *Philosophy* 37(141): 208–28.

Hall, Edward T. (1966) *The Hidden Dimension*. New York: Doubleday.

Hall, Stuart (1973/1980) 'Encoding/decoding', in Centre for Contemporary Cultural Studies (ed.) *Culture, Media, Language*. London: Hutchinson, pp. 128–38.

—— (1977) 'Culture, the media and the "ideological effect"', in James Curran, Michael Gurevitch, and Janet Woollacott (eds) (1977) *Mass Communication and Society*. London: Edward Arnold, pp. 315–48.

—— (1981) 'The determinations of news photographs', in Cohen and Young (eds) (1981), pp. 226–43.

Halliday, Michael A. K. (1978) *Language as Social Semiotic*. London: Arnold.

Halperin, David (1990) *One Hundred Years of Homosexuality*. New York: Routledge.

—— (2012) *How to be Gay*. Cambridge, MA: Harvard University Press.

Hariman, Robert and John Louis Lucaites (2007) *No Caption Needed: Iconic Photographs, Public Culture, and Liberal Democracy*. Chicago, IL: University of Chicago Press.

Harris, David (1996) *A Society of Signs?* London: Routledge.

Harris, Roy (1987) *Reading Saussure*. London: Duckworth.

—— (2003) *Saussure and his Interpreters* (2nd edn). Edinburgh: Edinburgh University Press.

Hastorf, Albert H. and Hadley Cantril (1954) 'They saw a game: a case study', *Journal of Abnormal and Social Psychology* 49: 129–34; reprinted in Robert Ornstein (1986) *The Psychology of Consciousness*. Harmondsworth: Penguin and in Robert Ornstein (ed.) (1973) *The Nature of Consciousness*. San Francisco, CA: W. H. Freeman.

Hauser, Nathan (1992) 'Introduction', in Peirce (1992), xix–xli.

Heath, Robert (2012) *Seducing the Subconscious.* Chichester: Wiley.

Henley, Nancy M. (1977) *Body Politics*. Englewood Cliffs, NJ: Prentice-Hall.

Hertz, Robert (1909/2004) *Death and the Right Hand*. London: Routledge.

Hine, Thomas (1995) *The Total Package*. Boston: Little, Brown.

Hirsch, E. D. (1967) *Validity in Interpretation*. New Haven, CT: Yale University Press.

Hjelmslev, Louis (1961) *Prolegomena to a Theory of Language* (trans. Francis J. Whitfield). Madison: University of Wisconsin Press.

Hockett, Charles F. (1958) *A Course in Modern Linguistics*. New York: Macmillan.

Hodge, Bob and Gunther Kress (1988) *Social Semiotics*. Cambridge: Polity.

Hodge, Bob and David Tripp (1986) *Children and Television*. Cambridge: Polity Press.

Holdcroft, David (1991) *Saussure: Signs, System, and Arbitrariness*. Cambridge: Cambridge University Press.

Holzner, Burkart (1968) *Reality Construction in Society*. Cambridge, MA: Schenkman.

Honderich, Ted (ed.) *The Oxford Companion to Philosophy*. Oxford: Oxford University Press.

Horigan, Stephen (1988) *Nature and Culture in Western Discourses*. London: Routledge.

Humboldt, Wilhelm von (1836/1999) *On Language*. Cambridge: Cambridge University Press.

Huxley, Aldous (1941) *Ends and Means*. London: Chatto & Windus.

Innis, Robert E. (1982) *Karl Bühler: Semiotic Foundations of Language Theory*. New York: Plenum Press.

Jackson, Leonard (1991) *The Poverty of Structuralism*. London: Longman.

Jacob, François (1982) *The Possible and the Actual*. New York: Pantheon.

Jakobson, Roman (1941/1968) *Child Language, Aphasia and Phonological Universals*. The. Hague: Mouton.

—— (1943) 'Franz Boas' approach to language', in Jakobson (1971b), pp. 477–88.

—— (1949a) 'Current issues of general linguistics', in Jakobson (1990), pp. 49–55.

—— (1949b) 'On the identification of phonemic entities', in Jakobson (1971a), pp. 418–25.

—— (1952) 'Pattern in linguistics', in Jakobson (1971b), pp. 223–8.

—— (1953) 'Aphasia as a linguistic topic', in Jakobson (1971b), pp. 229–38.

—— (1956) 'Two aspects of language and two types of aphasic disturbances', in Jakobson and Halle (1956), pp. 67–96; also in Jakobson (1971b), pp. 239–59 and Jakobson (1990), pp. 115–33.

—— (1958) 'On linguistic aspects of translation', in Jakobson (1971b), pp. 260–6.

—— (1960) 'Closing statement: linguistics and poetics', in Sebeok (ed.) (1960), pp. 350–77; first part reprinted as 'The Speech Event and the Functions of Language' in Jakobson (1990), pp. 69–79.

—— (1962) 'Results of the ninth International Conference of Linguists', in Jakobson (1971b), pp. 593–602.

—— (1963a) 'Efforts toward a means–end model of language in interwar continental linguistics', in Jakobson (1990), pp. 56–60; also in Jakobson (1971b), pp. 522–6.

—— (1963b) 'Parts and wholes in language', in Jakobson (1990), pp. 110–14; also in Jakobson (1971b), pp. 280–4.

—— (1963c) 'Visual and auditory signs', in Jakobson (1971b), pp. 334–7.

—— (1963d) 'Towards a linguistic classification of aphasic impairments', in Jakobson (1971b), pp. 289–306.

—— (1966) 'Quest for the essence of language', in Jakobson (1990), pp. 407–21; also in Jakobson (1971b), pp. 345–59.

—— (1968a) 'Language in relation to other communication systems', in Jakobson (1971b), pp. 697–708.

—— (1968b) 'Poetry of grammar and grammar of poetry', *Lingua* 21(1): 597–609.

—— (1970) 'Linguistics in relation to other sciences', in Jakobson (1990), pp. 451–88; also in Jakobson (1971b), pp. 655–96.

—— (1971a) *Selected Writings*, vol. 1, *Phonological Studies*. The Hague: Mouton.

—— (1971b) *Selected Writings*, vol. 2, *Word and Language*. The Hague: Mouton.

—— (1971c) 'Retrospect', in Jakobson (1971b), pp. 711–22.

—— (1972) 'Verbal communication', in *Scientific American* (eds) *Communication*. San Francisco, CA: Freeman, pp. 39–44 (originally in a special issue of *Scientific American*, September 1972).

—— (1973) 'Some questions of meaning', in Jakobson (1990), pp. 315–23.

—— (1976) 'The concept of phoneme', in Jakobson (1990), pp. 217–41.

—— (1980a) 'The concept of mark', in Jakobson (1990), pp. 134–40.

—— (1981) 'My favourite topics', in Jakobson (1990), pp. 61–6.

—— (1984) 'Language and parole: code and message', in Jakobson (1990), pp. 80–109.

—— (1985) *Verbal Art, Verbal Sign, Verbal Time* (eds Krystyna Pomorska and Stephen Rudy). Oxford: Blackwell.

—— (1990) *On Language* (eds Linda R. Waugh and Monique Monville-Burston). Cambridge, MA: Harvard University Press.

Jakobson, Roman and Morris Halle (1956) *Fundamentals of Language*. The Hague: Mouton.

Jakobson, Roman and Claude Lévi-Strauss (1970) 'Charles Baudelaire's "Les Chats"', in Lane (ed.) (1970), pp. 202–21.

James, William (1890/1950) *The Principles of Psychology*, vol. 1. New York: Dover.

Jameson, Fredric (1972) *The Prison-House of Language*. Princeton, NJ: Princeton University Press.

—— (1981) *The Political Unconscious*. Ithaca, NY: Cornell University Press.

—— (1991) *Postmodernism*. Durham, NC: Duke University Press.

Janis, I. L. and Hovland, C. I. (1959) 'An overview of persuasability research', in C. I. Hovland and I. L. Janis (eds) *Personality and Persuasability*. New Haven: Yale University Press, pp. 1–26.

Jenks, Chris (ed.) (1998) *Core Sociological Dichotomies*. London: Sage.

Jensen, Klaus Bruhn (1995) *The Social Semiotics of Mass Communication*. London: Sage.

—— (2001) 'Semiotics', in Neil J. Smelser and Paul B. Baltes (eds) *International Encyclopedia of the Social and Behavioral Sciences*, vol. 21. Oxford: Elsevier Science, pp. 13887–91.

Johnson, Harold G., Paul Ekman, and Wallace V. Friesen (1975) 'Communicative body movements: American emblems', *Semiotica* 15(4): 335–53.

Johnson, Richard (1996) 'What is cultural studies anyway?', in Storey (ed.) (1996), pp. 75–114.

Joseph, Michael and Dave Saunders (2000) *The Complete Photography Course*. London: Seven Dials.

Katz, Jonathan Ned (2007) *The Invention of Heterosexuality*. Chicago: University of Chicago Press.

Kennedy, John (1974) *A Psychology of Picture Perception*. San Francisco, CA: Jossey-Bass.

Kjørup, Søren (1974) 'George Inness and the battle at Hastings, or doing things with pictures', *The Monist* 58(2): 216–35.

—— (1977) 'Film as a meetingplace of multiple codes', in David Perkins and Barbara Leondar (eds) (1977) *The Arts and Cognition*. Baltimore, MD: Johns Hopkins University Press, pp. 20–47.

Korsmeyer, Carolyn (1985) 'Pictorial assertion', *Journal of Aesthetics and Art Criticism* 43(3): 257–65.

Korzybski, Alfred (1933) *Science and Sanity*. Lancaster, PA: Science Press.

Krampen, Martin (1983) 'Icons of the road', *Semiotica* 43(1/2): 1–204.

Krampen, Martin, Klaus Oehler, Roland Posner, and Thure von Uexküll (eds) (1987) *Classics of Semiotics*. New York: Springer.

Kress, Gunther and Theo van Leeuwen (1996) *Reading Images*. London: Routledge.

Kristeva, Julia (1970) *Le Texte du roman*. The Hague: Mouton.

—— (1973) 'The system and the speaking subject', *Times Literary Supplement* 12th October 1973: 1249–52.

—— (1974) *La Révolution du langage poétique.* Paris: Seuil.

—— (1980) *Desire in Language*. New York: Columbia University Press.

Lacan, Jacques (1977) *Écrits* (trans. Alan Sheridan). London: Routledge.

Lakoff, George and Mark Johnson (1980) *Metaphors We Live By*. Chicago: University of Chicago Press.

Langer, Susanne K. (1957) *Philosophy in a New Key*. Cambridge, MA: Harvard University Press.

Lanham, Richard A. (1969) *A Handlist of Rhetorical Terms*. Berkeley: University of California Press.

Lanier, Jaron (2011) *You Are Not a Gadget*. London: Penguin.

Larrucia, Victor (1975) 'Little Red Riding-Hood's metacommentary: paradoxical injunction, semiotics and behaviour', *Modern Language Notes* 90(4): 517–34.

Leach, Edmund (1964) 'Anthropological aspects of language: animal categories and verbal abuse', in E. H. Lenneberg (ed.) *New Directions in the Study of Language*. Cambridge, MA: MIT Press, pp. 23–6.

—— (1968) *A Runaway World?* London: BBC.

—— (1970) *Lévi-Strauss*. London: Fontana.

—— (1973) 'Structuralism in social anthropology', in Robey (ed.) (1973), pp. 37–56.

—— (1976) *Culture and Communication*. Cambridge: Cambridge University Press.

—— (1982) *Social Anthropology*. London: Fontana.

Lee, David Y. W. (2001) 'Genres, registers, text types, domains, and styles', *Language Learning & Technology* 5(3): 37–72.

Lévi-Strauss, Claude (1949/1969) *The Elementary Structures of Kinship* (trans. James Harle Bell, John Richard von Sturmer, and Rodney Needham). London: Eyre & Spottiswoode.

—— (1950/1987) *Introduction to the Work of Marcel Mauss* (trans. Felicity Baker). London: Routledge & Kegan Paul.

—— (1961) *Tristes Tropiques* (trans. John Russell). New York: Criterion.

—— (1962/1974) *The Savage Mind*. London: Weidenfeld and Nicolson.

—— (1964) *Totemism* (trans. Rodney Needham). Harmondsworth: Penguin.

—— (1968) 'The culinary triangle', in Counihan and van Esterik (eds) (1997), pp. 28–35.

—— (1969) *The Raw and the Cooked* (trans. John and Doreen Weightman). Chicago: University of Chicago Press.

—— (1972) *Structural Anthropology* (trans. Claire Jacobson and Brooke Grundfest Schoepf). Harmondsworth: Penguin.

Leymore, Varda Langholz (1975) *Hidden Myth*. New York: Basic Books.

Lidov, David (1998) 'Jakobson's model of linguistic communication', in Bouissac (ed.) (1998), pp. 330–2.

—— (1999) *Elements of Semiotics*. New York: St. Martin's Press.

Lippmann, Walter (1922/1997) *Public Opinion*. New York: Free Press.

Liu, C. H. and John M. Kennedy (1993) 'Symbolic forms and cognition', *Psyke & Logos* 14(2): 441–56.

Locke, John (1690/1974) *Essay Concerning Human Understanding*, vol. 2. London: Dent.

Lodge, David (1977/1996) *The Modes of Modern Writing*. London: Arnold.

Lopes, Dominic (1996) *Understanding Pictures*. Oxford: Clarendon Press.

Lotman, Yuri (1976) *Analysis of the Poetic Text*. Ann Arbor, MI: University of Michigan Press.

—— (1990) *Universe of the Mind* (trans. Ann Shukman). Bloomington, IN: Indiana University Press.

Lovell, Terry (1983) *Pictures of Reality*. London: BFI.

Lyons, John (1977) *Semantics*, vol. 1. Cambridge: Cambridge University Press.

MacCabe, Colin (1974) 'Realism and the cinema', *Screen* 15(2): 7–27.

MacGregor, Neil (2010) *A History of the World in 100 Objects*. London: Allen Lane.

Marion, Gilles (1994) 'L'apparence des individus: une lecture socio-sémiotique de la mode', *Protée* 23(2): 113–19.

Martin, Bronwen and Felizitas Ringham (2000) *Dictionary of Semiotics*. London: Cassell.

Mazzalovo, Gérald (2012) *Brand Aesthetics*. London: Palgrave.

McDonald, Edward (2012a) 'Aristotle, Saussure, Kress on speech and writing: language as paradigm for the semiotic?', *Language & Communication* 32(3): 205–15.

—— (2012b) 'Embodiment and meaning: moving beyond linguistic imperialism in social semiotics', *Social Semiotics* 23(3): 318–34.

McLuhan, Marshall and Quentin Fiore (1968) *War and Peace in the Global Village*. New York: Bantam.

McQuarrie, Edward F. and David Glen Mick (1992) 'On resonance: a critical pluralistic inquiry into advertising rhetoric', *Journal of Consumer Research* 19: 180–97.

Meisel, Perry and Haun Saussy (2011) 'Introduction: Saussure and his contexts', in Saussure (1916/2011), xv–xlviii.

Mepham, John (1973) 'The structuralist sciences and philosophy', in Robey (ed.) (1973), pp. 104–37.

Merrell, Floyd (1997) *Peirce, Signs, and Meaning*. Toronto: University of Toronto Press.

—— (2001) 'Charles Sanders Peirce's concept of the sign', in Cobley (ed.) (2001), pp. 28–39.

Messaris, Paul (1982) 'To what extent does one have to learn to interpret movies?', in Sari Thomas (ed.) (1982) *Film/Culture*. Metuchen, NJ: Scarecrow Press, pp. 168–83.

—— (1994) *Visual 'Literacy'*. Boulder, CO: Westview Press.

—— (1997) *Visual Persuasion*. London: Sage.

Metz, Christian (1968/1974) *Film Language* (trans. Michael Taylor). New York: Oxford University Press.

—— (1971/1974) *Language and Cinema* (trans. Jean Umiker-Sebeok). The Hague: Mouton.

—— (1977/1982) *The Imaginary Signifier* (trans. Celia Britton, Annwyl Williams, Ben Brewster, and Alfred Guzzetti). Bloomington: Indiana University Press.

Mick, David Glen and Laura G. Politi (1989) 'Consumers' interpretations of advertising imagery: a visit to the hell of connotation', in Elizabeth C. Hirschman (ed.) (1989) *Interpretive Consumer Research*. Provo, UT: Association for Consumer Research, pp. 85–96.

Miller, George A. (1956) 'The magical number seven, plus or minus two: some limits on our capacity for processing information', *Psychological Review* 63(2): 81–97.

Mitchell, W. J. T. (1987) *Iconology*. Chicago: University of Chicago Press.

Mitry, Jean (2000) *Semiotics and the Analysis of Film* (trans. Christopher King). Bloomington, IN: Indiana University Press.

Moeschberger, Scott L. and Rebekah A. Phillips DeZalia (eds) (2014) *Symbols that Bind, Symbols that Divide*. New York: Springer.

Morley, David (1980) *The 'Nationwide' Audience*. London: BFI.

—— (1981) '"The *Nationwide* Audience" – a critical postscript', *Screen Education* 39: 3–14.

—— (1983) 'Cultural transformations: the politics of resistance', in Davis and Walton (eds) (1983), pp. 104–17.

—— (1992) *Television, Audiences and Cultural Studies*. London: Routledge.

Morris, Brian (1991) *Western Conceptions of the Individual*. Oxford: Berg.

Morris, Charles W. (1938/1970) *Foundations of the Theory of Signs*. Chicago: Chicago University Press.

—— (1946) *Signs, Language and Behavior*. New York: Braziller.

—— (1964) *Signification and Significance*. Cambridge, MA: MIT Press.

—— (1971) *Writings on the General Theory of Signs*. The Hague: Mouton.

Morris, Pam (ed.) (1994) *The Bakhtin Reader*. London: Arnold.

Moss, Gloria (2014) *Why Men Like Straight Lines and Women Like Polka Dots*. Winchester: Psyche Books.

Murphy, Peter F. (2001) *Studs, Tools and the Family Jewels*. Madison, WI: University of Wisconsin Press.

Needham, Rodney (ed.) (1973) *Right and Left*. Chicago, IL: University of Chicago Press.

Neisser, Ulric (1976) *Cognition and Reality*. San Francisco, CA: W. H. Freeman.

Newcomb, Theodore M. (1952) *Social Psychology*. London: Tavistock.

Nichols, Bill (1981) *Ideology and the Image*. Bloomington, IN: Indiana University Press.

—— (1991) *Representing Reality*. Bloomington, IN: Indiana University Press.

Nöth, Winfried (1990) *Handbook of Semiotics*. Bloomington, IN: Indiana University Press.

Novitz, David (1977) *Pictures and Their Use in Communication*. The Hague: Martinus Nijhoff.

Ogden, Charles K. (1930/1944) *Basic English* (9th edn). London: Kegan Paul, Trench, Trubner & Co.

Ogden, Charles K. and Ivor A. Richards (1923) *The Meaning of Meaning*. London: Routledge & Kegan Paul.

Olson, David E. (ed.) (1994) *The World on Paper*. Cambridge: Cambridge University Press.

Oppé, A. Paul (1944) 'Right and left in Raphael's cartoons', *Journal of the Warburg and Courtauld Institutes* 7: 82–94.

Ortony, Andrew (ed.) (1979) *Metaphor and Thought*. Cambridge: Cambridge University Press.

Osgood, Charles E., George J. Suci, and Percy H. Tannenbaum (1957) *The Measurement of Meaning*. Urbana, IL: University of Illinois Press.

Oswald, Laura R. (2012) *Marketing Semiotics*. Oxford: Oxford University Press.

Packard, Vance (1957/2007) *The Hidden Persuaders*. New York: Ig Publishing.

Paoletti, Jo B. (2012) *Pink and Blue*. Bloomington, IN: Indiana University Press.

Passmore, John (1985) *Recent Philosophers*. London: Duckworth.

Pearce, W. Barnett (1989) *Communication and the Human Condition*. Carbondale, IL: Southern Illinois University Press.

Peirce, Charles Sanders (1931–58) *Collected Papers* (8 vols: vol. 1, *Principles of Philosophy*, ed. Charles Hartshorne and Paul Weiss, 1931; vol. 2, *Elements of Logic*, ed. Charles Hartshorne and Paul Weiss, 1932; vol. 3, *Exact Logic (Published Papers)*, ed. Charles Hartshorne and Paul Weiss, 1933; vol. 4, *The Simplest Mathematics*; ed. Charles Hartshorne and Paul Weiss, 1933; vol. 5, *Pragmatism and Pragmaticism*, ed. Charles Hartshorne and Paul Weiss, 1934; vol. 6, *Scientific Metaphysics* ed. Charles Hartshorne and Paul Weiss, 1935; vol. 7, *Science and Philosophy*, ed. William A. Burks, 1958; vol. 8, *Reviews, Correspondence and Bibliography*, ed. William A. Burks, 1958). Cambridge, MA: Harvard University Press.

—— (1966) *Selected Writings*. New York: Dover.

—— (1976) *The New Elements of Mathematics* (ed. Carolyn Eisele). The Hague: Mouton, vol. 4.

—— (1982–) *The Writings of Charles S. Peirce: A Chronological Edition.* Series in progress: vol. 1, *1857–1866*, ed. Max Fisch, 1982; vol. 2, *1867–1871*, ed. Edward C. Moore, 1984; vol. 3, *1872–1878*, ed. Christian Kloesel, 1986; vol. 4, *1879–1884* ed. Christian Kloesel, 1986; vol. 5, *1884–1886*, ed. Christian Kloesel, 1993; vol. 6, *1886–1890*, ed. Nathan Houser, 1993 vol. 8, *1890–1892*, ed. Peirce Edition Project, 2010; Bloomington IN: Indiana University Press.

—— (1991) *Peirce on Signs* (ed. James Hoopes). Chapel Hill, NC: University of North Carolina Press.

—— (1992) *The Essential Peirce: Selected Philosophical Writings* (2 vols: vol. 1, 1867–1893, ed. Nathan Houser and Christian Kloesel; vol. 2, 1893–1913, ed. Peirce Edition Project). Bloomington, IN: Indiana University Press.

Pelc, Jerzy (1994) 'Philosophy of language', in Sebeok (ed.) (1994b), vol. 2 (N–Z), pp. 708–14.

Pepper, Stephen C. (1942) *World Hypotheses*. Berkeley, CA: University of California Press.

Perry, Pamela (2001) 'Shades of white', in Jodi O'Brien (ed.) (2011) *The Production of Reality* (5th edn). Thousand Oaks, CA: Pine Forge Press, pp. 198–218.

Pettit, Philip (1977) *The Concept of Structuralism*. Berkeley, CA: University of California Press.

Petty, Richard E. and John T. Cacioppo (1986) *Communication and Persuasion*. New York: Springer-Verlag.

Piaget, Jean (1929) *The Child's Conception of the World*. New York: Humanities Press.

—— (1971) *Structuralism* (trans. Chaninah Maschler). London: Routledge & Kegan Paul.

Plato (1973) *Phaedrus and Letters VII and VIII* (trans. Walter Hamilton). Harmondsworth: Penguin.

—— (1998) *Cratylus* (trans. C. D. C. Reeve). Indianapolis, IN: Hackett.

Pollio, Howard R., J. Barrow, H. Fine, and M. Pollio (1977) *The Poetics of Growth*. Hillsdale, NJ: Lawrence Erlbaum.

Price, H. H. (1969) *Thinking and Experience* (2nd edn). London: Hutchinson.

Propp, Vladimir I. (1928/1968) *Morphology of the Folktale* (trans. Laurence Scott, 2nd edn). Austin: University of Texas Press.

Protevi, John (ed.) (2005) *The Edinburgh Dictionary of Continental Philosophy*. Edinburgh: Edinburgh University Press.

Quintilian (1969) *Institutio Oratoria/Institutes of Oratory*, vol. 1. London: Heinemann.

Reddy, Michael J. (1979) 'The conduit metaphor – a case of frame conflict in our language about language', in Ortony (ed.) (1979), pp. 284–324.

Reisz, Karel and Gavin Millar (1972) *The Technique of Film Editing*. London: Focal Press.

Richards, Ivor A. (1936) *The Philosophy of Rhetoric*. London: Oxford University Press.

Robertson, Keith (1994) 'On white space: when less is more', in Michael Bierut, William Drenttel, Steven Heller, and D. K. Holland (eds) *Looking Closer*. New York: Allworth Press, pp. 61–5; originally published in Keith Robertson (1993) 'On white space in graphic design', *Emigré* 26; also available online at: www.logoorange.com/white-space.php.

Robey, David (ed.) (1973) *Structuralism*. Oxford, Clarendon Press.

Rock, Irvin (1984) *Perception*. New York: Scientific American.

Rosenblum, Ralph and Robert Karen (1979) *When the Shooting Stops . . . The Cutting Begins*. New York: Da Capo.

Rudofsky, Bernard (1947) *Are Clothes Modern?* Chicago: Theobald.

Ruthrof, Horst (1997) *Semantics and the Body*. Toronto: University of Toronto Press.

Ryan, T. A. and C. B. Schwartz (1956) 'Speed of perception as a function of mode of representation', *American Journal of Psychology* 69(1): 66–9.

Sagan, Carl (1977) *The Dragons of Eden*. London: Hodder & Stoughton.

Sahlins, Marshall (1976) *Culture and Practical Reason*. Chicago: University of Chicago Press.

Salomon, Gavriel (1979) *Interaction of Media, Cognition, and Learning*. Hillsdale, NJ: Lawrence Erlbaum.

Sapir, Edward (1921/1971) *Language*. London: Rupert Hart-Davis.

—— (1929) 'The status of linguistics as a science', in Edward Sapir (1958) *Culture, Language and Personality* (ed. D. G. Mandelbaum). Berkeley, CA: University of California Press, pp. 65–77.

—— (1934) 'Symbolism', in Edwin R. A. Seligman (ed.) *Encyclopedia of the Social Sciences*. New York: Macmillan, vol. 14, pp. 492–5.

Sarup, Madan (1993) *An Introductory Guide to Post-Structuralism and Postmodernism*. Athens, GA: University of Georgia Press.

Saussure, Ferdinand de (1916/1995) *Cours de linguistique générale*. Paris: Payot.

—— (1916/2011) *Course in General Linguistics* (trans. Wade Baskin 1959, eds Perry Meisel and Haun Saussy). London: Fontana/Collins.

—— (1916/1983) *Course in General Linguistics* (trans. Roy Harris). London: Duckworth.

—— (1993) *Troisième cours de linguistique générale/Saussure's Second Course of Lectures on General Linguistics (1910–1911)*, ed. Eisuke Komatsu, trans. George Wolf. Oxford: Pergamon.

—— (1996) *Premier cours de linguistique générale/Saussure's First Course of Lectures on General Linguistics (1907)*, ed. Eisuke Komatsu, trans. George Wolf. Oxford: Pergamon.

—— (1997) *Deuxième cours de linguistique générale/Saussure's Second Course of Lectures on General Linguistics (1908–1909)*, ed. Eisuke Komatsu, trans. George Wolf. Oxford: Pergamon.

—— (2002) *Écrits de linguistique générale* (eds Simon Bouquet and Rudolf Engler). Paris: Gallimard.

—— (2006) *Writings in General Linguistics* (trans. Carol Sanders, Matthew Pires, and Peter Figueroa). Oxford: Oxford University Press.

Schank, Roger (1991) 'Johnny can't read (and neither can his old man)', in John Brockman (ed.) *Ways of Knowing*. New York: Prentice Hall, pp. 31–69.

Schier, Flint (1986) *Deeper into Pictures*. Cambridge: Cambridge University Press.

Schramm, Wilbur (1973) *Men, Messages and Media*. New York: Harper & Row.

Schudson, Michael (1984) *Advertising: The Uneasy Persuasion*. New York: Basic Books.

Scribner, Sylvia and Michael Cole (1981) *The Psychology of Literacy*. Cambridge, MA: Harvard University Press.

Scruton, Roger (1983) *The Aesthetic Understanding*. London: Methuen.

Sebeok, Thomas A. (ed.) (1960) *Style in Language*. Cambridge, MA: MIT Press.

—— (ed.) (1977) *A Perfusion of Signs*. Bloomington, IN: Indiana University Press.

—— (1986) *I Think I Am a Verb*. New York: Plenum Press.

—— (1994a) *Signs*. Toronto: University of Toronto Press.

—— (ed.) (1994b) *Encyclopedic Dictionary of Semiotics* (2nd edn), 3 vols. Berlin: Mouton de Gruyter.

Sedgwick, Eve Kosofsky (1990) *Epistemology of the Closet*. Berkeley, CA: University of California Press.

Seiter, Ellen (1992) 'Semiotics, structuralism and television', in Robert C. Allen (ed.) (1992) *Channels of Discourse, Reassembled*. London: Routledge, pp. 31–66.

Shannon, Claude E. and Warren Weaver (1949) *A Mathematical Model of Communication*. Urbana, IL: University of Illinois Press.

Short, T. L. (2007) *Peirce's Theory of Signs*. Cambridge: Cambridge University Press.

Silverman, David and Brian Torode (1980) *The Material Word*. London: Routledge & Kegan Paul.

Silverman, Kaja (1983) *The Subject of Semiotics*. New York: Oxford University Press.

Simpkins, Scott (1998) 'Postsemiotics', in Bouissac (ed.) (1998), pp. 509–12.

Slater, Don (1983) 'Marketing mass photography', in Davis and Walton (eds) (1983), pp. 245–63.

Sloane, Thomas (ed.) (2001) *Encyclopedia of Rhetoric*. Oxford: Oxford University Press.

Sonesson, Göran (1989) *Pictorial Concepts*. Lund: Lund University Press.

Sontag, Susan (1979) *On Photography*. London: Penguin.

Sperber, Dan and Deirdre Wilson (1995) *Relevance: Communication and Cognition*, 2nd edn, Oxford: Blackwell.

Stam, Robert (2000) *Film Theory*. Oxford: Blackwell.

Sturrock, John (ed.) (1979) *Structuralism and Since*. Oxford: Oxford University Press.

—— (1986) *Structuralism*. London: Paladin.

Taft, Charles (1997) 'Color meaning and context: comparisons of semantic ratings of colors on samples and objects', *Color Research and Application* 22(1): 40–50.

Tagg, John (1988) *The Burden of Representation*. Basingstoke: Macmillan.

Tallis, Raymond (1995) *Not Saussure* (2nd edn). Basingstoke: Palgrave.

Tapper, Richard (1994) 'Animality, humanity, morality, society', in Tim Ingold (ed.) *What is an Animal?* London: Routledge, pp. 47–62.

Thellefsen, Torkild and Bent Sørensen (eds) (2014) *Charles S. Peirce in his own Words*. Berlin: De Gruyter Mouton.

Thibault, Paul J. (1991) *Social Semiotics as Praxis*. Minneapolis, MN: University of Minnesota.

—— (1997) *Re-reading Saussure.* London: Routledge.

—— (1998a) 'Binarism', in Bouissac (ed.) (1998), pp. 76–82.

—— (1998b) 'Code', in Bouissac (ed.) (1998), pp. 125–9.

Thomas, William I. and Dorothy Swaine Thomas (1928) *The Child in America*. New York: Knopf.

Thwaites, Tony, Lloyd Davis, and Warwick Mules (1994) *Tools for Cultural Studies*. South Melbourne: Macmillan.

Tolkien, J. R. R. (1939) 'On fairy stories', in C. S. Lewis (ed.) (1947) *Essays Presented to Charles Williams*. Grand Rapids, MI: Eerdmans.

Trifonas, Peter (ed.) (2015) *International Handbook of Semiotics*. Dordrecht: Springer.

Tuchman, Gaye (1978) *Making News*. New York: Free Press.

Valentine, Virginia (nd): 'The "notness" principle' [WWW document] www.semioticsolutions.com/media/notness.doc [no longer available].

van Leeuwen, Theo (2005) *Introducing Social Semiotics*. London: Routledge.

Veblen, Thorstein (1899/2007) *Theory of the Leisure Class*. Oxford: Oxford University Press.

Vico, Giambattista (1744/1968) *The New Science* (trans. Thomas Goddard Bergin and Max Harold Finch). Ithaca, NY: Cornell University Press.

Voloshinov, Valentin N. (1973) *Marxism and the Philosophy of Language* (trans. Ladislav Matejka and I. R. Titunik). New York: Seminar Press.

Vygotsky, Lev S. (1939) 'Thought and speech', *Psychiatry* 2: 29–54.

—— (1962) *Thought and Language*. Cambridge MA: MIT Press.

—— (1978) *Mind in Society*. Cambridge, MA: Harvard University Press.

Watt, W. C. (1998) 'Semiotics', in Edward Craig (ed.) (1998) *Routledge Encyclopedia of Philosophy*. London: Routledge, vol. 8, pp. 675–9.

Watzlawick, Paul (1976) *How Real is Real?* New York: Vintage.

—— (ed.) (1984) *The Invented Reality*. New York: Norton.

Watzlawick, Paul, Janet Beavin, and Don D. Jackson (1967) *The Pragmatics of Human Communication*. New York: Norton.

Weinberg, Jonathan (2005) *Male Desire*. New York: Harry N. Abrams.

White, Hayden (1973) *Metahistory*. Baltimore, MD: Johns Hopkins University Press.

Whittock, Trevor (2009) *Metaphor and Film*. Cambridge: Cambridge University Press.

Whorf, Benjamin Lee (1940) 'Science and linguistics', *Technology Review* 42(6): 229–31, 247–8. Also in Whorf (1956), pp. 207–19.

—— (1956) *Language, Thought and Reality* (ed. John B. Carroll). Cambridge, MA: MIT Press.

Wierzbicka, Anna (1997) *Understanding Cultures Through Their Key Words*. New York: Oxford University Press.

Wilde, Oscar (1891) *Intentions*. London: Osgood McIlvaine and Co.

Wilden, Anthony (1972) *System and Structure*. London: Tavistock.

—— (1987) *The Rules Are No Game*. London: Routledge & Kegan Paul.

Williams, Raymond (1974) *Television: Technology and Cultural Form*. London: Fontana.

—— (1977) *Marxism and Literature*. Oxford: Oxford University Press.

Williamson, Judith (1978) *Decoding Advertisements*. London: Marion Boyars.

Wimsatt, William K. and Monroe C. Beardsley (1954) *The Verbal Icon*. Lexington, KY: University of Kentucky Press.

Wittgenstein, Ludwig (1922/1974) *Tractatus Logico-Philosophicus* (trans. D. F. Pears and B. F. McGuinness). London: Routledge.

—— (1953/2007) *Philosophical Investigations*, 4th edn (trans. G. E. M. Anscombe, P. M. S. Hacker, and Joachim Schulte). Oxford: Blackwell.

Wölfflin, Heinrich (1940) *Gedanken Zur Kunstgeschichte*. Basel: Benno Schwabe.

Wollen, Peter (1969) *Signs and Meanings in the Cinema*. London: Secker & Warburg.

Wolterstorff, Nicholas (1980) *Works and Worlds of Art*. Oxford: Clarendon Press.

Worth, Sol (1981) *Studying Visual Communication*. Philadelphia, PA: University of Pennsylvania Press.

Young, Brian M. (1990) *Television Advertising and Children*. Oxford: Clarendon Press.

Zeman, J. Jay (1997) 'Peirce's theory of signs', in Sebeok (ed.) (1977), pp. 22–39.

Zerubavel, Eviatar (1993) *The Fine Line*. Chicago: University of Chicago Press.

Zettl, Herbert (1990) *Sight–Sound–Motion* (2nd edn). Belmont, CA.

Zlatev, Jordan (2012) 'Cognitive semiotics: an emerging field for the transdisciplinary study of meaning', *Public Journal of Semiotics* 4(1): 2–24.

INDEX

 Taylor & Francis eBooks

Helping you to choose the right eBooks for your Library

Add Routledge titles to your library's digital collection today. Taylor and Francis ebooks contains over 50,000 titles in the Humanities, Social Sciences, Behavioural Sciences, Built Environment and Law.

Choose from a range of subject packages or create your own!

Benefits for you

>> Free MARC records
>> COUNTER-compliant usage statistics
>> Flexible purchase and pricing options
>> All titles DRM-free.

REQUEST YOUR **FREE** INSTITUTIONAL TRIAL TODAY

Free Trials Available
We offer free trials to qualifying academic, corporate and government customers.

Benefits for your user

>> Off-site, anytime access via Athens or referring URL
>> Print or copy pages or chapters
>> Full content search
>> Bookmark, highlight and annotate text
>> Access to thousands of pages of quality research at the click of a button.

eCollections – Choose from over 30 subject eCollections, including:

Archaeology	Language Learning
Architecture	Law
Asian Studies	Literature
Business & Management	Media & Communication
Classical Studies	Middle East Studies
Construction	Music
Creative & Media Arts	Philosophy
Criminology & Criminal Justice	Planning
Economics	Politics
Education	Psychology & Mental Health
Energy	Religion
Engineering	Security
English Language & Linguistics	Social Work
Environment & Sustainability	Sociology
Geography	Sport
Health Studies	Theatre & Performance
History	Tourism, Hospitality & Events

For more information, pricing enquiries or to order a free trial, please contact your local sales team: www.tandfebooks.com/page/sales

 Routledge
Taylor & Francis Group

The home of
Routledge books

www.tandfebooks.com

ICS

THE BASICS

Praise for *Semiotics: The Basics*:

'A very useful book, not only for those who wish to find out about semiotics, but also for those interested in finding out how language or any other sign system is far from being a neutral means of communication.' – *Juan A. Prieto-Pablos, University of Seville, Spain*

'The book is well written and up-to-date, without unnecessary verbosity or jargon, and yet reflects the complexity of the field and its problems.' – *Journal of Pragmatics*

'It is no small task to present semiotics in a manner that makes it accessible to the beginning student, and Chandler achieves this, describing difficult concepts clearly and thoroughly.' – *Donald J. Cunningham, Indiana University, USA*

Praise for the third edition:

'In this book that is, at once, highly accessible, extremely interesting, encyclopedic in its scope, and authoritative, Daniel Chandler's third edition of *Semiotics: The Basics* answers the question: how do you improve on a classic? Highly recommended for all courses involving semiotics and its applications to media, culture and society.' – *Arthur Asa Berger, San Francisco State University, USA*

The third edition of this bestselling textbook has been fully updated. In response to popular requests, this edition has many more illustrations and includes study suggestions at the end of each chapter. Using jargon-free language and lively up-to-date examples, *Semiotics: The Basics* demystifies this highly interdisciplinary subject and addresses questions such as:

- What are signs and codes?
- How does connotation work?
- What can semiotics teach us about representation and reality?

- What tools does it offer for analysing texts and cultural practices?
- Who are Saussure, Peirce, Jakobson, and Barthes – and why are they important?

This new edition of *Semiotics: The Basics* provides an engaging and accessible introduction to this field of study, and is a must-have for anyone coming to semiotics for the first time.

Additional resources for Language and Communication can be accessed on the Routledge Language and Communication Portal (www.routledgetextbooks.com/textbooks/languageandcommunication).

Daniel Chandler is an Emeritus faculty member at Aberystwyth University and a consultant in marketing semiotics. He is also the senior compiler of *A Dictionary of Media and Communication* and *A Dictionary of Social Media* (Oxford University Press 2016).